THE
EMPLOYEE
RIGHTS
HANDBOOK

ANSWERS TO
LEGAL QUESTIONS—
FROM INTERVIEW
TO PINK SLIP

Steven Mitchell Sack

Facts On File
New York • Oxford

||||||||||||||||

To Gwen,
with all my love

**The Employee Rights Handbook: Answers to Legal Questions—
From Interview to Pink Slip**
Copyright © 1991 by Steven Mitchell Sack

Facts On File, Inc.
460 Park Avenue South
New York NY 10016
USA

Facts On File Limited
Collins Street
Oxford OX4 1XJ
United Kingdom

Library of Congress Cataloging-in-Publication Data
    Sack, Steven Mitchell, 1954–
The employee rights handbook: answers to legal questions—from interview to
  pink slip / Steven Mitchell Sack.
      p. cm.
  Includes bibliographical references and index.
  ISBN 0-8160-2064-7
  1. Labor laws and legislation—United States—Popular works.
  2. Employee rights—United States—Popular works. I. Title.
KF3455.Z9S23 1991
344.73'014—dc20
[347.3041]   90-44731

A British CIP catalogue record for this book is available from the British Library.

Text design by Donna Sinisgalli
Jacket design by James Victore
Composition by Facts On File, Inc.
Manufactured by the Maple-Vail Manufacturing Group
Printed in the United States of America

10 9 8 7 6 5 4 3 2

This book is printed on acid-free paper.

CONTENTS

ACKNOWLEDGMENTS

S pecial thanks are extended to my agent, Bert Holtje of James Peter Associates, for his efforts in obtaining the "green light" for this project.

I also wish to thank Robert Davidson III for his generous assistance in reviewing and drafting selected portions of the manuscript. I am truly grateful to Charles A. Alessandrini, president, and I. Gregg Van Wert, executive vice president of the National Association of Printers and Lithographers, for permitting me to use extensive material from articles I furnish to NAPL as general labor counsel in *Printing Manager* magazine and from publications I have drafted for NAPL, including the *NAPL Employee Handbook* and the *Hiring and Firing Guide*. Without permission to reuse this material, this book could not and would not have been written. In addition, a special word of thanks is given to Rhona Bronson at NAPL for her constant support, assistance, and competent skills.

I also thank J. Robert Connor, editor-in-chief of *Graduating Engineer* magazine, for permitting me to include materials previously furnished in articles written for the magazine on the rights of pregnant workers and minorities (i.e., race discrimination). Kudos also go to Marilyn Stephens, executive director of the Manufacturers' Representatives Educational Research Foundation, for allowing me to reproduce text I previously drafted on litigation concerns in the *Operations Manual for Manufacturers' Representative Firms*.

Special thanks go to Henry Bergson, executive director of the National Electrical Manufacturers Representatives Association (NEMRA), for permitting me to include a copy of the association's *Guidelines for Negotiating Agreements between Sales Representatives and Manufacturers* and compendium of salient elements of the various state sales rep protection laws.

In addition, I offer my warmest appreciation to friend and fellow attorney Stanley M. Spiegler, who taught me more about the practice of labor law than he could ever realize. I also acknowledge the friendship and expertise of Shirley and Larry Alexander, who helped me develop and hone my legal writing skills.

Acknowledgments are also extended to my brother and associate Jonathan Scott Sack, Esq. at my law firm for drafting the Glossary of Terms. Of course, personal thanks are extended to Joan and Sidney Pollack for their wonderful support and help while I wrote this book, and to my wife, Gwen, for giving me the desire to complete the project. I also thank Dr. Jack and Cynthia Plawner and Dr. Robert and Stacey Sack-Zuckerman, Esq. for their constant love and encouragement.

Finally, as always, I wish to express my appreciation and gratitude to my mother, Judith, and my father, Bernard, whose insights and dreams helped make the idea for this book a reality; and to my son, Andrew, for future dreams.

AUTHOR'S NOTE

The information in this book is my attempt to reduce complex and confusing law to practical general labor strategies. These strategies are meant to serve as helpful guidelines—concepts to think about—when you experience job-related problems. They are *not* intended as legal advice per se, because laws vary considerably throughout the 50 states and the law can be interpreted differently depending upon the particular facts of each case. Thus, it is important to consult experienced labor counsel regarding the applicability of any strategy or point of information contained herein.

Additionally, this book is sold with the understanding that the publisher is not engaged in rendering legal, accounting or other professional service. If legal advice or other expert assistance is required, the services of a competent professional must always be sought.

Finally, fictitious names have been used throughout the work and any similarity to actual persons, places or events is purely coincidental.

PREFACE

This book was written to save you money and aggravation.

Like most Americans, you are probably unaware how strongly the law affects your life. But without an understanding of the law, there is a good chance you will be exploited, especially in your job and business relationships.

A job is like a romance. Companies woo applicants with promises of security, fulfillment and riches. Then, when the honeymoon is over, even highly qualified people often find themselves being treated unfairly. Many don't receive promised benefits such as year-end bonuses, commissions, health insurance and overtime. Others are fired without cause or notice through no fault of their own.

However, most people are unaware that dramatic changes are occurring in the workplace regarding their legal rights. Years ago, the law favored employers when it came to resolving employment disputes. It used to be that employers could fire workers with or without cause or notice with little fear of legal reprisal. Fortunately, this is changing. For example, federal and state rulings now grant some employees access to their personnel records, permit them to be represented by counsel when accused of disciplinary violations, and protect them in many other ways. Both men and women are receiving protection from on-the-job discrimination, sexual harassment, unfair parental leave policies, drug testing, unfair discharge and mandatory lie detector tests.

Millions of independent salespeople are also receiving protection from principals who fail to pay commissions due them in a timely fashion. This is because in the past few years more than 28 states have passed sales rep protection laws which guarantee prompt payment of commissions upon termination or resignation and award double and triple damages, plus reasonable attorney fees and costs of litigation, in the event companies fail to comply with the appropriate provisions of each applicable state law.

More and more terminated workers are successfully arguing and proving that company promises made at the time of the hiring interview are binding on the employer. Years ago, terminated employees would merely bow their heads and shuffle out the door after hearing they had been fired. Now, terminated workers are questioning these decisions and negotiating better severance packages and other post-termination benefits.

No company, regardless of its size or industry, is immune from this growing trend. The evolution of new laws, and the philosophy that a job is an integral part of a person's life and not just a vehicle for earning a living, are giving workers ammunition to fight back. Statistics indicate that 3.8 of every 100 employees are fired or resign from their jobs each month. Experts suggest that more than 350,000 workers each year are terminated unjustly. The vast majority of these individuals do not belong to unions and work without written contracts and basic job security.

However, you are not powerless. A story in *The New York Times* recently reported that "in almost every industry, unfair discharge litigation has proliferated and the amount of money involved in settlements runs into hundreds of millions of dollars annually." *The Wall Street Journal* confirmed in a 1987 article that more than one-third of the New England companies interviewed indicated they were involved in legal actions with terminated employees, and most cases were settled for cash payments ranging from $1,000 to $50,000, which did not include other benefits such as continued medical, dental, and life insurance coverage, office space, use of telephone, secretarial help, resumé preparation and outplacement guidance while looking for a new job.

The idea for *The Employee Rights Handbook* began in the fall of 1984 when I was interviewed by *The Wall Street Journal* for an article about the rights of terminated workers. Hundreds of terminated employees who read the article began calling me at my New York City office to determine if they had any legal rights after being fired. I began negotiating post-termination benefits for a large number of clients and was surprised to learn that cash settlements and other perks were obtained *a large majority of the time* through my intervention. This has convinced me that the vast majority of private employers are fearful of the repercussions of most firings and are anxious to explore amicable solutions to avoid additional legal expenses, bad publicity and potential damages that sometimes arise.

In one case I obtained a cash settlement of $37,500 for a man who was fired after being falsely accused of drinking too much at lunch. Another executive with nine-plus years of accumulated work time was fired suddenly one late November day. During negotiations, I argued that the firing was unjustified and deprived him of a large year-end bonus he was anticipating and a pension due to vest at the beginning of his tenth year of service. The company eventually paid me a bonus of $50,000 plus severance pay totalling $75,000 (representing one month's salary for each year of service) on my client's behalf and agreed to keep him on unpaid leave for the duration of the year so he would qualify for his vested pension.

Regardless of your experience or the type of job or industry you work in, this book offers practical advice and hundreds of preventive steps to take to help you avoid problems. For example, you will learn how to be hired properly to reduce the chances of exploitation later. You will also understand your on-the-job rights and how companies are obligated to deal fairly and in good faith with long-time workers. In many cases this prohibits them from terminating workers in retaliation after they tattle on abuses of authority—i.e., whistleblowing—and prohibits employers from firing workers merely to deny an economic benefit such as a pension, commission or bonus that has been earned or is about to become due.

The book will instruct you on how to resign properly so you do not forfeit valuable benefits. Additionally, you will learn the correct steps to take when you are fired to protect your rights and increase the chances of obtaining severance compensation and other post-termination benefits. The material will reduce the odds of your being fired unfairly and give you ammunition to maximize claims if you are fired. For example, some states allow terminated workers to sue in tort (as opposed to asserting claims based in contract) and recover punitive damages and money for pain and suffering arising from the firing. Employees who assert tort claims for wrongful discharge sometimes recover large six-figure jury verdicts as a result. Also, innovative lawyers are asserting federal racketeering (RICO) claims seeking criminal sanctions and treble (triple) damages against companies. This is in addition to fraud and misrepresentation claims against individuals responsible for making wrongful termination decisions. Thus, by reading this book, you may be able to recognize when to assert such theories and maximize your claims in the process.

As a practicing labor lawyer, I am consulted by hundreds of individuals each year. To make the book as relevant and useful as possible, I have focused my attention on key topics on which my clients typically seek guidance. Consequently, the practical strategies contained in this book cover areas in which people are commonly exploited and misinformed, and are particularly applicable for:

- College students and those entering the job market for the first time who need to know what negotiating points to discuss and what to ask for before being hired
- Seasoned workers experiencing on-the-job sex harassment, discrimination, invasion of privacy, defamation and other problems
- Long-time workers suddenly fired for no apparent reason
- Loyal employees denied expected benefits and compensation
- Individuals recently fired and denied reasonable severance, favorable job references or unemployment benefits
- Individual sales reps and traditional non-union employees who wish to learn how to protect their jobs and earnings
- People interested in knowing all of their rights before working, while on the job, and after their employment relationship has ended

This book was written to give you the edge. In the following pages you will find hundreds of valuable legal tips pertaining to job-related rights. Armed with this advice, you will become aware of the right steps to take before you accept a job, while you are working, and after an employment relationship has ended. This information will help protect your benefits and your job. In addition, by utilizing this information, you will be able to anticipate and avoid legal hassles before they occur.

To make the book as relevant and useful as possible, I have included numerous questions to ask and points to consider to protect your rights. I have used tables to analyze important subjects on a state-by-state basis. You will also note that I have included actual sample letters and agreements so you can implement many of my suggestions and guidelines. The glossary at the end of the book will help you understand the meaning of many legal terms and concepts and apply them properly.

This book was not meant to replace a lawyer, but it will help you determine whether your problem requires a lawyer's assistance. If you currently have a lawyer, the information will help you make that lawyer work more effectively on your behalf, and it will help you make more intelligent choices and avoid being pressured into making decisions you may not wish to make. I also suggest courses of action to take before consulting a lawyer; such advice may prove invaluable to your lawyer once one has been retained. Finally, you will discover that many of my suggestions can be followed without the help of a lawyer.

Whatever your background, education, age, job skills and work experience, the information in this book will help you detect problems before they occur and will make you aware of the legal consequences of your boss's actions. If litigation becomes necessary, your chances of success and the value of your claim will increase substantially because you will recognize potential exploitation and know what to do about it.

I have provided you with all the practical information my clients receive, but at a fraction of the cost. Thus, you should keep this guide in an accessible place. Read the applicable sections before making a decision, such as when you are offered a job, when you have a problem on the job, before you resign from a job or after you are fired. That is what "preventive law" is all about. Just as wealthy businesspeople and companies keep lawyers on retainer, so you too will now have access to ongoing advice.

The benefits of applying this information can be significant. The following true stories demonstrate what can happen if you don't know your rights.

A 55-year-old man recently came to my office for a consultation after I had been recommended by a friend. The man had spent 20 years working as a middle manager at a financial institution in New York City and was currently earning a salary of $60,000 per annum. Several months before he was fired, my client's supervisor was replaced by another individual and the parties did not seem to hit it off. For the first time in many years, my client received a poor performance evaluation; he was suddenly fired by the bank. The employer offered no severance; my client was told he had been fired "for cause."

The client sought my advice. I advised him that although I could probably not get him his job back, he was entitled to long-term severance pay based on his many years of service. After being retained, I immediately contacted his former employer by letter and implied that legal action would be taken if the matter was not immediately settled in an amicable fashion.

During negotiations, I informed the employer that it had not treated my client fairly. He was a long-time worker who was well-respected within the company, and he had received excellent performance appraisals (except for this last one) and had received regular salary increases and merit bonuses during his tenure. Also, he was never warned that his job was in jeopardy and had passed up other job offers from other employers due to his loyalty and dedication to the current job. In essence, I demonstrated that the firing was caused by unfair, subjective criteria and implied that if the bank hired a person under 40 to take his place, they could be liable for age discrimination.

Almost immediately, the bank offered me a lump sum settlement of $46,153, representing two weeks' pay for each year my client worked for the company. The client accepted this offer and was thrilled with the result.

I later learned that the man initially did not think he had a case and was prepared to go away meekly after being fired. Fortunately, he spoke to the friend who suggested that he consult me "just to be sure." That made all the difference; as a result of the conversation with his friend, my client was richer and more satisfied.

In another case, I recently represented an employee who worked a full year and was expecting a bonus of $7,500 to be paid on February 15 of the following year. The company had a policy of requiring workers to be employed on the date of payment in order to receive the bonus. My client was fired on February 10 for alleged misconduct due to an unauthorized absence taken the day before. The employer refused to pay the bonus or severance and I was hired to collect these monies.

During negotiations, I demonstrated that my client had a valid excuse for missing work on the day in question. Furthermore, I argued that the employer's policy of paying earned bonuses only if the worker was still employed the following year was unfair. Although I was unable to obtain his reemployment with the company, I did manage to obtain a very generous severance pay arrangement plus the expected bonus.

No one should take a job expecting the worst. However, this book will help you recover money for your efforts when you have been wronged. I have reduced complicated court rulings, regulations and labor laws into simple strategies you can understand and follow. For the millions of workers who think they have no job security or protection in the working world, think again—you are about to learn that knowledge is power and that you have more rights in the workplace than you think!

Steven Mitchell Sack, Esq.
New York City

PART I

▌▌▌▌▌▌▌▌▌▌▌▌▌▌▌▌▌▌▌▌▌▌▌▌▌▌▌▌▌▌▌▌▌

HOW TO BE HIRED
PROPERLY

People are exploited in many ways when looking for a job. Some are victimized by discriminatory advertisements and brochures during job recruitment. Others are asked illegal questions during the job interview. Still others rely on phony promises or are subjected to various forms of job misrepresentation.

This first chapter covers problems sometimes encountered before hiring and suggests steps that can be taken to avoid such problems. The information will assist you in discovering how to reduce your chances of being misled by a job offer or being abused during the hiring interview. For example, you will learn when it is illegal for a potential employer to ask you to submit to a lie detector or drug test. You will understand just how far a potential employer can go in obtaining private credit and background information to verify your job qualifications. Additionally, you will learn answers to such questions as: Do you have the right to review and respond to inaccurate information discovered during the hiring process? Can you rely on statements of job security and other promises before you begin working? Are such promises binding? What effect, if any, do disclaimers have in employment applications, job descriptions and letter offers?

This chapter also offers strategies to help you learn how to properly investigate an employer before accepting a job. Many individuals rush too quickly into jobs they know nothing about, often *after* resigning from a good job. They then discover that the new job is not what they expected in terms of remuneration or job duties. This chapter examines ways to investigate potential employers and get answers to simple questions so this does not happen to you.

The second chapter in this section discusses how to be hired properly. The hiring phase is probably the most important part of the employment relationship. During this phase you can increase your job security, acquire additional compensation and benefits, reduce misunderstandings and protect your rights. Unfortunately, most workers do not understand or know

1

how to accomplish this. They accept work without clearly defining the terms of their employment or negotiating for additional terms. Others forget to ask for a written contract; they shake hands with the new employer and assume that everything will go smoothly. Later when problems develop, they learn that their failure to negotiate properly has placed them at a serious legal disadvantage.

In this second chapter you will gain valuable information on how to negotiate for a job. You will discover why it is best to obtain a written contract and how to protect yourself when you don't receive one. I have provided a detailed checklist of key negotiating points to ask and *insist upon*, whatever job you are seeking. You will also learn how to clarify confusing points regarding bonuses, advances and other compensation terms. Sample employment contracts and letter agreements are included for your review and analysis.

The chapter also contains strategies pertaining to points to avoid in any agreement. These include discussion regarding restrictive covenants (also known as covenants not to compete) and other onerous contract provisions.

Finally, the chapter stresses the right questions to ask and correct steps to take *before* accepting any job. Clients typically pay me hundreds of dollars for this advice and I am delighted to share this information with you in this section.

1

■■

AVOIDING PREHIRING
ABUSES

TYPICAL ABUSES

Most employers train and advise staff in charge of hiring applicants to correctly design advertisements and brochures, screen people carefully, avoid misrepresenting any job, and conduct the hiring interview legally to avoid charges of discrimination. Additionally, staff members are taught how to properly investigate a candidate's references and statements on the employment application to avoid charges of defamation and invasion of privacy. Unfortunately, however, some employers do not follow the law. Typical abuses will now be explored in greater detail.

Illegal Advertisements and Brochures

The prospective employee's first exposure to a company sometimes begins after reading an advertisement or brochure. Applicants should be concerned with two potential forms of exploitation in this area.

First, employers may use descriptions in ads and brochures implying that the job is secure. Common words used often include "long-term growth," "permanent," "secure" and "career path." Such words may create an inference that the employer is offering a job which cannot be terminated except for notice or cause. However, most employers have no intention of giving workers additional job security despite such words in ads and brochures. (Note: You will learn in the next chapter that the issue of job security is a point which should be negotiated and confirmed at the hiring interview so you know what kind of job protection, if any, you will be receiving.)

Secondly, employers often draft advertisements and brochures which fail to comply with various federal and state discrimination laws. For example, employers are prohibited from publishing advertisements indicating any preference, limitation, specification or discrimination based on age. The Department of Labor recently published an "Interpretive Bulletin"

3

stipulating that help wanted notices or advertisements containing phrases such as:

- "age 25 to 35 preferred"
- "recent college graduate"
- "sales trainee, any recent degree"
- "sales executive, 2–4 yrs. out of college"

or others of a similar nature discriminated against the employment of older persons when used in relation to a specific job and were illegal.

Such laws apply equally to advertisements which favor men over women, whites over blacks, or any other class of people to the detriment of protected minorities.

■ ■

STRATEGY: *If you read such an ad and believe it discriminates by denying you access to any job interview, contact your nearest Department of Consumer Affairs office, Equal Employment Opportunity Commission office, Division of Human Rights office or the state attorney general's office. You may be able to file charges and obtain damages or force the employer to rewrite the ad as a result.*

■ ■

Employment Applications and Applicant Screening

Proper screening procedures begin with an accurate, detailed job description so that applicants know what type of job is being offered. Generally, candidates are requested to complete a formal application form which contains information pertaining to the candidate's educational background, work experience, references and other pertinent information.

Many employers require candidates to sign lengthy employment applications. Be aware that most employment applications are used to undercut job security, reduce an employer's exposure when investigating your past employment and credit information, and give the employer added grounds for immediate termination when false statements contained in the application are discovered.

The following language was taken from an employment application I recently reviewed for a client:

> I acknowledge that I have given (name of company) the right to make a thorough investigation of my past employment, education and activities without liability, and understand that any false answer, statement or implication made by me in my employment application or at any job interview shall be considered grounds for my immediate discharge.
>
> If hired, I agree to conform to the rules and regulations of (name of company) in all respects. I understand that my employment with and compensation from (name of company) can be terminated at any time

without notice or cause at the option of either of us. I also acknowledge that no representations or promises regarding continued employment for any specified period of time have been made to me during job discussions.

Just as I am free to resign any time without notice, so may the (name of company) terminate me at any time with or without cause and with or without notice. Upon my resignation or termination, I agree to return all company property in my possession or under my control at the company's request.

Most employment applications typically contain a space for the applicant's signature and date, particularly when disclaimers similar to the above are included. Be aware that if you do not allow the potential employer to investigate the private facts of your life or if you refuse to sign such an application, you will probably not be considered for the job. Employers can insist on this requirement and it is legal in most situations.

However, always review employment applications before signing them. Question ambiguous or misleading language. Recognize that particular clauses in the application can and may be used against you at a later date. That is why you should request a copy of the employment application after you have signed it. This can minimize a frequent problem that arises when the application becomes a part of a job dispute or firing but you cannot locate (and the employer won't give you) the application in question.

Finally, be careful not to embellish your past work experience and qualifications. Most employers thoroughly investigate all statements made on job applications these days. Material misstatements are usually dealt with by immediate discharge when discovered, no matter how long or success-fully the person has worked for the company.

Illegal Questions at the Hiring Interview

Twenty years ago, employers could ask almost any question they wanted of an applicant or employee. Questions could be asked about marital status, past arrests, alcohol and drug use, credit history, childbearing plans or age. Now such questions are illegal.

The law has taken great strides to protect female applicants in this area. Questions pertaining to child care and marital status (For example, "Who will look after your child if you are hired? Do you have children? What form of birth control, if any, do you use? If you became pregnant while working would you continue to work? Are you married? Does your husband support your decision to work?") and related matters are illegal.

Generally, employers may ask questions to learn about a candidate's motivation and personality. Such questions can relate to former job respon-sibilities and outside interests.

However, inquiries into an applicant's race, color, age, sex, religion and national origin which further discriminatory purposes are illegal under Title VII of the Civil Rights Act of 1964, as amended. This law applies to private employers, employment agencies, labor organizations and training programs.

Additionally, each state has its own discrimination laws, which often go even further in protecting the rights of applicants during job interviews. Companies must conduct preemployment interviews properly to avoid liability, since innocent questions can often cause employers to face costly and time-consuming charges of discrimination filed with the federal Equal Employment Opportunity Commission and with various other agencies such as the Human Rights Commission, the Civil Liberties Union and the state attorney general's office. If discrimination is found, an applicant may be awarded damages, which may include being offered a job, reimbursement for fees spent for hiring a lawyer and other benefits.

The following chart gives you a better understanding of the kinds of questions that are illegal under federal Equal Employment Opportunity Commission guidelines and state regulations. This chart should be used only as a guide since some questions that are indicated as being illegal can be asked in certain situations (for example, where the applicant is applying for a security-sensitive job).

The potential illegality of such questions must always be examined in the context in which they are asked. However, the chart is instructive since most applicants generally know nothing about their rights in this area.

INTERVIEW QUESTIONS AND THE LAW		
SUBJECT	**LEGAL**	**ILLEGAL**
NAME	What is your full name? Have you ever worked under a different name? If so, what name? What is the name of your parent or guardian? (*but only in the case of a minor job applicant*) What is your maiden name? (*but only to check prior employment or education*)	What are the names of friends and relatives working for the company? Have you ever changed your name by court order or other means?
RESIDENCE	What is your address? How long have you been a resident of this state? of this city? What is your phone number?	Do you rent or own your home? How long have you lived in the U.S.? Do you live with someone? If so, what is your relationship with that person? Do you live in a foreign country?
COLOR		What is your skin coloring?

NATIONAL ORIGIN		What is your ancestry? place of birth? What is your mother's native language? What is your spouse's nationality? What is your maiden name?
CITIZENSHIP	Are you a citizen of the U.S.? If not, do you intend to become one? Do you have a legal right to be employed in this country?	Of what country are you a citizen? Are your parents or spouse naturalized or native-born citizens? When did they acquire citizenship? Are you a native-born citizen?
AGE	Are you old enough to work? Are you between 18 and 65 years of age? If not, state your age.	How old are you? What is your date of birth? Why did you decide to seek employment at your age?
RELIGION		What is your religion? Are you available to work on the Sabbath? What religious holidays do you observe? What church do you attend?
MARITAL STATUS	What is your marital status?	Where does your spouse work? What does your spouse do? When do you plan to marry? Do you plan on having children? Who will care for the children while you work? What is your spouse's health insurance coverage? How much does your spouse earn? What is your view on ERA? Are you a feminist? Do you advocate the use of birth control or family planning? Are you married, single, divorced, separated, engaged or widowed? Are you the head of the household? Are you the principal wage earner? Should we call you Mr., Mrs., Miss, or Ms.?

DISABILITY	Do you have any impairments that interfere with your ability to work in this job? Would you submit to a company physical or provide a doctor's certificate of health after this interview?	Do you have a disability? Have you ever been treated for any of the following diseases? Have you ever been compensated for injuries? How much time have you lost because of illness in the past two years?
ARREST RECORD	Have you ever been convicted of a crime? Do you have a valid driver's license?	Have you ever been arrested? Have you ever pled guilty to a crime? Have you ever been in trouble with the law?
CHILD-CARE RESPONSI-BILITIES	Is there any reason that you will not be able to come to work every day, on time? (only if asked of all applicants)	Do you have any young children at home? Do you have a babysitter? How old are your children?
LANGUAGE	Do you speak a foreign language? If so, which one?	What is your native tongue? How did you acquire the ability to read, write and speak a foreign language?
RELATIVES	Names of relatives already employed by this company.	Names, addresses, age and other pertinent information concerning your spouse, children or relatives not employed by the company. What type of work does your mother/father do?
ORGANIZA-TIONS	List all organizations in which your membership is relevant to this job.	List all clubs, societies and lodges to which you belong.

Based on the preceding chart, you can now understand how often job applicants are exploited in this area (since many illegal questions are typically regarded as routine).

You should also be aware that illegality sometimes arises when employers:

1. Ask applicants for photographs before hiring.
2. Ask applicants for references from clergy before hiring.
3. Ask questions of females which are not asked of males.
4. Ask questions about the applicant's military service in countries other than the U.S.
5. Ask questions about the applicant's military record or type of discharge.

Additionally, employers are not permitted to ask questions about past arrests, since these often end in acquittal, dismissal, withdrawal of charges or overturning of the conviction. Under the Fair Debt Credit Reporting Act, employers are also forbidden to use credit reports for hiring or employment decisions. When such reports are made, you have the right to receive a copy of the report, including the name and address of the credit agency supplying it.

Be aware that employers sometimes design medical history forms which contain discriminatory questions. If you are asked discriminatory questions on a medical form or during a physical exam, you have the right to refuse to answer such questions.

Finally, recognize that discriminatory questions are often asked after the formal interview has concluded (for example, during lunch after the interview but before the decision to hire has been made). Answers to such questions may *not* be considered in the hiring process, and the ramifications of asking illegal questions in such informal settings are just as serious as when they are asked during a formal interview.

Thus, be sure to review all employment applications and forms which contain discriminatory questions and be aware of improper questions during the interview. If you feel that a question is discriminatory, point this out to the interviewer. Be tactful. Explain that you believe the question is illegal and that you decline to answer it for that reason.

Some employers will appreciate your candor and may be impressed by your knowledge of the law. Others may feel you are a threat and may decline to offer you the job. However, if you feel you were denied a job based on a refusal to answer discriminatory questions, contact an appropriate agency to protect your rights. This includes a regional office of the Division of Human Rights in your state, a local chapter of the Civil Liberties Union or a regional office of the Equal Employment Opportunity Commission.

The letter on the following page is an example of how such a complaint may be made.

After sending such a letter, contact the agency to confirm that action is being taken to protect your rights. Speak to a lawyer to determine your rights and options if you are not satisfied with the progress of the investigation. In some states, significant money damages and attorney fees have been awarded to individuals who proved they were denied a job because of refusing to answer discriminatory questions or based on answers to illegal questions.

Job Misrepresentation and Phony Employment Schemes

People are often exposed to phony advertisements and employment schemes promising large income for part-time work or offering jobs with unlimited earning potential. The following is an example of a typical ad:

OVER $1000 PER WEEK possible by working at home. Manage your own time—no prior experience necessary.

Date

Name of Official
Title
Name of Agency
Address

Dear (Name of Official),

This letter is a formal protest against certain hiring practices of (name of Employer) which I believe are illegal.

On (date), I was interviewed by (name and title of employee) for the position of (state). The interview took place at (specify). During the interview, (name of employee) asked the following questions which I believe were illegal under federal and state law (specify):

I explained to the interviewer that such questions were improper and refused to answer them. The interviewer told me such questions were routinely asked of all job candidates and that the interview would be terminated immediately if I chose not to answer them.

The interviewer then told me I had "an attitude problem" and that the position was no longer available. Based on this, I believe I have been victimized by discrimination since I am highly qualified for the job in question and was never given an adequate opportunity to display my qualifications.

I authorize you to investigate this matter on my behalf if it is determined that my charges have merit. You may also institute legal proceedings if appropriate. I am available to meet with you at your office at a mutually convenient date to furnish you with additional details and can be reached at (home address and telephone number).

Thank you for your cooperation and attention in this matter.

Very truly yours,

Your name

SENT CERTIFIED MAIL, RETURN RECEIPT REQUESTED

Newspapers are filled with ads for such jobs. However, the vast majority of these ads are misleading. Applicants sometimes travel great distances (at their own expense) to apply. They then learn that a large amount of some product (for example, $10,000 worth) must be purchased in order to sell for the company and be hired!

Job offers that require people to buy a product before working are not the only common illegal employment scheme. Applicants are sometimes misled by interviewers who oversell by making exaggerated guaranteed earnings claims. For example, applicants are told, "If you come to work for us you will make $100,000 in commission this year, based on what our other salespeople make." People then accept the job based on such representations, not realizing that the statements may be illegal. This is because according to the Federal Trade Commission, a promise of earnings that exceed the average net earning of other employees or sales reps is an unfair and deceptive trade practice.

■ ■

STRATEGY   *Always be on the alert when a potential employer makes claims regarding guaranteed earnings. You have the right to see copies of the wage statements (for example, W-2's or 1099's) of other employees of the company to confirm such claims. If the employer tells you such information is confidential, tell him or her to remove the names of the employees. If the employer refuses to do this or cannot provide ample factual information to support such claims, think twice before accepting the job.*

■ ■

To avoid misleading potential employees, prudent employers hedge by using the following types of phrases when advising applicants of potential earnings. "It is possible you may make $100,000 this year since three out of eight sales reps achieved that figure last year," or "Although not typical, we have had employees who earned as much as $100,000 in a given year."

Some employers also misrepresent the amount and quality of assistance to be rendered. The law is violated when false promises of support are made or when other material terms (for example, exclusive sales territories) are offered which do not exist.

■ ■

STRATEGY   *To protect yourself in this area, always speak directly to the people who will supposedly assist you. Find out what their functions and duties are and how long they have worked for the employer. Talking to people directly will help you form a "gut" opinion and make it easier to determine when false claims have been made.*

■ ■

As a general rule, always be skeptical of work-at-home employment ads. Many ads turn out to be envelope-stuffing pyramid schemes requiring people to purchase introductory mailing lists. These lists typically cost more than people can possibly earn from work-at-home activities.

If you believe you have been victimized by an employment scheme or a work-at-home advertisement, you have many options. Obviously, you can contact a lawyer or Legal Aid service to protect your rights and take action on your behalf. Such action could include filing a private lawsuit based on fraud and misrepresentation. Some lawsuits even allow you to sue the officers of an employer in their individual capacities.

Additionally, you can contact the nearest regional office of the Federal Trade Commission, the Better Business Bureau or the U.S. Post Office. Numerous federal and state laws have been enacted, including the Uniform Deceptive Trade Practices Act, the Racketeer Influenced and Corrupt Organizations Act (RICO), and other labor statutes, preventing employers from engaging in a variety of phony employment schemes or using the mails to further such schemes.

For example, the Federal Trade Commission has the authority to investigate claims and impose cease and desist orders prohibiting the continuation of illegal activity by phony employers. Each state's attorney general's office maintains a division for labor fraud and other related deceptive employment practices. The U.S. Post Office can be of great assistance by issuing a court order preventing employers from using the mails or receiving mail.

■ ■

STRATEGY   *Whenever you are in doubt about a particular employer or an individual representing the employer, contact your local Better Business Bureau. Most Better Business Bureaus maintain lists of employers and individuals accused of engaging in phony employment-related practices. Obtaining such information before accepting employment or participating in a dubious venture can save you a great deal of aggravation and expense down the road.*

■ ■

Try to recognize phony employment schemes and advertisements before problems develop and take immediate action when appropriate.

Abuses by Employment Agencies, Search Firms or Career Counselors

In your anxiousness to find a job, you may risk being exploited by unscrupulous persons or organizations promising to help you find employment. The required placement fee may be exorbitant, you may pay nonrefundable fees for so-called job leads that do not lead to employment, you may be asked illegal discriminatory questions at the initial interview or you may be told that you must register in prescribed training for which the agency gets a fee.

How can you avoid such skullduggery? Here are a few of the ways you can protect yourself from unethical or illegal employment practices:

1. **Know who you are dealing with**. The main purpose of an employment agency is to find a job for you. Career counselors and search firms offer additional services such as resumé and letter preparation and training in interview techniques, as well as providing job-opening leads. Career counselors do not, however, obtain jobs for applicants.

2. **Understand the terms of the arrangement**. Must the agency or counselor be licensed? If so, is it licensed? What services are you to receive? What are the fee terms and who pays the fee (you or the employer)? What must you do? Who pays costs involved? What if you do not take the job that is offered? Does the agency check the history and reliability of the hiring firm? Does the agency have exclusive rights to represent you? And more.

3. **Confirm everything in writing**. While the law says an oral contract is just as binding as a written contract, oral contracts are often difficult to prove. Thus, reduce the arrangement to writing. If you have questions, don't sign a contract until you understand what it will mean to you. If the contract is long and complicated, you may need the advice of a lawyer before signing.

4. **Don't pay money in advance of results**. While it is illegal for employment agencies to charge fees *before* they have found a job for you, career counselors and search firms are allowed to charge up-front fees. Resist such requests because all too often, promised services are not received.

5. **Know in advance what is prohibited**. Check with your local bar association or library for a description of what employment agencies, career counselors and search firms are allowed to do, and what prohibitions exist. In New York State, for example, it is illegal to induce a person to quit a job so that the agency can find new employment for the person, to make false representations or promises, to charge a placement fee for a job where the employer pays the fee, and more.

6. **Seek immediate relief if you have been exploited**. Don't procrastinate if an employment agency or career service takes advantage of you. The longer you wait, the harder it is to prove your case. If the exploitation involves major dollars, contact your attorney immediately. If your loss is of less urgent importance, you can send a certified letter (return receipt requested) to the offending firm. State the reasons for your dissatisfaction and how you would like to see the problem resolved. If the problem is not resolved to your satisfaction, contact your local Department of Consumer Affairs or Better Business Bureau, outlining your complaint in detail. If you are still dissatisfied with the outcome, you can then consider action in a Small Claims Court (see Chapter 8), or you can contact your attorney, or both.

Unfair Job Requirements

Are you a member of a protected minority (for example, black, female, person over 40) who has been barred from applying for a job on the basis of your education or skills? If so, is the education or skills requirement specified in the ad, recruiting brochure or employment opportunity notice really necessary to do the job properly? If not, you may have a valid discrimination claim.

When employers set a higher requirement than is needed for a job just to attract a different kind of applicant, they sometimes inadvertently discriminate against a particular class of applicant; *this is illegal.*

For example, in the case of the *United States* v. *Georgia Power Company,* the requirements of a high school diploma and aptitude test scores by the employer raised a question as to whether such requirements were really related to successful job performance. The diploma requirement was found to be unlawful since it did not measure an individual's ability to do the job. In fact, the court determined that since blacks, as opposed to whites, were more likely not to have completed high school in Georgia in the late 1960's and early 1970's, such a requirement essentially excluded them from working for the company.

Thus, if you are a member of a protected minority and believe you are being unfairly excluded from applying for employment due to unfair job requirements, you may wish to speak to a representative from a regional office of the federal Equal Employment Opportunity Commission or state Division of Human Rights.

Applicant References

The majority of states limit an employer's ability to make preemployment inquiries regarding criminal arrests and convictions more than ten years before and restrict the use of such information. However, many employers conduct thorough background checks of applicants before hiring. In fact, when companies fail to investigate an applicant's background and they hire a person unfit for the position who causes harm or injury to another, they are sometimes liable under a legal theory referred to as negligent hiring and retention.

Employers may also be liable to the applicant and employee under legal claims (including defamation, intentional infliction of emotional distress and violations of the implied covenant of good faith and fair dealing) when references are not investigated properly or are leaked to nonessential third parties. (Note: Libel suits filed by discharged employees and job applicants now account for approximately one-third of all defamation actions, and the average winning verdict exceeds $100,000 for such cases.)

Be aware that you may have rights in the event that harmful confidential information (for example, credit references) is communicated to nonessential third parties to your detriment. For more information and strategies on this subject, consult the section in Chapter 8 which discusses defamatory job references.

Preemployment Drug Testing

Experts suggest that as many as 25% of the major corporations in the United States now engage in drug screening before hiring new employees; such tests are on the rise, particularly in high technology and security-conscious industries.

Drug tests have generally been upheld as legal, particularly with respect to job applicants (as opposed to employees who are asked to submit to random tests as a requisite for continued employment). Applicants have fewer rights to protest such tests than employees. The reason is that drug tests are generally not viewed as violating people's privacy rights since applicants are told in advance they must take and pass the test to get the job and that all applicants must submit to such tests even to be considered for employment.

However, the right to test does not give potential employers the right to handle test results carelessly. Unwarranted disclosure of this information can result in huge damages, so be aware that you have rights in this area. You may also have rights in the event you are refused a job because you allegedly failed a test and it is determined later that there was a mistake in the test results (in other words, that the test results were really negative).

Speak to a lawyer immediately if you are denied employment for allegedly failing a drug test when you know this cannot be so, if you are fired shortly after accepting employment for allegedly failing a test, or if the results of a failed test are conveyed to nonessential third parties, causing you humiliation and embarrassment. (Note: Chapter 3 in Section II, dealing with on-the-job rights of employees, covers the legality and strategies of drug and alcohol tests for workers in more detail.)

Preemployment Lie Detector Tests

Drug testing is not the only new hurdle confronting job applicants. Polygraph, personality and so-called honesty tests are now being offered by more companies each year.

The use of polygraph or lie detector exams by private employers has become the subject of increased scrutiny and criticism. In the past, employers resorted to such tests to verify statements on job applications and to reduce employee theft and other forms of dishonesty. However, the tests generally came to be viewed as violating a person's fundamental rights regarding free speech, privacy, self-incrimination and the right to be free from illegal search and seizure.

On December 27, 1988, the federal Polygraph Protection Act of 1988 was enacted. Prior to that date, 24 states and the District of Columbia either limited or forbade the use of lie detectors in the employment context. Some states prohibited an employer from demanding or requiring that employees and applicants take a lie detector exam; other jurisdictions adopted broader prohibitions preventing employers from even suggesting, soliciting or requesting submission to such tests.

The new law now forbids the use of such tests in all states which previously allowed them. Additionally, it prohibits use of such tests (defined as any mechanical or electrical device used to render a diagnostic opinion regarding honesty) in all *preemployment screening* as well as in discharge and disciplinary proceedings. Thus, applicants generally cannot be asked to submit to such tests.

Most states have also enacted strong laws protecting job applicants from stress tests, psychological evaluation tests and other honesty tests. If you are asked to submit to such a test as a condition of being offered a job and believe that the test is either unfair, harmful or distasteful, it may be a good idea to investigate the particular law in your state before acting in this area.

TIPS TO AVOID BEING HIRED BY A DECEITFUL EMPLOYER

No matter what type of job you are considering, you should *investigate* the potential employer even if you desperately need the job. This should always be done *before* accepting employment. Typical information you would like to learn includes facts regarding the employer's business reputation, credit rating, financial status, rate of employee turnover, morale problems with workers, whether the company has been involved in any employee-related lawsuits recently (and if so, did the employee win or lose?) and commitments to the community in which the company is located.

For example, if you are being hired to replace someone in an important position, try to obtain the name of the person you might be replacing and find out why the individual is no longer there. Better still, by speaking to that person you could learn valuable information to influence your decision. Many applicants who follow this advice discover that the individual decided to resign because he or she was being harassed on the job by a supervisor, the job was long and tedious, or promised commissions, bonuses, raises and promotions were not given.

It is particularly important to do your homework when you are being offered an important position that includes long-term employment, stock options, profit sharing and other valuable financial benefits. Such an investigation should be made to assess the chances that the employer has sufficient assets to pay these benefits or that the employer will still be in business when you retire.

Most lawyers and accountants who represent successful business clients obtain the following kinds of financial information from credit reporting agencies (such as Dunn & Bradstreet) and the banks with whom the company does its business. The following list of questions is a good starting point in this area.

1. What is the legal form of the employer? Is it a corporation, an S corporation, a partnership or a sole proprietorship? (Note: You should know the legal distinctions among these terms for additional protection.)
2. What are the names of the principal shareholders or partners?
3. What is the financial history of the employer? Is it a recently established business or has it been in existence for a while? (Note: Many new businesses fail within the first few years, hurting employees in the process by firing them suddenly and not paying adequate severance benefits. I always instruct clients wishing to join nonestablished employers to proceed with caution because such a move may be risky.)
4. With whom does the employer maintain banking relations? For how long has it done so? What is the average balance on deposit? Does the employer have a line of credit? If so, for how much?
5. How many people work for the company? Do any of them belong to a union? Is the employer opposed to union participation? Could you join a union if asked? What additional benefits would you receive if you joined a union? Has the employer recently been involved in any litigation with any of its employees? What was the lawsuit about? Did the employer win? What was the effect on employee morale? What is the rate of employee turnover?
6. Does the employer offer generous benefits? These include such items as liberal sick day and vacation policies, paid maternity and paternity leaves, etc., and will be discussed in greater detail in the next chapter.
7. Has the employer filed a recent financial statement? Was it a certified statement? (Note: Certified financial statements are usually more accurate and verifiable than regular financial statements.) What are the company's assets and liabilities? Does it have an unusually high late-paying accounts receivables problem? (Note: This might indicate a cash flow problem and potential bankruptcy situation if the receivables aren't paid.)
8. What are the employer's assets? Does it own real estate, patents, inventions, licenses and other tangible assets?
9. What does the latest balance sheet reveal? This is an important document. It shows the employer's financial status on the last date of the reported fiscal year. For example, you can learn what the employer owns in terms of cash, marketable securities, accounts receivable, inventory, property and equipment. The balance sheet will also indicate money owed for unpaid bills and taxes, loan repayments to banks, bondholders and other lenders. You may also be able to determine the amount of the employer's working capital, costs of doing business, and other pertinent

information. If you are being hired for an important position and are given stock or stock options, be sure that you obtain copies of such documents for the current year and several past years of the employer's operations.

10.   What are the liabilities of the employer? Are there any outstanding encumbrances, judgments or liens?

11.   Has the business been sold recently? Did the new owners assume the liabilities or just purchase the assets? *This is important.* Suppose you are owed bonuses which the old employer refuses to pay. The new owners may be able to step away from this obligation if they only purchased the company's assets and not its liabilities.

12.   Who administers the employer's pension plan? Is it a reliable company?

You should never accept a new job blindly, particularly when a high salary and other substantial benefits are offered. Negotiating a job is a two-way street. The employer spends much time and expense verifying the personal background, job qualifications and prior references of job applicants. You should try to gather as much information as possible on the employer's history, management style and financial stability as well. In certain instances, what you learn may give you second thoughts—you may come to suspect that you will not be promoted properly or even that the company may not be around in the future.

Thus, try to gather as much information as possible before making your decision. Talk to fellow workers; listen to what they say. Many are accessible and honest and will give you a true picture of the way the employer really runs its business (as opposed to what you're told at the interview).

Better still, speak to friends and business associates in the industry to learn more about the employer's business reputation. For example, if you learn names of customers, suppliers or distributors of the employer, it may be a good idea to inquire discreetly to learn their opinions about the company. What you learn may surprise you. The same is true for reputable employment agencies who have dealt with the employer in the past and can tell you about the company's reputation and business methods.

Finally, if you are about to work for a large company, you may be able to locate written information in the business press. Check the microfiche files in a good library for articles in leading business publications. Major general news magazines usually have extensive business coverage for your edification.

Remember, ask questions and do your homework. You may learn information that will save you money and aggravation in the future.

2

NEGOTIATING THE JOB

S mart applicants never accept employment until they have carefully discussed and clarified all key terms, conditions and responsibilities of the job up front, no matter what type of job is being offered. You risk being exploited when you fail to do so. When key terms (including the compensation arrangement and benefits package) are not agreed on before the hiring, the law will not generally impute such rights and you cannot force an employer to give valuable benefits not promised before the start date after you begin working.

Never be afraid to negotiate. Remember that a successful job negotiation is one of give and take. Obviously, the more points you insist on, the more benefits and protections you will obtain. Be aware, however, that certain employer policies may not be negotiable. Salary, title, duties, authority and such are fair game for negotiation. On the other hand, fringe benefit, profit sharing and pension programs usually are fixed and not open to negotiation. Reviewing your prospective employer's employee handbook or personnel manual will give you a good idea of where the flexibilities and inflexibilities are. Types of negotiations and strategies you can use are discussed in the following pages.

Most well-run companies respect applicants who thoroughly negotiate their jobs. Thus, use the following checklist of negotiating points wisely. Even if you cannot negotiate many of the points cited below, you can minimize disappointment and confusion by knowing what to expect after you begin working. Thorough negotiations can also reduce potential litigation claims arising from breach of contract, wrongful discharge and other legal problems which frequently arise during and after the employment relationship has ended.

Finally, do not expect to get everything you request. However, by understanding the nature of successful job negotiations and the many options that are available, you can receive additional benefits and protection merely by recognizing what to ask for.

CHECKLIST OF KEY NEGOTIATING POINTS TO COVER DURING THE HIRING INTERVIEW

The following checklist is divided into three main sections: (A) The Job; (B) Job Security, and (C) Salary and Benefits. Where appropriate, detailed "strategies" have been inserted into the checklist for further information. (Additional negotiating points for salespeople and others who earn commissions are provided in Chapter 8.)

The Job

1. *Job description* (Understand the nature of the job being offered.)
2. What is your *title*?
3. What will be your *job functions*? Will you report to a superior? If so, who?
4. When are you expected to *begin working*? (start date)
5. What is your *employment status*?
    a. Are you considered a regular full-time employee eligible for all employer-provided fringe benefits? (as opposed to a part-time or exempt employee paid on an hourly basis with limited fringe benefits)
    b. Are you considered an employee or an independent contractor? (As an independent contractor, you may be required to pay all federal, state and local withholding taxes, social security and other taxes. However, there are certain advantages to being hired as an independent contractor which will be discussed later in this chapter.)
    c. Are you being hired as a *consultant*? If so, can you work for other companies, have outside work and sidelines, etc.? This too will be discussed later in the chapter.

Job Security

1. Will you be given *job security*? (As opposed to merely being hired at will, which gives the employer the right to fire you at any time with or without notice and with or without cause.)
2. If so, what kind of job security is being offered?

■ ■

STRATEGY 1   *Your objective in negotiating for job security is to avoid being fired suddenly at the employer's discretion.*

■ ■

The best job security to obtain is to be employed for a definite term—for example, two years. This means that the employer cannot fire you prior to the expiration of that term except for a compelling reason—that is, for cause. Most employers are reluctant to hire people for a definite term because it reduces their ability to fire employees at any time. Thus, always ask for a definite term when being hired. Use your discretion as to the amount of job security you request. Your request can range from six months to several years. Tell the employer you want an *X* year contract; the employer will know what you mean.

STRATEGY 2 *If the employer refuses to hire you for a definite term, ask for a guarantee that you cannot be fired except for cause or as long as you achieve certain goals (for example, a minimum sales quota if you are being hired as a salesperson). This request can give you needed protection without locking the employer into a time frame.*

STRATEGY 3 *If this request is refused, ask to be guaranteed a written warning within a definite period of time (for example, 30 days to cure alleged deficient performance) before being fired. This will protect you from a sudden firing, and some employers will accept this. Or you can ask for a written notice of termination (for example, 30 days before the contract will end) before the effective termination date so that you can plan ahead and look for other employment while still collecting a paycheck.*

STRATEGY 4 *If the employer refuses #3, request pay in lieu of notice in the event you are fired without warning; for example, ask to receive two weeks' additional pay at your current salary level in the event you are fired suddenly. (Note: This is in addition to severance pay more fully discussed below.)*

STRATEGY 5 *Be sure you understand if you are being hired for a probationary period. Some employers establish a probationary period (for example, the first 90 days of employment) ranging from 30 to 120 days to evaluate an employee's performance. If you are hired for a probationary period but are fired before the end of the period, you may be entitled to receive salary and other benefits until the end of the probationary period in certain situations.*

Salary and Other Benefits

1. What is your *base salary* and when is it payable? Understand all deductions from your paycheck.
2. When does the *pay week* start and end?

3. If payday falls on a holiday, when are paychecks distributed?
4. Is *overtime offered*? If so, at what rate? Is there a seniority basis for offering overtime (for example, a policy that overtime is first offered to long-time workers). Note: Most states, in addition to federal law, require that overtime must be paid whenever a part-time or hourly employee works in excess of 40 hours per week. Special employees working in government contracting or subcontracting work may also be required to be paid overtime if they work more than eight hours on any given day. Discuss this if relevant.
5. Will you be required to outlay *expenses*? If so, are expenses reimbursable? Be sure you know the kind and amount of expenses that are reimbursable. Be sure you understand the kind of documentation to be supplied to the employer for reimbursement and how long you must wait before reimbursement.
6. Are you entitled to *commissions*? If so, understand how commissions are earned, the commission rate and when commissions are paid. (See Chapter 8.)
7. Are you to receive a *bonus*? If so, how is it calculated and when is it paid? Is the bonus gratuitous (in other words, merely paid at the employer's whim and discretion in an amount determined solely by the employer) or is it enforceable by contract with a verifiable sum linked to some specific formula (profits, revenue, output, etc.)?

Many people fail to understand their rights regarding bonuses and are later disappointed or exploited. For example, while some people work a full year counting on a bonus and don't receive it, others receive bonuses that are not even closely related to what they were expecting. But that is not the worst problem that frequently arises. Employers sometimes fire individuals after the bonus has technically been earned (at the end of the year) but before it is distributed (on February 15 of the following year). They then tell the ex-employee that he or she must be working for the company at the time the bonus is paid in order to collect!

These common abuses can be avoided by understanding and negotiating the following:

■ ■

STRATEGY 1   *Request a verifiable bonus that is not subject to the employer's discretion. Specify the amount, when it will be paid, and that there are to be no strings or conditions attached. In other words, treat the bonus as part of your salary package; this will increase your legal rights in the event you are not paid.*

■ ■

STRATEGY 2   *Request a pro rata bonus in the event you resign or are fired prior to the bonus being paid. For example, if the bonus is computed on sales volume and you work a full year and resign or are fired on December 1 of that year, you should be able to receive eleven-twelfths of the expected bonus. Many employers will accept this provided you give ample notice before the resignation and you are not fired for misconduct (that is, for cause).*

STRATEGY 3   *Avoid allowing the employer the right to arbitrarily determine when and if a bonus will be paid and in what amount. This arrangement is considered a gratuitous bonus which may not be enforceable by contract. When an employer controls the timing, amount and whether or not to pay a bonus at all, or states that the money is paid in appreciation for continuous, efficient, or satisfactory service, employees have a weaker chance to recover an expected bonus from the employer when they are not paid.*

STRATEGY 4   *Resist arrangements which require you to be on the job after a bonus is earned in order to receive it. If the employer insists on this condition, negotiate the right to receive a bonus if you are fired due to a business reorganization, layoff or for any reason other than gross misconduct.*

STRATEGY 5   *Get it in writing. Verbal promises to pay bonuses are not always enforceable. Confirm your understanding in writing for additional protection. (Note: You will learn how to do this effectively in another section of this chapter.)*

STRATEGY 6   *Are additional services required in order to earn the bonus? If so, promises to pay a bonus for work, labor or services already completed at the time the promise is made may not be valid.*

STRATEGY 7   *Try to link the bonus to some verifiable formula (for example, gross profits or sales volume). Such an arrangement can give you extra legal protection; in the event you are not paid a correct amount, you would be able to verify the bonus from the company's books and records. In fact, if a bonus-enforceable-by-contract arrangement could be proved in court, you would have the right to inspect the employer's books and records in a lawsuit.*

Many employers are reluctant to base bonuses on verifiable components because they are aware of the vulnerability to exposure in a lawsuit. However, you should leave nothing up to chance when negotiating a bonus.

You want to know precisely how the bonus is to be earned and steps to take (for example, the right to be given company records for review) in the event you are not paid what you believe you are owed. Insist on nothing less.

8. What *fringe benefits* will you receive?

Most employees fail to properly negotiate extra compensation in the form of fringe benefits. Many forms of fringe benefits are even more valuable than salary because they are nontaxable. Don't forget to ask for fringe benefits during the negotiating process.

The following detailed summary of fringe benefits will be helpful in this area:

> *Insurance benefits:* These include basic group term life insurance, basic accidental death and dismemberment coverage, optional group term life insurance, dependent term life insurance, optional accidental death and dismemberment insurance, business travel accident insurance, weekly income accident and sickness plans, illness payment plans, short- and long-term disability insurance plans, medical benefit plans, dental benefit plans and legal benefit plans.

This list is not meant to be all-inclusive. Rather, it gives you an idea about the kinds of benefits that are available. However, most insurance benefits are not negotiable since employers must offer them to all employees so as not to be liable for charges of discrimination.

> *Other benefits:* These can include the use of an automobile, free parking, car insurance, gasoline allowance, death benefits, prepaid legal services, credit cards, loans at reduced rates of interest with favorable repayment schedules and other perks. Be sure you know *all* the elements of your benefit package and don't be afraid to negotiate extra benefits when appropriate.

> *Pensions and profit-sharing plans:* Are you entitled to additional compensation in the form of tax qualified plans including defined benefit, profit-sharing, money purchase and pension plans? Other benefits you should also be aware of are social security benefits, Individual Retirement Accounts (IRA's), 401(k) plans, thrift plans, stock bonus plans and employee stock ownership plans (ESOPs).

All of these plans are extra financial perks to help you accumulate additional revenue for financial security and your retirement. Be sure you understand what benefits the employer offers in this area and what contributions will be made on your behalf. Other questions to ask are:

- Are you required to contribute matching sums of money? If so, how much will this cost you? Can you increase or decrease matching contributions at your discretion? If so, is notice required and how much?

- Does the investment accumulate tax-free?
- Can the money be taken prior to your retirement? If so, is there a penalty?
- What happens if you resign or are fired for cause? Is the money forfeited?
- What happens if the company is sold or goes bankrupt? Is the money protected?
- Who administers the plan benefits? How can you be sure that there are no funding liabilities—in other words, how can you be sure that monies will be set aside as promised? Are the plan benefits invested in such a manner as to preclude large losses?
- If as a result of an acquisition through the purchase of the company you are laid off, how will COBRA and ERISA laws apply? ERISA (Employee Retirement Income Security Act) as modified by COBRA (Consolidated Omnibus Budget Reconciliation Act of 1986) is a federal law designed to protect your (and your beneficiaries') pension and other benefit rights when you are laid off. Note that ERISA does not apply to employment by churches or federal, state, or local governments, or by companies with 20 or fewer employees, and may not apply if it can be proven that your termination was for gross misconduct. However, in most situations, these laws ensure that money previously set aside on your behalf will be given to you, regardless of internal changes or organizational restructuring in your company.

All of these points and many more should be explored and explained to your satisfaction. Since these financial benefits can account for a large part of additional compensation, never overlook their importance. Always negotiate to receive the maximum amount of benefits available.

Raises and job advancement: Are periodic raises given? What is the procedure for merit raises and job advancement?

■ ■

STRATEGY   *Employees are sometimes disappointed by the size of annual or periodic merit increases or the speed of job advancement. To avoid problems in this area, be sure you know how such increases are determined. Avoid situations where the amount of the raise or promotion is determined by one person's subjective decision. If it is, request the right to appeal the supervisor's decision and discuss how this may be accomplished.*

■ ■

Relocation expenses: This is money often paid to employees who are required to relocate.

Points to discuss and negotiate include questions like: How much relocation pay will be given?; When is it payable and who will pay for it?; Are taxes taken out of the payments? Be sure to determine whether you need to furnish supporting documentation (copies of bills for legal fees incurred in a house closing, etc.) in order to receive reimbursement. Also, ask what arrangements will be made if you resign or are terminated within a short period of time.

■ ■

STRATEGY   Do not *allow the employer to unilaterally cancel reloca-tion expenses if the job doesn't work out, because you may have relocated yourself and your family thousands of miles at great expense with no protection. If you are planning to relocate to a distant location, always receive assurances in writing that relocation expenses will be paid regardless of how long you work for the company.*

■ ■

Severance pay: Does the employer have a definite stated policy regarding severance? (e.g., two weeks of severance for each year of employment).

Inquire whether severance is paid if you resign as opposed to being fired. Some companies do not pay severance upon resignations and do not pay severance when the termination is for cause.

Vacation pay: How much vacation pay you get often depends on your salary grade, type of job offered and how well you negotiate.

Be sure you understand how vacation pay is computed and other important matters regarding the granting of vacation time. Consider the following as starting points:

- Must vacation days be used in the year they are granted, or can they be carried over to the next year? If they can't, can a prorated share, for example, one-half the days, be carried over?
- How long must you work in order to be qualified?
- Does the amount of vacation time increase depending on the number of years with the company? (for example, two weeks of vacation pay for the first five years, increasing to three weeks of paid vacation from years 6–10).
- Must vacation days be taken all at once, or can they be staggered? If so, how?
- How much notice are you required to give before you can take vacations?
- Are there times during peak seasonal demands when requests will not be granted?

- If the employee leaves or is terminated, will you be paid for all unused vacation time?

This last point should be considered carefully. Employees frequently leave their jobs expecting to receive large payments for unused vacation (carried over for several years) but are denied payment in this regard. Some states, including California, require companies to pay accrued vacation pay in all circumstances, even when the employee is fired for cause. Thus, check with the Department of Labor in your state or speak to competent legal counsel where applicable.

Personal days: Personal days give you a chance to attend to personal business, religious observances or special occasions. Some companies add them to vacation time with pay. Others only allow personal days without pay. In addition, inquire about absences due to medical and dental appointments, bereavement pay, military leave, paternity leaves, appearance in court and jury duty.

Employers are not required by law to allow employees personal leaves of absence, but must apply such practices consistently to all employees if they do. If you are considering taking an extended leave, what about the continuation of medical benefits during this period? Ask whether medical and other benefits terminate at the end of the month when the leave becomes effective. Can you keep those benefits in effect during the absence period by continuing to pay your payroll deductions?

Also, be aware that federal law prohibits companies from requiring employees to work an extended period of time (such as 12 months) before being allowed to take unpaid personal leaves. The Equal Employment Opportunity Commission (EEOC) has ruled that such a policy has a disparate impact on women who desire to nurse their newborn children. Also, ask if your job is guaranteed when you return from an an extended leave.

Disability leave: If you will be a full-time employee you are entitled to disability leave should you become unable to work due to a nonoccupational illness.

Note: A company cannot treat pregnancy-related disability or maternity leave differently than it treats other forms of disability leaves of absence. This is explained in greater detail in Chapter 5.

Disability: What happens in the event you are disabled? Can you receive salary and other benefits for a predetermined period of time? Define the meanings of temporary disability and permanent disability and know what ramifications will ensue in the event of such disability to reduce misunderstandings.

Other Matters of Concern

In addition to financial benefits, job security and duties, there are many other matters to discuss at the hiring interview. The following checklist will cover concerns often enunciated by the employer (which may or may not be relevant depending upon your particular situation):

1. Are you required to protect confidential information and trade secrets acquired while working for the company? If so, agree how this can be accomplished.
2. Can you have side ventures in a noncompeting business or must you work exclusively for the company on a full-time basis?
3. Who owns inventions and processes created by you during employment?
4. Will disputes be resolved by litigation or binding arbitration? Can the prevailing party recover attorneys' fees and court costs from the losing party?
5. To perform your job better and reduce misunderstandings, it is also wise to receive information regarding the following policies:

- Time clock regulations
- Rest periods
- Absences
- Safety and accident prevention
- Authorized use of telephones
- Reporting complaints
- Making suggestions
- Resolving disputes
- Personal appearance rules
- Solicitation rules
- Conflict of Interest and Code of Ethic Rules

Restrictive Covenants   Does the company require you to sign a contract containing a restrictive covenant prohibiting you from working for a competitor or calling on customers previously solicited during your employ? If so, does the company require all new employees to sign similar contracts?

Restrictive covenants are provisions in employment agreements that prohibit a person from directly competing or working for a competitor after leaving his or her employer. The effect of such clauses varies greatly. For example, they can:

1. Restrict an employee from working for a competitor of the former employer.

2. Restrict an employee from starting a business or forming a venture with others that competes against the former employer.

3. Restrict an employee from contacting or soliciting former or current customers or employees of the employer.

4. Restrict an employee from using confidential knowledge, trade secrets and other privileged information learned while working for the former employer.

5. Restrict an employee from any of the above both in geographic or time limitations.

The above points are illustrated by the following clauses taken from employment agreements:

"For a period of one (1) year following the termination of your employment for any reason, it is agreed that you will not contact or solicit any person, firm, association or corporation to which you sold products of the Company during the year preceding the termination of your employment."

"Upon termination of the Doctor's employment under this Agreement for any reason, the Doctor shall not engage in the practice of neurology or open his own office for the practice of neurology or associate himself with other physicians within a five (5) mile radius of the office of the Corporation or a five mile radius of any hospital for which the Doctor has worked on behalf of the Corporation for a period of one (1) year after the effective date of termination."

"In consideration of compensation paid to me as an employee, I hereby recognize as the exclusive property of the employer and agree to assign, transfer and convey to the employer, every invention, discovery, concept, idea, process, method and technique which I become acquainted with as a result or consequence of my employment and agree to execute all documents requested by the employer to evidence its ownership thereof."

You may be surprised to learn, however, that such clauses are not always enforceable. Although every case is different, judges have been taking dimmer views of such attempts to restrict an employee's livelihood. Consult Chapter 8 for more information about the weight such clauses can carry once you are fired or resign.

Whether or not such covenants are legal, however, defending lawsuits involving restrictive covenants is time-consuming and expensive, so you should avoid signing such agreements in the first place. Many employers have a tendency to "hang" such a clause over individuals by threatening to institute legal action after a person's resignation or termination. This can discourage you from contacting prospective employers and customers in your industry and trade or establishing your own business. Thus, consider the following strategies for help in this area:

■ ■ ■ ■ ■ ■ ■ ■ ■ ■ ■ ■ ■ ■ ■ ■ ■·■ ■ ■ ■ ■ ■ ■ ■ ■ ■ ■ ■ ■ ■ ■ ■ ■ ■ ■

STRATEGY 1   *Carefully review and resist signing contracts containing restrictive covenants. An employee who works without an employment contract and who leaves without taking any trade secrets has total freedom to work elsewhere in the same industry. This generally includes the right to solicit the ex-employer's customers. However, you may be subjecting yourself to a lawsuit (even when no valid grounds exist) by signing an agreement containing such a clause.*

Always read your employment contract carefully before signing it. What does the restrictive covenant say? For example, does it prohibit you from working for a competitor or calling on customers you previously sold for the company for an excessive period (i.e., two years)? If so, make the employer aware of this. Negotiate to reduce the covenant to a reasonable period you can live with (e.g., three months) and insist on the right to receive continued salary and other benefits while the restrictive covenant is in effect. Remember, everything is negotiable before you sign on the bottom line. Once the agreement is signed, however, you may be bound by its terms.

■ ■

STRATEGY 2   *Always obtain a copy of the agreement after it is signed. Many people forget to do this. After they resign or are discharged and receive a formal demand requesting them to refrain from certain acts (usually in the form of a written cease and desist letter), they cannot locate the agreement containing the restrictive provision. This places them at a disadvantage. For example, they may be unable to obtain an accurate opinion from a lawyer if he or she cannot review the contract or may be forced to spend unnecessary legal fees trying to obtain a copy from the employer. Thus, request a copy of all documents that you sign and store them in a safe place for later review.*

■ ■

Confirming These Points in Writing

Once you and the company have agreed to key terms, it is essential to confirm the deal *in writing*. Legal disputes often arise when people are hired on a handshake. A handshake, or oral agreement, indicates only that the parties came to some form of agreement; it does not say what the agreement was. Failure to spell out important terms often leads to misunderstandings and disputes. Even when key terms are discussed, the same spoken words that are agreed upon have different meanings from the employee's and company's perspective. Written words limit this sort of misunderstanding.

Although a written contract cannot guarantee you will be satisfied with the company's performance, it can provide additional remedies in the event of the employer's nonperformance. Once the agreement is signed, the law presumes that the parties incorporated their intentions into the contract. The instrument "speaks for itself" and courts will not hear testimony about understandings or discussions before the contract was signed unless the information is necessary to interpret ambiguous terms or establish particular trade customs.

Additionally, be aware that clauses in written contracts can give you negotiating strength. For example, some employment contracts state that terms cannot be changed without the written consent of both parties. If such a clause was included in your contract and an employer attempted to reduce your salary or other benefits, this could not be done without your written approval.

Written contracts also protect employees who are fired in a manner prohibited by the contract. The following is an example of a situation that could occur:

> Andrew received a one-year contract to work as an advertising executive. The contract stated that it would be automatically renewed for an additional year if notice of termination was not received at least 90 days prior to the expiration of the first year. Andrew's company gave him notice that the contract would not be renewed one week prior to the start of the next year. Andrew sued for damages; the court ruled that he was entitled to additional compensation since the employer failed to abide by the terms of the agreement.

Working on a handshake for an indefinite period of time is a risky proposition. In most states, the law says that if you are hired without a written contract and for a nonspecific period of time, you are *hired at will.* This means that, subject to various exceptions outlined in later chapters of this book, your employer can fire you at any time without notice and without cause.

The at-will doctrine developed in the 1800's during the transition from the master–servant relationship of employment to the application of contract law. The legal concept was "mutuality of obligation." It was reasoned that if an employee could quit his job without notice, the employer also had the right to terminate an employee for any reason or for no reason.

A number of states have recognized the inequality of power between the employee and the employer, and have found ways to modify the at-will doctrine. These are listed in the table in Chapter 5, entitled COMPENDIUM OF STATES RECOGNIZING EXCEPTIONS TO THE EMPLOYMENT-AT-WILL DOCTRINE.

Due to the unfairness of the at-will doctrine, which affects hundreds of thousands of employees each year, many more people are no longer accepting being hired on a handshake. Now, they are recognizing that they can be better protected by including favorable clauses in clearly drafted contracts and are insisting on receiving written agreements whenever they accept a job.

A good employment contract should describe in specific detail all important aspects of your employment, such as term of the contract, duties, authority and responsibility, job description and title, compensation and reimbursement, benefits, termination, and methods for resolving disputes, such as arbitration, mediation, and more.

There are three purposes for every written contract. First, the act of writing helps ensure that both parties to the contract understand and agree to its terms. Second, the written word provides a reminder to both parties of the terms of the agreement. Third, the written, signed, and witnessed contract can serve as evidence if legal action is required to enforce the terms. Each employment contract must be drafted to meet specific situations, needs and understandings for both the employee and the employer.

Everything in the contract should be very specific. Anything that is vague or open for later negotiation creates a potential misunderstanding, and may fail to carry weight in a court of law. So be sure to cover everything that is important to you, and be sure that all understandings based on your discussions and negotiations are included in the written words of the contract. Consider, for example:

- Compensation: salary, salary increases, bonus program and requirements, profit sharing, etc.
- Job description: statement of job duties, authorities, responsibilities, title, etc.
- Terms of employment: contract period and provision for renewal, at-will, etc.
- Fringe benefits: pension plan (and when vested), life and health insurance, savings plan, company contribution, etc.
- Vacation time: number of days, when earned, carryover, etc.
- Sick leave: number of days, conditions for allowance, salary and benefits continuance during extended health-based absences, etc.
- Arbitration: provision for arbitration or mediation in the event of unreconcilable disagreements affecting the basis of a term in the employment agreement.
- Termination/resignation: terms leading to employment termination or allowing no-fault resignation, with terms for payment and continuation of benefits upon leaving the company's employment, etc.
- Special provisions: office facilities, parking space, dining room rights, recreational facilities, health-maintenance programs, medical examinations, company car or equivalent, bonding, liability coverage (and indemnification), etc.

Don't stop here, however. Consider all of the things that are important to you related to the job, its benefits, its responsibilities and its expectations, both positive and potentially negative. Consider what will happen if the economic fortunes of the company fade. What if your job or department is abolished? What if the firm is taken over by another firm? Will you, as the newest employee, be the first to be laid off? Or do you have employment protection? If not, are there provisions for termination payments if you are invited to leave?

Following is an example of a special type of contract, one between a professional sales representative and a company seeking help in selling its product or service. Note that this contract is written in "plain English" in contrast to "legalese." A growing number of states now require that all contracts must be written in language that is clearly understood by those not trained in the legal profession.

The terms in the example contract are as appropriate for an individual sales representative as they are for an incorporated organization providing sales representation services. The essence of this type of agreement is that the sales representative is an independent contractor (non-employee) engaged by a principal (company seeking sales representation from the independent contractor).

Note that in paragraph 9, the agreement provides that it may not be terminated except upon 60 days' written notice. This is the kind of protection you should negotiate for and include in a written agreement for protection, regardless of the type of job or industry. Since this agreement is included for illustrative purposes only, do *not* use such an agreement without first consulting with a competent labor attorney.

Whenever you obtain an employment contract or any business document, read it carefully. Question all ambiguous and confusing language. Consult a lawyer if you do not understand the meaning of any terms. Remember that contracts prepared by employers usually contain clauses which work to your disadvantage. Thus, you should review the agreement thoroughly before signing.

SAMPLE SALES REPRESENTATION CONTRACT

This AGREEMENT dated the _____ day of June, 19XX, is between XYZ Company, Inc. (the "COMPANY") and SMS Trading Corp. ("SMS"). The purpose of this AGREEMENT is for SMS to provide sales representation services for the COMPANY in the apparel industry. The COMPANY and SMS agree that:

1. SMS will perform managerial and supervisory services for the selling activities of a new division (the "DIVISION") of the COMPANY to be formed, such services to be for a term starting on _____, _____ 19XX, and ending on _____, _____ 19XX.

2. The selling management and supervision provided by SMS will apply to the selling activities of all of the DIVISION's sales representatives, both COMPANY employees and independent-contractor sales representatives under contract to the DIVISION. SMS's services are to be subject to the control and direction of the principal executive officers of the COMPANY and the President of the DIVISION.

3. SMS agrees to provide adequate, experienced personnel to carry out the terms of this AGREEMENT, including [executive].

4. SMS agrees that its employees and its representatives will not perform services of any kind for any apparel company that is competitive with the COMPANY or which has business relations with the COMPANY without prior permission by the Chairman, President or Vice Chairman of the COMPANY.

5. The COMPANY agrees to pay SMS the amount of eighty thousand dollars ($80,000.00) per annum in return for the services provided by SMS. Payment shall be made on a weekly basis, or in any other manner agreed to by both SMS and the COMPANY.

6. All persons employed by or associated with SMS, including [executive], will be paid by SMS and are considered to be independent contractors under contract to the COMPANY, and shall not be considered as employees or agents for the COMPANY. No officer, employee, or associate of SMS will be entitled to participate in or benefit from any pension, profit sharing, medical health plan, life insurance or similar plan of the COMPANY. If so requested by the COMPANY, each of the persons associated with SMS will confirm the same in writing to the COMPANY.

7. SMS will assume full responsibility for its officers, employees, and associates with respect to all federal, state, and local obligations including, but not limited to, tax withholding, social security payments, employees' liability, workmen's compensation, unemployment insurance, and other employee benefit laws.

8. SMS represents that it has the exclusive right to the services of [executive] and has an employment agreement with [executive] employing [executive] as a principle executive officer of SMS. The COMPANY may with written notice terminate this agreement with SMS if [executive] violates her employment agreement with SMS, or dies, or is unable to perform her duties for a period of more than two (2) months because of physical or mental illness or incapacity, or is found to possess or use illegal drugs or other prohibited materials, or uses alcoholic beverages excessively so as to impair her ability to perform for SMS as contemplated by this AGREEMENT, or appears to be under the influence of such drugs, substances, or alcohol during business hours. As of the date of such written notice, the COMPANY shall pay all amounts to which SMS is entitled under Paragraph 5 of this AGREEMENT.

9. During the term of this AGREEMENT, either party may terminate this AGREEMENT with sixty (60) days prior written notice to the other party.

10. SMS agrees that during the term of this AGREEMENT or for a period of twelve (12) months following completion or earlier termination of this AGREEMENT SMS will not:

   a. Employ, hire, engage, or act as a co-venturer with any employee of the COMPANY or any of its subsidiaries, or with any independent contractor doing business with the COMPANY or its subsidiaries;

   b. Induce any person connected with or employed by the COMPANY or any of its subsidiaries to leave the employ of such entities; or

c. Solicit the employment of such person on behalf of SMS or any other business enterprise.

The provisions of this paragraph shall survive the termination or expiration of this AGREEMENT.

11. In the event that SMS shall violate any of the provisions of Paragraph 10 of this AGREEMENT, SMS consents to the granting of a temporary or permanent injunction against it by any court of competent jurisdiction prohibiting SMS from violating any such provision. In any such proceeding SMS agrees that its own ability to claim damages from the COMPANY shall not be a bar or defense to the granting of such temporary or permanent injunction against SMS. SMS agrees that the COMPANY will not have an adequate remedy at law in the event of any such breach of contract by SMS, and that because of the breach the COMPANY will suffer irreparable damage and injury. The foregoing shall not limit any other remedies that the COMPANY will have under this AGREEMENT or under any applicable law.

12. This AGREEMENT shall continue from month to month subsequent to its effective starting date of _____, _____ 19XX, unless a new written agreement between the parties shall be drafted and executed.

13. This AGREEMENT shall not be modified or amended except in a writing signed by both parties to this AGREEMENT.

14. This AGREEMENT shall be binding upon and inure to the benefit of the parties to the AGREEMENT and their respective successors and assigns, and shall be governed by the laws of the State of _____

IN WITNESS WHEREOF, the parties have duly executed this AGREEMENT as of the date written above.

For XYZ COMPANY, INC.

_____

For SMS TRADING, INC.

_____

Witnesses

_____

When written agreements are used, be sure that all changes, strikeouts and erasures are initialled by both parties and that all blanks are filled in. If additions are necessary, include them in a space provided or attach them to the contract itself. Then, note on the contract that addenda have been added and accepted by both parties. This prevents questions from arising if addenda are lost or separated, because it is difficult to prove there were any without mention in the body of the contract.

Also, be sure that the contract is signed by a bona fide officer who has the legal authority to bind the employer to important terms. Finally, always obtain a signed copy of the executed agreement for your files and keep it in a safe place where you store other valuable documents.

Turning an Oral Contract into a Written Agreement

A formal agreement similar to the above is not always required to serve your purposes; in some cases an oral contract confirmed in writing can be an acceptable substitute. Before I describe how this may be accomplished, a few words about oral contracts are appropriate. An oral contract is a verbal agreement between the employee and the company defining their working relationship. Such contracts may be binding when the duties, compensation and terms of employment are agreed to by both parties.

There are certain types of contracts that must be in writing to be legally binding. The rule requiring this is called the Statute of Frauds. While there are a number of items covered in the Statute of Frauds, the one of direct interest to you regarding employment states that any contract agreement that will require more than a year to complete must be in writing. Each state has its own version of the Statute of Frauds, and various courts interpret its provisions differently. However, remember that most courts do not support indefinite employment agreements based on an oral contract because employment could be terminated at any time prior to the elapse of a year. Thus, to ensure enforceability of a working arrangement in excess of one year, you must include such an arrangement in writing.

Many workers have oral agreements because their companies refuse to give them a written contract. In fact, companies like to operate under oral agreements because there is no written evidence to indicate what terms were discussed and accepted by both parties when they entered into the employment arrangement. If disputes arise, it is more difficult for the employee to *prove* that the company failed to abide by the terms of the agreement. For example, if a bonus totalling $10,000 to be paid was accepted orally, a dishonest employer could deny this by stating that a gratuitous bonus arrangement had been accepted which was substantially less than $10,000. The employee would then have to prove that both parties had agreed upon the higher bonus figure.

When a legal dispute arises concerning the terms of an oral contract, a court will resolve the problem by examining all the evidence that the employee and company offer and weighing the testimony to determine who is telling the truth. Thus, to avoid problems, all employees should try to obtain a written contract to clarify their rights. However, if your company refuses to sign a written agreement, there are ways to protect yourself if you have an oral contract. Your chief concern should be directed toward obtaining written evidence that indicates the accepted terms, including information that defines your compensation, additional benefits, job security concerns, notice of termination requirements and other considerations.

If your company refuses to sign a written agreement, it is advisable to write a letter whenever you reach an oral agreement relating to your job. Whatever deal is agreed upon, a letter should be drafted similar to the following:

SAMPLE LETTER AGREEMENT

Date

Name of Corporate Officer
Title
Name of Employer
Address

Dear (name of officer),

I enjoyed meeting you on (date). This letter confirms that I agree to be employed by (name of company) as a (specify job title or position) for an initial term of one (1) year commencing on February 10, 1991 and terminating on February 9, 1992.

As compensation for my services, I agree to accept an annual salary of $40,000 payable in equal weekly installments in the sum of (specify). Additionally, I shall be paid an annual bonus of at least $10,000 payable on or before December 1 of each year, commencing in 1991.

According to our agreement, the company shall also reimburse me up to a maximum of $500 per month for all business-related travel expenses, and I shall receive this reimbursement by a separate check within two (2) weeks of my presentation of appropriate vouchers and records.

This agreement cannot be shortened or modified without the express written consent of both parties. Additionally, in the event notice of termination is not received no later than one (1) month prior to the expiration of the original term, this agreement shall be automatically renewed, under the same terms and conditions, for an additional one (1) year period.

Upon termination of this agreement for any reason, I shall be entitled to receive my bonus and salary for the remaining period of the quarter in which my termination occurs.

If any terms of this letter are ambiguous or incorrect, please reply within (specify) days from your receipt hereof. Otherwise, this letter shall set forth our entire understanding in this matter.

I look forward to working for (name of company).

Very truly yours,

Name of employee

SENT CERTIFIED MAIL, RETURN RECEIPT REQUESTED

After being hired, *always* write a letter similar to the above confirming the points you and the company agreed upon if you cannot obtain a written contract. Be aware that in many instances the letter you write to the company can serve in place of a formal employment contract. You may find that your letter holds you to your stated understanding of the employment terms, so be very careful, specific and accurate in your wording. If the company replies in agreement, particularly if it replies in writing, or does not argue with your stated understanding, a court may rule that these terms are also binding on the company. Another way that a company may be bound to certain terms of employment is through statements published in their employee handbook or personnel manual. This aspect is discussed in detail in Chapter 5.

Write the letter with precision, since ambiguous terms are resolved against the letter writer. Be sure to keep a copy of the letter for your own records and save the certified mail receipt. If at a later date the terms of the oral agreement are changed (for instance, additional compensation is paid to you or your duties are expanded) write another letter specifying the new arrangement that has been reached. Keep a copy of this letter and all correspondance sent to and received from your company for your protection.

Part II

████████████████████████████

HOW TO PROTECT YOUR ON-THE-JOB RIGHTS

Most employees are unaware of the numerous rights that exist in the workplace. These rights are frequently violated by executives, security personnel, private investigators, and owners of businesses that hire them, and the law allows people to recover damages when employees, agents, and their companies act improperly.

This section of the book covers your rights on the job. Chapter 3 discusses privacy and other basic freedoms of employees. This includes searches, interrogations, wiretapping, eavesdropping and other forms of surveillance that are often perpetrated on employees. It also discusses such diverse subjects as a person's right to work in a smoke-free environment, new federal legislation dealing with the right to be warned of a mass layoff 60 days prior to a plant closing, and whether employees can have access to their personnel records.

Additionally, you will learn about your rights regarding lie detector tests, voice stress analyzers, psychological stress evaluators and other tests, and whether or not you can lawfully refuse to submit to such tests while working. AIDS, drug and alcohol testing will also be discussed so you will know your rights in this area.

Finally, you will learn how workers are protected under the Occupational Safety and Health Act (OSHA), a law which requires all employers to provide a safe and healthful workplace.

Chapter 4 is devoted to how workers can protect themselves from discrimination. In this chapter you will learn what constitutes age, sex, race, handicap and religious discrimination and how to enforce your rights and protect yourself if you are a victim in this area. For example, if you are being forced to work in a hostile and offensive environment (if, for example, you are the victim of sex harassment) you will learn how to prove your claim by sending letters to document such exploitation.

You will also learn how to file a formal complaint with the Equal Employment Opportunity Commission or other appropriate agency to start the ball rolling. Additionally, the chapter provides strategies to help you win your case. More than 50,000 charges of on-the-job discrimination are filed with various agencies each year; this chapter will help you know when you are being victimized, how to fight back and how to successfully prove your case and collect damages when you are being treated unfairly.

3

RECOGNIZING EMPLOYEE
RIGHTS

B eing properly hired is only the first step in the employment relationship. It is also important to know your rights in the event that
problems develop on the job. Recent changes in the law are protecting
workers throughout the United States from illegal invasions of privacy,
dangerous working conditions, defamation and many other areas.

(Note: Although the vast majority of the rights discussed pertain to
non-union employees, some explanation of the genesis of your on-the-job
rights as a union member are included here.)

▌ UNION RIGHTS OF EMPLOYEES

To understand your rights under modern labor law, it helps to understand
the source of the laws and regulations that serve to protect workers who
belong to unions. Labor law as we know it today began in 1935 with the
Wagner Act, created by Congress to protect union members from the
excesses of employers. The three main objectives of the Wagner Act were
to end labor conflict (including conflict among labor unions themselves),
to create a system for fair collective bargaining and to create a concept to
identify unfair labor practices. The National Labor Relations Board
(NLRB) was created to interpret and enforce the Wagner Act.

The NLRB acts as a court, hearing disputes related to labor law. It
oversees labor-union representation elections and union representation,
and it determines or defines appropriate bargaining units. By definition, the
NLRB enters the picture when employees seek to protect themselves by
"concerted action" for "mutual aid and protection."

In 1947 the Taft-Hartley Act was passed by Congress to protect employers from the excesses of unions. The act outlawed the closed shop, in which
an employer would agree to hire only union members, but allowed what is
called an agency shop. In an agency shop, a person coming to work for a
unionized shop does not have to join the union, but must within a certain

time start paying union dues. While federal law allows the agency shop, state right-to-work laws can outlaw them.

The Taft-Hartley Act added to labor law prohibitions against union coercion, unreasonable union dues and featherbedding. It also allowed the President of the United States to stop a strike that endangered health or safety. The 80-day cooling-off period was another result of the Taft-Hartley Act.

The next step in labor law was the Landrum-Griffin Act of 1959, which was enacted for the purpose of protecting union members from the unions themselves. Most notable in the act was what is known as a "Bill of Rights" for union members. Elements of this act guaranteed union members that they would receive equal treatment, could criticize the union (free speech and assembly), and could sue the union. It provided for fair union discipline hearings, fair and open elections, review of union financial information and fair representation.

If you belong to a union, much of your protection as a union member derives from the powers and actions of the NLRB, but the U.S. Department of Labor also has a protective role (together with state law). Federal law is more powerful than state law with regard to minimum legal requirements. States can, however, have even more restrictive laws, as noted earlier in the discussion of the agency shop.

If your complaint involves an employer, your relief will come from the NLRB. Unfortunately, if you have a complaint against a small company (definition unclear), the NLRB will not act. And the law does not apply to state or local government jobs. However, if your complaint is against a union (or your union), it must go through the NLRB or the Department of Labor; for example, a safety complaint would be filed with OSHA (Occupational Safety and Health Administration).

Regardless or your union or non-union status, Title VII of the Civil Rights Act of 1964 is the basis of the EEOC (Equal Employment Opportunity Commission), to which you can appeal if you are being discriminated against because of your race, color, religion, sex or national origin. Through the EEOC, you can sue an employer who discriminates if the employer has at least 15 employees for at least 20 weeks out of the year. You cannot, however, sue a religious organization for religious discrimination, but you can sue federal, state and local governments, as well as labor unions and employment agencies. Discrimination based on job seniority or performance merit cannot be the basis for a suit.

Proceedings under the EEOC can be long and tedious. If you win, however, you may receive up to two years' back pay and reinstatement in your job. An especially important aspect of the law is that if you win, the loser must pay your attorney's fees. Strategies to prove and win discrimination cases are included in far greater detail in Chapter 4.

The following material will explore many issues pertaining to employee rights for your benefit.

▌ PRIVACY RIGHTS OF EMPLOYEES

Lie Detector Tests

Prior to December 27, 1988, only 24 states regulated the use of polygraph (lie detector) tests. More than two million tests were given to employees annually and many people were abused by being asked outrageous questions during the test (for example, Are you in debt? Have you ever had an abortion?) or being subjected to improper interpretation of the test results by unqualified or unlicensed examiners. Others were victims of defamation when incorrect test results were communicated to third parties, or when they were fired for failing the test (suggesting they were guilty of theft).

Common abuses such as these caused Congress to enact the Polygraph Protection Act of 1988. This federal legislation bans lie detector tests (including polygraphs, deceptographs, voice stress analyzers, psychological stress evaluations and similar devices) in *most* situations (for example, employers cannot regularly test employees as a matter of policy or in cases of continuing investigations where no suspects have been found, or use the test as a "fishing expedition" to intimidate or harass individuals or to determine whether an employee has used drugs or alcohol).

The law restricts most companies, regardless of size, in the areas of applicant screening, random testing of employees and lie detector use during investigations of suspected wrongdoing. (Note: federal, state and local governments are exempt from the law; also exempt are certain federal contractors engaged in intelligence and security work, employers authorized by law to manufacture, distribute or dispense controlled substances, and employers providing security services in some circumstances.)

Additionally, the law restricts employers from taking action against employees who refuse to submit to such tests. For example, if an employee refuses to take the test, he or she cannot be fired as a result. Although tests *can* be used in connection with the investigation of workplace thefts, embezzlement, sabotage, check-kiting, and money laundering, employers must now follow detailed safeguards to avoid the imposition of fines and penalties. Also, there must be a reasonable suspicion that the tested employee was involved in the activity being investigated and the employer must provide the subject with a statement detailing the incident in question and the basis of the suspicion of wrongdoing. Fines and penalties include back pay, job reinstatement and related damages, attorneys' fees and costs to successful litigants, and civil penalties up to $10,000 and injunctive relief for actions brought by the U.S. Secretary of Labor within three years from the wrongful act.

Here is a thumbnail sketch of the relevant portions of this new law:

Effect on state laws   In those states which currently have stronger laws prohibiting lie detector tests (defined as any mechanical or electrical device used to render a diagnostic opinion regarding honesty), the federal law is of no consequence. This is because the federal law sets minimum standards for private employers in each state to follow. Thus, for example, employers in states such as Florida and Illinois which have few restrictions are required to follow the new federal law.

Prohibited uses   Generally, employers are prohibited from directly or indirectly requiring, requesting, suggesting or causing an applicant or employee to take any lie detector test. Tests can be administered in connection with an investigation, but only *after* reasonable suspicion has been established and many procedural safeguards have been carefully followed. The procedural safeguards are as follows:

1.   The individual must be given the opportunity to consult with and obtain legal counsel before each phase of the test;
2.   The individual must be provided with at least 48 hours' notice of the time and place of the test;
3.   The individual must receive notification of the evidentiary basis for the test (i.e., the specified incident being investigated and the basis for testing);
4.   The individual must be advised of the nature and characteristics of the test and instruments involved, (i.e., two-way mirrors or recording devices);
5.   The individual must be provided an opportunity to review all questions to be asked at the examination; and
6.   The individual must be given a copy of the law which advises rights and remedies for employees and which gives him or her the right to stop the test at any time.

Additionally, all employers are required to post notices on bulletin boards which advise workers of the existence of this federal law and their rights thereunder.

Accepted uses   Although the federal law restricts the circumstances under which the tests can be given, it does allow for lie detector use to investigate serious workplace improprieties. However, employees who submit to such a test must be given the test results together with a copy of the questions asked. Additionally, employers are now forbidden from administering more than five tests per day, and each test must not run beyond 90 minutes. All persons administering such tests must be qualified by law (i.e., bonded with at least $50,000 of coverage or an equivalent amount of professional liability insurance) and are forbidden from asking questions regarding religious, racial or political beliefs, matters relating to sexual behavior, affiliations with labor organizations, or any matter not presented in writing to the examinee prior to the actual test. Also, they cannot recommend action to employers regarding test results.

Since employers must now have a reasonable basis for suspicion of wrongdoing to order the test, companies must be sure that such suspicions are *well-founded* lest they face liability. Additionally, all results of the exam and actions taken as a result of the test must be carefully guarded against careless dissemination to nonessential third parties. It is also interesting to note that the federal law forbids companies from allowing nonsuspects to voluntarily take the test to "clear their own name."

Finally, refusal to submit to such a test and the results of the test alone may not serve as a basis for adverse employment action. Employers must possess other evidence, including admissions by the examinee or evidence indicating that the employee was involved in the activity being investigated, to justify a firing or denial of promotion.

If you believe you are being asked to submit to such a test in violation of federal or state law (or a collective bargaining agreement if you are a union member), were fired as a result of taking such a test, or that proper procedural safeguards were not followed, speak with a representative of your local Department of Labor, Civil Liberties Union, attorney general's office or private labor lawyer immediately to protect your rights. All private employers must be mindful of the law to avoid problems, and workers now have many rights in this area.

Obviously, lie detector, voice stress analyzer, psychological stress evaluator and other tests can no longer be given as part of a "fishing expedition" to uncover facts. Now, employers may use the test only as part of an ongoing investigation, must be able to demonstrate the suspected employee's involvement in the matter under investigation, and must be careful to follow all pre-test, test and post-test procedures; the failure to follow any of the above can lead to serious legal repercussions.

Access to Personnel Records

Each state has its own laws regarding an employee's or ex-employee's right to inspect his or her personnel file. In some states, including California, Connecticut, Delaware, Illinois, Maine, Michigan, Nevada, New Hampshire, Ohio, Oregon, Pennsylvania, Washington and Wisconsin, employees or their representatives have the right to review their personnel records pertaining to employment decisions. However, they generally cannot inspect confidential items such as letters of reference, information about other employees, records of investigation, information about misconduct or crimes that have not been used adversely against them.

If you need legal help in your efforts to inspect the personnel file your employer (or past employer) has on you, and you don't have a personal attorney upon whom you can call, your local or state bar association most likely will have a referral service. Ask for an attorney experienced in employment law. Statutes of this sort are often modified and are constantly changing; only those who specialize in employment law in your state will be up to date on the finer points that may affect you.

Do you have the right to include a rebuttal statement in your personnel file if incorrect information is discovered? Some states, including Connecticut, Delaware, Illinois, Michigan, New Hampshire, Washington and Wisconsin permit workers to do this when the employer will not delete such comments. In fact, Connecticut, Delaware, Illinois, Michigan and New Hampshire have laws which require employers to send copies of rebuttal statements to prospective employers or other parties when information pertaining to you or your employment history is conveyed.

Some states (e.g., Illinois and Michigan) prohibit employers from gathering and maintaining information regarding an employee's off-premises political, religious and other nonbusiness activities without the individual's written consent. In these states, employees and former employees can inspect their personnel file for the purpose of discovering if any such information exists. If their file contains such information, the employer may be liable for damages, court costs, attorney's fees and fines.

■ ■

STRATEGY   *Always try to review the contents of your personnel file, especially when you believe that the employer is treating you unfairly (for example, denying you a promotion or raise). If damaging or false information is discovered, try to photocopy such information if possible. Don't forget to inquire whether a rebuttal can be included in your file. Finally, if the employer refuses your request, investigate whether the law in your particular state permits you to review the contents of your file.*

■ ■

Access to Credit Reports and Medical Records

Employers can conduct a *credit check* if this serves a legitimate business purpose. However, the Fair Credit Reporting Act, federal legislation enacted in 1971, gives employees the right to know what's in their credit file and to challenge inaccurate information. This law is beneficial in many areas. For example:

- If an applicant is rejected from a job because of a consumer report prepared by a retail credit bureau or similar agency, that person must be so informed and given the name and address of the agency. The person can then write or visit the agency directly to investigate the accuracy of the report.
- An employer requesting an investigative consumer report must notify an employee that the report is being ordered within three days and, upon request, must make a complete and accurate disclosure of the nature and scope of the investigation.

- If you are denied credit, you are entitled to know what's in your file within 30 days of receiving a rejection letter. That notice will contain the name and location of the credit-reporting bureau contacted in evaluating your file.
- If you apply for a federal job, you may have even greater protection under the law. For example, the Fair Credit Reporting Act requires most federal agencies to furnish applicants with the reasons why such credit information is requested, the purpose for which the information will be used, who the information can be released to, whether the applicant is obligated to answer questions and the consequences for refusing to supply such information. Aggrieved individuals may sue the agency in federal court for alleged violations, and damages are recoverable when an agency misrepresents or illegally uses requested information for a different purpose.

Many states prohibit the unauthorized disclosure of an employee's *medical records* as well as the unauthorized acquisition of medical information. In Colorado, for example, the unauthorized acquisition of medical records or information is punishable as felony theft. In Maryland, an employer cannot inquire into physical or mental conditions of a job applicant which do not bear a "direct, material and timely relationship" on the person's ability to do the job in question.

Some states require that an applicant or employee not be charged the cost of an employer-requested physical or that they be given a copy of the results. In other states (California, for example), the physician must obtain the job applicant's or employee's written consent *before* disclosing examination results to the employer. It is probably permissible for an employer to require you to take a physical as the last part of the screening process to get a job, provided all applicants are requested to participate in this process. However, be aware that company doctors sometimes are not trained properly and ask discriminatory questions during the examination, or request answers to discriminatory questions contained on poorly drafted medical history forms; being denied employment on the basis of answers to such questions is illegal.

Thus, recognize that you may have rights in the event that confidential credit or medical information is conveyed to outsiders by your employer without your consent or knowledge or is used to your detriment. In fact, only relevant, accurate information should be maintained by the employer, and reasonable procedures should be adopted to assure the accuracy, timeliness and completeness of such information. With respect to medical data, all information regarding an employee's health, diagnosis and treatment of illnesses or other personal information revealed during medical consultations *must* be maintained in the strictest confidence to avoid violations of state privacy laws.

▪ ■

STRATEGY   *Employers should give applicants and employees the oppor-tunity to review their records and correct mistakes before inaccurate information is disseminated. In many well-run companies, requests for information from law enforcement agencies, government agencies, unemployment insurance offices, credit agencies, security investigators and search firms must typically be accompanied by subpoenas or official documents. This insures the reliability of the identity of the source requesting such information. Additionally, unless prevented by injunction, it is a good idea for employers to advise employees of the source of the subpoena, the date when the information will be given and an explanation of the person's rights.*

▪ ▪

If you have any questions regarding your rights in this area, consult an experienced attorney or review applicable state law where appropriate.

Employee Searches

The law regarding employee searches involves a careful balancing of the employer's right to manage his or her business and the privacy rights of employees. For example, the Fourth Amendment to the United States Constitution provides protection for all persons against unreasonable search and seizure of their persons, homes and personal property, and this doctrine applies when the employer is the government. However, most private employers are exempt from this doctrine (unless the private employer does extensive business with or is heavily regulated by the government) and are generally permitted to use a variety of techniques when suspecting a worker of misconduct. These include searching the employee's office or locker without his knowledge or consent and requesting the employee to open his or her briefcase or package upon leaving a company facility.

Although each case is decided on its own merits, the law generally states that office searches *are* permissible if an employer has a reasonable basis for suspecting the employee of wrongdoing and the search is confined to nonpersonal areas of his or her office. The reason is that the office and documents relevant to company business are the property of the employer and can be searched anytime.

However, clearly visible personal items cannot be searched, and employers *cannot* conduct a search if there is no reasonable ground for suspicion. Legitimate searches of an employee's briefcase, locker or packages depend upon whether the employee had a reasonable expectation of privacy.

The absence or presence of any regulation or policy placing employees on notice that routine searches would be conducted is the primary factor in determining whether or not searches of employees or their work areas or property are legal. For example, when signs are posted throughout a company reminding workers that personal property is subject to search, when memos are distributed stating that surveillance measures will be taken on a regular basis, and when handbooks are disseminated stating that personal property is subject to search in company lockers, case decisions indicate such measures reduce claims of illegal privacy invasions (particularly when such policies explain the necessity for conducting searches, set forth procedures minimizing personal intrusion, and advise employees that their refusal to cooperate may lead to discipline or discharge).

For example, with such policies in place, one court found that packages may be searched. Another court decided that searching vehicles on company property was legal. One court even found a search valid on the basis that an employee had voluntarily accepted and continued employment notwithstanding the fact that the job subjected him to searches on a routine basis. This, the court concluded, demonstrated his willingness and implied consent to be searched (thereby waiving the claim that his privacy rights had been violated).

However, when the employer does not have such policies in place, the lack of published work rules and regulations may actually *encourage* an expectation of privacy claim. For example, in one recent case the employer searched an employee's purse, which was contained in a company locker. The court ruled that this violated the employee's reasonable expectation of privacy since she was permitted to use a private lock on her locker and there was no regulation authorizing searches without employee consent.

You should also recognize that the expectation of privacy is greatest when a pat-down or other personal search of an employee is conducted. Knowledgeable employers are reluctant to conduct personal searches, especially if they are random or done without specific, probable cause with respect to the individual involved.

Recently, an employer's security guards detained and searched an auto worker leaving a plant because he was suspected of stealing auto parts. According to testimony at the trial, the guards yelled at the employee in addition to shoving him. Although serious inventory shortages had been reported in the area where the employee was seen wandering shortly before leaving the plant, he was awarded $27,000 in damages after proving he had been singled out and treated unfairly by being subjected to the search; also, no stolen parts were found on his person during the search.

If you believe you are the victim of an employer's illegal search, ask yourself the following questions:

- Have similar searches been conducted on you or your property before? If so, did you acquiesce in the search?
- Have similar searches been conducted on other employees?
- Were you given a warning that the employer intended to conduct a search?
- Was the object of the search company property?

- Did the search have an offensive impact? Were you grabbed, jostled, struck or held? Were you coerced, threatened physically or mentally abused in order to make you cooperate?
- Were you held against your will? Were you so intimidated by the experience that you were afraid to leave?
- Were you chosen at random for a pat-down search with no actual suspicion of wrongdoing?
- Did the employer search your belongings in an area that was truly private?
- Were you stigmatized (e.g., fired) by a search when in fact you did nothing wrong?
- Did the employer search you in front of nonessential third parties and was your business reputation harmed by such action?

If you answered yes to the last six questions, speak to a labor lawyer immediately to discuss your rights. You may have a strong case, especially if you were fired, placed on probation, suspended or given an official reprimand after the search and you did nothing wrong. The tort actions most frequently alleged as a result of an improper employer search include assault, battery, defamation (in particular, slander), false imprisonment, invasion of privacy and abusive discharge. For example, if you are detained against your will during the search, you may be able to allege a valid cause of action for false imprisonment.

This happened recently to a checkout clerk who was accused of failing to ring up merchandise purchases. The employee was searched and interrogated by security personnel and told to accompany them to another location for additional questioning. At the trial, the company proved that the woman failed to ring up purchases. However, a jury awarded the employee $25,700 on the grounds of false imprisonment, because the woman was never told she could leave the room where she was being questioned and was forced to remain there for several hours.

Cases such as these illustrate that you may have rights which are violated during or after a search. For example, you may be able to sue the employer for slander and invasion of privacy if a search is conducted in front of nonessential third parties in a way which is suggestive that you are a thief.

Employee Interrogations

Employers can question workers in an effort to discover illegal acts. However, employees have rights during these interviews. Depending on the particular state where the act occurs, these may include:

- The right to receive an explanation regarding the purpose of the interrogation (e.g., are you a suspect?)

- The right to insist on the presence of a union representative at the interview if the worker is a union member and has reason to suspect it may result in disciplinary action
- The right to limit questions to relevant matters
- The right to refuse to sign any written statements
- The right to remain silent
- The right to speak to a lawyer before speaking
- The right to leave the room at any time

All of the above points must be carefully reviewed if you are wrongly accused or treated improperly in an interrogation. If the employer conducts the interrogation incorrectly, grave legal consequences can ensue. The following recent case demonstrates this:

> Three company representatives kept a supervisor in a manager's office for several hours until he finally signed a resignation notice and "admitted" his guilt concerning certain money given to him for driving duties. The man sued the company for false imprisonment and won. Additionally, the court found that the facts supported the tort of intentional infliction of emotional distress.

All employees should recognize that an employer may be violating your rights during an interrogation in the event you are restrained or confined by force or threat of force, thereby denying your freedom of movement (i.e., false imprisonment). It is no defense if you are detained during working hours; confinement cannot be done for the purpose of extracting a confession.

Do not hesitate to assert your rights if you believe you are being treated unfairly; if you are falsely accused of misconduct in front of others or are intimidated into answering questions at an interrogation, you may have a good case for defamation or false imprisonment.

Wiretapping and Eavesdropping

Although technological developments have enhanced surveillance capabilities and employers are increasingly using electronic monitoring devices to keep tabs on employee conduct during the workday (primarily designed to combat employee theft), confidential information about an employee is also sometimes acquired.

Wiretapping and eavesdropping policies are generally regulated and to some degree prohibited by federal and state law. Title III of the Omnibus Crime Control and Safe Streets Act of 1968 prohibits the deliberate interception of oral communications, including telephone conversations. Thus, conversations between employees uttered with the expectation that such communications are private (for example, in a ladies' bathroom) are confidential and employers are forbidden from eavesdropping under this statute. Employers who fail to comply with this federal law are liable for actual and punitive damages and criminal liability for willful violations.

State law varies with respect to wiretapping, eavesdropping and surveillance practices. In Colorado, New York and Texas, for example, it is legal for individuals and companies to record telephone or in-person conversations with another person without first obtaining the other person's consent (note: you only need the approval of one of the two parties to tape). In such states, the recording may subsequently be used as evidence in a civil or criminal trial under proper circumstances (e.g., that the tape was not tampered with or altered and that the voices on the tape can be identified clearly).

However, other states are not as liberal. For example, California and Massachusetts forbid the interception of oral or wire communications unless both (or all) parties are advised and give their consent. Connecticut laws prohibit employers from operating any electronic surveillance device, including sound recording and closed circuit television cameras, in employee lounges, restrooms and locker rooms (note: surveillance *is* permitted in actual work areas). Laws in these states make it virtually impossible for employers to lawfully engage in surreptitious eavesdropping.

One Georgia company placed wiretaps on business telephones in certain stores. The court ruled that this was a violation under federal law and a violation of the employees' privacy rights under Georgia law. In another recent case, a company monitored the calls of one of its sales representatives. A supervisor overheard the sales representative say she was going to accept another employer's offer. The supervisor told the employee what he had learned and tried to dissuade her from leaving. The employee left anyway and sued the company for invasion of privacy. The court ruled that the employer had violated the law by listening to her personal calls, and awarded her damages.

In another case, a company president installed wiretapping machines on four business telephone lines. When a vice president learned about this, he spoke with the company's lawyer and had the machines removed. He was later fired, and he sued the former employer; the court ruled he had a recognizable claim under Title III of the Omnibus Crime and Control Act of 1968.

Thus, in order to know your rights in this area, it is essential to know the laws of your particular state (since such laws vary widely).

Employers frequently maintain microphones between counter areas and the boss's office or instruct the office operator to listen in and monitor suspicious or personal telephone calls by employees. This is illegal in many situations. However, if the conversation is in a public area, if one of the parties consents to a taping, or if the employer had a genuine suspicion of wrongdoing and only monitored business calls and not personal calls, the eavesdropping or taping may be legal.

Also be aware that in certain instances "extension phone" monitoring (in which microphones are placed near a customer service desk to measure a worker's productivity and communication with the public or detect nonbusiness telephone use) has been upheld as legal. One employer did this and was sued by an employee claiming illegal interception of her conversations. The court ruled in favor of the employer, finding that the monitoring was done "for a legitimate business purpose" with the knowledge of the affected employee. This was proved, since written notification of the monitoring program was given to employees beforehand (who were monitored for training purposes).

In another recent case, the legality of extension phone monitoring was also upheld when a supervisor used an extension phone to listen in on an employee suspected of disclosing confidential information to a competitor. The court found the supervisor's conduct (which was spurred by a customer's tip) to be legal.

Thus, it is best to research appropriate state law or speak to an experienced labor lawyer if you believe your rights in this area have been violated. This is because if an electronic surveillance law in your state imposes greater restrictions than federal law, an employer must comply with the requirements of *both* laws.

You should also know that photographing employees without their knowledge or consent for surveillance purposes has been held not to violate any federal or state laws regarding invasions of a worker's privacy rights. However, if the pictures are released to nonessential third parties and are strongly suggestive of guilt which defames a person's reputation, you may have a valid cause of action for defamation.

AIDS and Genetic Testing

The fear of AIDS has been rampant in the workplace, but state legislatures and the courts are only beginning to define the rights of employees who have the disease. For example, the United States Supreme Court recently ruled that Section 504 of the Rehabilitation Act of 1973 prohibits recipient-businesses of federal money from discriminating against people afflicted with contagious diseases. Additionally, more than 34 states have enacted laws protecting handicapped or disabled workers from being discriminated against on the job as long as they can perform their duties.

Employers can be liable for refusing afflicted workers access to their jobs. This recently happened to one employee with AIDS in California who sued an employer when he was told he could not report back to work after a two-week hospital absence. Although he subsequently died, the California Fair Employment and Housing Commission found the company liable and ordered it to pay back wages totalling $4,359 to the man's estate. In another case in New York, a mailroom clerk was fired after returning from a four-week absence when his employer confronted him about his health problems. The man contacted the AIDS discrimination unit of the state

Human Rights Division and settled the case for $8,000 and full health benefits for a five-year period.

AIDS testing of employees is now mandated in some cities and localities, including Florida's Dade County (which requires all restaurant and other food workers to obtain and carry certificates indicating that they are free from AIDS, venereal disease and tuberculosis), government agencies and the military. California and Wisconsin mandate AIDS testing in blood donations.

However, at present the law is not well settled in this area. While civil liberties groups claim such tests unjustifiably discriminate and invade workers' rights to privacy, they are opposed by other groups who argue that legislation should protect the safety of innocent members of society who face exposure to the deadly AIDS virus.

The issue of genetic testing is even more unsettled. More than 18 major corporations are now testing the relationship of inherited genetic traits to occupational disease to determine if there are certain predisposing risks to employees and job applicants. More and more companies are considering using such tests.

Until recently there were no reported case decisions involving employment discrimination against persons with infectious or contagious conditions. And, while the Justice Department ruled that certain employers may legally fire AIDS patients if their motive is the protection of other employees, it qualified this ruling by stating that it would not release employers from compliance with appropriate state laws protecting the rights of the handicapped (which are in force in over 40 states—see Chapter 4). Most of the laws in these states provide full civil protection from firings to persons with AIDS who can perform their jobs.

Related problems are also emerging. For example, to what extent may employers require HIV testing as a condition of employment? May insurers require AIDS testing as a condition of issuing life or disability insurance? May they deny insurance or charge an additional premium for the individual who tests positively? How can the company be sure that the results of such tests will remain confidential to avoid charges of slander or libel and other invasions of privacy?

Thus, since the law in this area is unsettled, it is important to consult an experienced labor attorney to determine your rights, obligations and options if applicable.

Drugs and Alcohol Testing

The fight against drug and alcohol abuse in the workplace often results in drug tests of employees. There has been a sharp rise in employer interest in drug and alcohol testing, fueled in part by high-profile drug deaths and publicity surrounding the marketing of drug tests. More employers are resorting to such tests, especially pre-employment testing, to identify drug users and reduce the incidence of on-the-job accidents and absences.

Critics argue that indiscriminate testing violates employees' rights of privacy, due process and freedom from unreasonable search and seizure, and that test results are often incorrect, unreliable or disseminated to nonessential third parties. Proponents of testing cite its success (for example, the military's program has dramatically lowered drug use in the armed forces) and the growing confidence in the reliability of current testing methods.

Recent statistics reflect the magnitude of the problem within the applicant pool and existing workplace. For example:

- At least 20 million Americans use marijuana/hashish
- At least 6 million Americans are cocaine users and 100 million are alcohol users
- The typical recreational drug user in the workplace is late 3 times as often as fellow employees and has 2.5 as many absences of 8 or more days per year
- A recreational drug user is 5 times more likely to file a workers' compensation claim and is involved in accidents 3.6 times more frequently than other workers

Generally, since private employers are *not* held to the same constitutional standards as local, state and federal government employers, private employers *may* implement and conduct drug and alcohol tests provided certain procedural safeguards are followed which minimize potential offensiveness. This typically includes adopting a comprehensive testing policy and putting it in writing, periodically reminding employees of the stated drug or alcohol testing policy, reducing the incidence of errors, treating test results carefully (i.e., confidentially) to avoid improper dissemination, and following local, state and federal laws and decisions in this area.

Despite the general legitimacy of such tests, some state and local governments have passed laws prohibiting the testing of employees for drugs or alcohol. This includes a blanket prohibition in Florida and certain restrictions in San Francisco and some cities in Oregon. You should also know that under federal law, employers whose workers are represented by unions are *not* free to unilaterally implement a testing program without bargaining with the union over changes and conditions in employment; to do so violates the National Labor Relations Act.

Perhaps the most important change to occur *legitimizing* such tests results from the recent passage of the federal Drug Free Workplace Act of 1988, effective March 18, 1989. This law requires certain employers who do business with the federal government to publish strict statements prohibiting drugs in the workplace and educating employees on substance abuse. It also requires employers to report to the procuring agency any workers convicted of workplace-related drug activities and to certify that they will not condone unlawful drug activity during the performance of a contract with a government agency.

Companies who fail to follow such rules will be subject to suspension of payments due under their contract with the federal agency, or termination of the contract. Thus, there is great incentive for companies dealing with the government to comply with the requirements of this law. However, although the law goes a long way towards creating a heightened drug-awareness policy, it does not mandate drug testing either for job applicants or for employees. Nor does the law explicitly sanction such testing. Thus, the decision to test is still basically an individual one, particularly for private employers that do not deal with the government.

■ ■

STRATEGY   *If you work for a private employer, and are not a member of a union, what concerns should you have when advised that the employer intends to test you for drugs and alcohol? First, if the employer has decided to test, you are probably entitled to* advance notification *in work rules, policy manuals and employment contracts to reduce perceived privacy rights in this area. For example, the manual should outline the steps management would take when it suspected that an employee was impaired on the job, such as immediate testing, with a description of how the test will be administered and the consequences flowing from a positive result, such as immediate discharge with no severance or other benefits. If no such notice was received before the test was administered, you could have a valid claim that your privacy rights were violated, especially when there was no rational reason for asking you to submit to the test (e.g., you were randomly selected) and you were requested to take the test without warning.*

Second, even if your privacy rights are not violated, all tests must be administered in a consistent, evenhanded manner. For example, if you are black or a woman, and employees belonging to your classification of race or sex are being tested and fired as a result of such tests in far greater numbers than other classifications, a charge of race or sex discrimination might be valid under certain circumstances.

Third, how the employer handles the test results is another important consideration. Results must be treated in the same manner as other confidential personnel information. Unwarranted disclosure of this information (even within your company) when made with reckless disregard for the truthfulness of the disclosure, or excessive publication, can allow you to sue for damages. One employee in Texas was recently awarded $200,000 for defamation after his employer internally and externally published written statements regarding drug screening results allegedly showing a trace of methadone.

Additionally, a firing based on a positive test finding which later proves inaccurate could lead to a multitude of legal causes of action including wrongful discharge, slander and invasion of privacy. Thus, if the employer fails to hire a reputable testing company or the test's results are inaccurate, you can challenge the test on this basis; be aware that six-figure verdicts are routinely being awarded for violations in this area.

■ ■

Note: Recent surveys cited by the National Institute on Drug Abuse reveal that the percentage of Fortune 500 companies screening employees or applicants for drug use rose from 3% in 1982 to almost 30% in 1985, and the trend appears to rising dramatically. Additionally, the Centers for Disease Control recently reported that the most common test, the EMIT urine test, is plagued by a high degree of false positive results (sometimes as high as 69%) due to human error and inexperienced testing personnel. Other problems with this test are that it does not prove intoxication (i.e., the inability of the employee to perform his or her job duties) at the time the test is taken (which should always be the governing factor in any discharge decision) and may also indicate positive results for employees who have only used legal over-the-counter drug medications.

Thus, recognize that there may be ample ways to challenge the test results in the event you are fired or treated unfairly. You should speak to an experienced labor lawyer immediately if you believe that:

- The test was not administered fairly; i.e., no advance warnings were given or there was inconsistent enforcement;
- The penalty for violations was too severe (e.g., an employee was fired for possessing marijuana in his locker but proved he did not smoke the drug on company property);
- The reliability of test procedures and/or results is suspect;
- The employer cannot prove the identity of the illegal drug allegedly found in the test;
- The specimen was not properly identified as belonging to the accused worker;
- The test was given randomly with no expectation that an employee had an impairment caused by persistent on-the-job drug or alcohol use (i.e., no observation of disorientation was present);
- No confirmatory tests were made following positive preliminary screening; and
- The company engaged in discriminatory practices relating to its testing procedures.

Note: federal workers, employees engaged in security-conscious industries (for example, those who are required to carry firearms), employees who handle money or engage in transporting members of the public (bus drivers, train engineers, etc.) have fewer legal rights to oppose drug and alcohol tests, because of the nature of their jobs. Random drug testing was even recently upheld for horse jockeys. The court ruled that horse racing was one of a special class of industries accustomed to heavy state regulation, and that the need for safety and honesty to promote the integrity of the industry outweighed the jockeys' significantly diminished expectations of privacy.

However, as stated above, even when testing is legal, employers must follow proper procedures to be sure that results are accurate and are not disseminated carelessly. Additionally, such tests are being challenged all the time and the law is constantly changing in this area. For example, one New York court recently held that probationary schoolteachers could not be compelled to submit to urinalysis on the whim of the Board of Education without a reasonable suspicion that the teacher being tested was or ever had been a drug user. In the absence of such suspicion, the court determined that the ordering of a urine test was "an act of pure bureaucratic caprice."

The same concerns that apply to drug tests are also applicable to alcohol tests. For example, instead of drawing blood, companies should use accurate breath-testing devices whenever possible to minimize offensiveness. Test procedures should insure reliable test results. Results should be handled on a strict need-to-know basis inside and outside the company. Employees should be given an opportunity to explain any result and the test results should be reconfirmed if possible.

Additionally, employers must be aware that former alcoholics and drug users whose substance use is controlled and which does not prevent them from performing the duties of the job in question may be characterized as handicapped individuals and *protected* under federal law and the laws in some 45 states and the District of Columbia. As handicapped individuals, they could be protected from being discharged under various handicap discrimination laws, even in the presence of positive test results. (See Chapter 4.)

The line between reasonable and unreasonable requests to undergo drug and alcohol testing will continue to be more clearly drawn as court decisions and state legislatures articulate specific policies on this issue. There is no doubt that more drug policy and testing cases will reach the courts because of the strong desire in government and political circles to eliminate drug and alcohol abuse in the workplace. However, the information in this section should help you recognize that you may have rights before, during and after any test is administered to you.

Smoking in the Workplace

More workers than ever before are demanding the right to work in a smoke-free environment. This right is being upheld with increasing regularity through federal legislation, state laws, city ordinances and case decisions.

In December 1986, the United States government concluded that environmental or secondary smoke posed a threat to nonsmokers and ruled that federal agencies must take reasonable steps to permit smoking only in expressly designated areas. This federal ruling follows a national trend (in 75 localities and at least 12 states including New York, New Jersey, Connecticut, Colorado, Minnesota, Montana, Nebraska, Oregon, Utah, Florida, Maine and New Hampshire) to pass laws recognizing the rights of nonsmokers to work in a smoke-free environment.

Various federal agencies, including the Merit Board and the Equal Employment Opportunity Commission, have ruled that employers must take reasonable steps to keep smoke away from workers who are sensitive to it, and the Occupational Safety and Health Administration (OSHA) has begun issuing similar requirements to enhance safety in the workplace. All of these developments are now causing most employers to reevaluate their smoking policies and implement either formal or voluntary rules, depending upon applicable state and local laws.

Critics contend that such policies violate an individual's right to privacy. However, because of increased public sentiment and awareness in favor of such policies, and since in virtually all states an employer has a common-law duty to provide a reasonably safe workplace for its employees, the enforceability of on-the-job bans is increasingly being upheld throughout the country.

As a result, many employees have successfully eliminated smoking in the office where they work. Others are suing for and receiving unemployment compensation after resigning from their jobs. Still others are seeking disability pay. In one recent case, a woman was awarded $20,000 in disability pay because she developed asthmatic bronchitis after being trans-ferred to an office with several smokers. The court also ruled that unless her employer (a government agency) transferred her to a job in a smoke-free office within sixty days, she would be eligible for disability retirement benefits of $500 per month.

Some employers have even enacted policies denying jobs to applicants who smoke! And companies have become more tolerant and responsive to complaints by nonsmokers and are now more willing to accommodate their needs. It should be noted that such accommodations make sense since employers are fearful of formal litigation, OSHA investigations, union intervention or EEOC involvement (which is being brought with increasing regularity in this area).

According to a recent survey by the Bureau of National Affairs, approx-imately 38% of all employers have put flexible smoking guidelines into place since 1985. Such policies have included permitting employees to vote on whether smoking will be permitted in conference rooms and common areas (such as cafeterias and lounges) with a supervisor working it out if the vote is close. Some companies have even instituted inflexible no-smoking poli-cies for all staff, visitors and customers in response to recent legal and health trends.

Some manufacturers, prompted by the discovery that materials used in their plants can be hazardous to smokers, are announcing that workers will be discharged unless they stop smoking in warehouses and factories. Such policies are being enacted with the approval of OSHA, since management has the right to designate rules pertaining to work assignments to insure an employee's health and safety.

For example, it was reported that one major U.S. corporation introduced an absolute ban on smoking after the company discovered that mineral fibers used in nine of its acoustical-products plants could have adverse health effects on both smokers and nonsmokers. To date, such a policy has gone unchallenged from workers at its plants.

If you desire to work in a smoke-free environment, the following strategies may help you protect your rights and increase the chances of a successful lawsuit.

▪ ▪

STRATEGY 1   *Gather the facts. Document the environmental condition of your work location to support your request. For example, it is important to determine the number of smokers, type of ventilation, physical arrangement of desks, how often people around you smoke, etc.*

▪ ▪

STRATEGY 2   *Acquire medical proof. Visit a doctor if you suffer an illness from working in a smoke-filled environment. Note the prescriptions and the amount of time lost from work. It is also a good idea to visit your employer's medical department (if one exists) to document your condition.*

▪ ▪

STRATEGY 3   *Speak to management. Present management with a letter from your personal doctor stating your need to work in a smoke-free area. If possible, request the transfer collectively with other workers.*

▪ ▪

STRATEGY 4   *Confirm all grievances in writing. After the initial discussion, it is a good idea to document your request by presenting management with a letter similar to the one at the top of the opposite page:*

▪ ▪

Wait a few days after sending such a letter. Then, if a satisfactory response is not made, you may wish to send an additional letter similar to the one at the bottom of the opposite page:

▪ ▪

STRATEGY 5   *Speak to a lawyer. If you receive a negative response, you may wish to consult a lawyer to determine your rights. The lawyer can assert several options on your behalf. For example, she can assist you in presenting demands directly to the employer or union representative, file an action in court, contact OSHA or sue the employer under the Equal Employment Opportunity Act. Legal fees are sometimes awarded to successful litigants under these acts. (Note: Although such action may be illegal, be aware that your employer may fire or penalize you for enforcing your rights. This possibility should be considered before you decide to hire a lawyer.)*

▪ ▪

Date

Name of Supervisor
Title
Name of Company
Address

Dear (Name of Supervisor):

This will confirm the conversations we have had regarding the need to provide me (us) with a work environment free of tobacco smoke. Enclosed is information to support the request to eliminate smoking in work areas.

Also enclosed is a petition signed by employees in our work location. As my (our) ability to work is constantly undermined by the unhealthy, toxic pollutants to which I (we) am (are) chronically exposed, I (we) will appreciate your giving this request priority and your prompt attention.

Thank you for your cooperation in this matter.

Very truly yours,

Your name

cc: Copies to your personal physician, union delegate, other management personnel, etc.

Date

Name of Supervisor
Title
Name of Company
Address

Dear (Name of Supervisor):

As of this date, I (we) have received no reply to my (our) request of (date).

[If temporary or interim measures have been tried but are not successful, identify them. For example, if the employer took steps to improve the ventilation but the air has not been cleaned and you are now being exposed to cold drafts, state this.]

To protect my (our) health while in your employ it is vital that the company provide me (us) with a smoke-free work area to comply with OSHA and other requirements of this state. If this is not done immediately, I (we) will request intervention by experts in occupational health.

I (we) am (are) most appreciative of your immediate response in this matter.

Very truly yours,

Your name

cc: president of the Company, medical director, your doctor

▪ ▪

STRATEGY 6   *Contact an appropriate agency for further information. Your regional Department of Labor, Department of Health, or OSHA office will provide you with more information. In addition, you may wish to contact an organization called GASP, which stands for the New Jersey Group Against Smoking Pollution. GASP has been an advocate of the rights of nonsmokers and maintains a list of nationwide pertinent cases, regulations and lawyers who are knowledgeable in this area.*

▪ ▪

STRATEGY 7   *Speak to a doctor about Worker's Compensation. If you incur medical expenses due to a smoke-related on-the-job illness, discuss filing a Worker's Compensation claim with your doctor.*

▪ ▪

OTHER RIGHTS OF EMPLOYEES

Confidential Information and Trade Secrets

Employees often resign from a job or are lured away to a rival company to compete directly against their former employers. Sometimes they take valuable customer lists, trade secrets and confidential information (such as prices and requirements of key customers) with them. When the former company discovers this, a lawsuit may be filed to stop the employee from using such information. In other instances, a former employer may attempt to stop the individual from using information which was learned and acquired while working. Can this be done? The following information can decrease the chances that such problems will occur and give you a better understanding of the legalities in this area.

Understand what constitutes a trade secret.   A trade secret may consist of any formula, pattern, device or compilation of information used in business that gives a company an opportunity to obtain an advantage over competitors that do not know or use it. Although an exact definition is not possible, trade secrets are usually involved when:

- An employer takes precautions to guard the secrecy of the information
- The employer has expended significant money and effort in developing the information
- It is difficult to acquire the information outside of the company (that is, it isn't generally known to outsiders)
- Employees are warned that trade secrets are involved and that they are obligated to act in a confidential manner

The most frequently disputed issue concerning trade secrets involves customer lists. A "secret" list is not a list of companies or individuals that can be compiled from a telephone directory or other source that anyone can examine. A list becomes confidential when the names of customers can be learned only by someone through his employment—for example, when a salesperson secretly copies a list of customers that the company spent considerable time, effort and money compiling and kept under lock and key.

When employees have become friendly with customers in the course of their previous employment, they are allowed to call on them for new employers. However, the law generally states that they are prohibited from using their knowledge of customer buying habits, requirements or other special information when soliciting their former employers' accounts. If a salesperson knows that a particular customer will be in short supply of a product, for instance, he should not solicit that account, because he may expose himself to a lawsuit. This is because the law imposes a fiduciary duty of good faith and loyalty on all employees, sales and non-sales alike.

An employee cannot make deals with customers in which he or she promises to perform favors in return for secret kickbacks involving money or other benefits such as vacations. If you engage in such conduct without the company's knowledge and consent, the employer can terminate your employment and sue you for damages.

Has a climate of confidentiality been created?   When an employer has made a special effort to remind employees of their obligation to protect the company's trade secrets, employees are sometimes held to a higher standard. For example, if posters are displayed in prominent areas reminding workers of their obligation to protect company secrets and this is published on a continuing basis in company journals, work rules, policy manuals and memos, this reduces a person's argument that he or she didn't know it was wrong to convey confidential information to a competitor.

Be aware that the transfer of confidential information may constitute a crime.
Many states have passed laws making it a criminal offense to steal trade secrets. Recent legislation was enacted in New Jersey, for example, making it a high misdemeanor to steal company property, including written material. Other states such as Arkansas, California, Colorado, Maine, Michigan, Minnesota, Nebraska, New Hampshire, New Mexico, Ohio, Oklahoma, Pennsylvania, Tennessee, Texas and Wisconsin have similar laws. The state of New York has gone even further in addressing this problem by declaring it a felony for anyone to steal company property consisting of secret scientific material.

In addition, if valuable written material is stolen and transported to another state, the Federal Bureau of Investigation and the Justice Department can assist employers in apprehending workers because it is a federal crime to sell or receive stolen property worth more than $5,000 that has been transported across state lines.

Employee Inventions and Suggestions

Workers frequently create valuable suggestions, comments, ideas, designs, manufacturing processes and inventions. These suggestions often lead to money-saving and money-making devices. If the invention is created while on the job or is used by an employer, is the company obligated to pay the employee for the use of such an idea? Who owns the device or invention created?

This section will clarify ambiguous law and give you a better understanding of how to avoid problems and protect yourself in this area. To be able to implement many of the strategies contained herein, it is important to first understand the following basic concepts:

Work for hire   A work for hire is defined as a work prepared by an employee within the scope of his or her employment or work specifically ordered or commissioned by the employer which the employee creates in reliance upon an express agreement. Thus, for example, when an employee is specifically engaged to do something (e.g., solve a problem, develop a new product, process or machine), he or she is provided with the means and opportunity to resolve the problem or achieve the result *and* is paid for that work, then the employer is generally entitled to the fruits of the employee's labors. Thus, for example, if a worker creates an invention while on the job, the invention may be owned by the employer under this legal principle.

The shop right concept   If an employee is not hired to invent or solve a particular problem, does the employee have the right to claim any rights to his or her discoveries? Maybe, depending upon the particular facts involved.

For example, under the shop right concept, when an employee makes an invention or discovery that is outside the scope of his employment but utilizes the employer's resources (equipment, labor, materials or facilities in making the invention), that invention may be owned by the employee subject to a "shop right" on the part of the employer. This "shop right" in certain instances may give the employer a nonexclusive, irrevocable license to use the invention indefinitely, without having to pay a royalty.

Valuable ideas as opposed to patentable inventions   Using a hypothetical case, Gwen develops a manufacturing process during nonworking hours which she thinks will save the company money. She tells her boss and the idea is incorporated into the company's production process. Gwen is not compensated for the idea. She resigns and sues to recover a percentage of the money saved by the idea's use.

Gwen's case is not as strong as it appears. The reason is that ideas, plans, methods and procedures for business operations cannot normally be copyrighted. This is also true with respect to certain ideas as intellectual property. The law generally states that ideas belong to no one and are there for the taking.

Additionally, an idea is presumed to be a work made for hire and the property of the employer if an employee offers it voluntarily without contracting to receive additional compensation. Thus, for example, Gwen would have a stronger case if she could prove that the idea was her own original, unique creation not requested or developed while working on company time or on the employer's premises, *and* that it was furnished because of a specific promise or understanding that she would be promoted or compensated once it was implemented by the employer.

Many workers are unknowingly exploited because they give away their ideas without understanding their rights. Review the following strategies if you wish to avoid being exploited in this area.

■ ■

STRATEGY 1   *Articulate your idea, method or process in writing. This is essential because it is difficult to prove you are the creator of a valuable idea unless it is set down on paper.*

■ ■

STRATEGY 2   *Be sure the writing is detailed and specific. This can increase your chances of proving the idea is a protectable property interest. For example, if you write a proposal for a unique and original television show, be sure to fully describe the characters, budget, and script dialogue rather than briefly discussing the concept of the show.*

■ ■

STRATEGY 3   *Avoid volunteering ideas. In one famous case, a homemaker mailed an unsolicited cheesecake recipe to a baking company. The recipe was used and became a popular money-maker. Although the woman sued the company for damages, she lost. The court ruled that no recovery was obtainable because the homemaker voluntarily gave her idea to the company.*

The lesson to be learned from this case is clear. Since employers generally have no obligation to compensate employees for ideas, inventions or suggestions which are conveyed voluntarily, think twice before doing this, particularly if company policy states that there is no obligation to pay anything if the idea is used, or that any payments made will be purely discretionary (that is, not linked to any predetermined formula such as a percentage of specific company savings, revenue or profits generated from the idea).

■ ■

▪ ▪

STRATEGY 4   *Avoid signing any agreement or contract with work for hire provisions. Some companies request job applicants and employees to sign agreements which state that all inventions authored or conceived by the employee belong to the employer. Avoid this whenever possible.*

▪ ▪

STRATEGY 5   *Negotiate a predetermined method of compensation and articulate your understanding in writing. For example, the agreement should mention the type of idea being conveyed and the manner of compensation for its use, and should stipulate that the employer will maintain the confidentiality of the idea and will not disclose, assign or transfer the idea or its value to anyone else without your consent.*

▪ ▪

The sample agreement below illustrates these points in greater detail.

(Note: If compensation is difficult to ascertain at the time the acknowledgment is negotiated, the agreement can state that the employee will be compensated in a manner mutually agreed upon by the parties and that the idea will remain the property of the employee or individual until such formula is determined.)

ACKNOWLEDGMENT OF RECEIPT OF IDEA

Received on this day from (name of employee or individual) an idea concerning (specify) which was presented in the form of (specify) and which is hereby acknowledged.

The employer confirms that it has not used or implemented this idea in the past, that it is sufficiently original and has been conveyed with the expectation of receiving payment thereof, and, if used or implemented in any manner, shall cause the (name of employee or individual) to be compensated according to the following: (specify).

The employer agrees to maintain the confidentiality of the material submitted herein by (name of employee or individual) and agrees not to disclose it, or the ideas upon which it is based, to any person, firm or entity without the (name of employee or individual's) consent.

Accepted and consented to: Name of Employer

Date: _____   By: _____
                                        Name of Officer and Title

Date: _____   By: _____
                                        Name of Employee or Individual

■ ■

STRATEGY 6   *Get a receipt. If you are unable to receive a signed acknowledgment similar to the above, you must be able to prove delivery of a valuable idea to another in order to protect your rights. For example, it is often wise to send a certified letter indicating that your idea was submitted in confidence with the expectation of being paid for its use. The letter below illustrates this concept:*

■ ■

(Note: Although a letter like the one shown below cannot guarantee protection of your idea, it can increase the chances that you will not be exploited in this area. Try to send the materials by certified mail, return receipt requested, to prove delivery, and follow up the letter with a

---

Date

Name of Officer
Title
Name of Employer
Address

Re: The submission of my original idea regarding (specify) consisting of (specify)

Dear (Name of Officer),

Per our earlier telephone conversation on (specify date), I have enclosed, per your request, my original idea regarding (specify) consisting of (specify).

You indicated an interest in this concept and advised me that the materials would be reviewed in confidence with no disclosure to any other person, firm or entity without my prior written consent.

Finally, it was agreed that these materials are submitted with the expectation of furnishing appropriate acknowledgment of my authorship and payment to me in the event they are used after my written consent has been given.

Thank you for your interest and attention in this matter and I look forward to hearing from you after you have completed your review.

Very truly yours,

Your Name

SENT CERTIFIED MAIL, RETURN RECEIPT REQUESTED

telephone call or another letter in the near future if you do not receive an immediate response. Finally, insist on receiving all materials returned, plus copies, if you receive an unfavorable reply; you don't want the materials floating around so other people can look at them and steal your idea).

■ ■

STRATEGY 7   *Avoid signing releases. Many employers and individuals request that creators sign releases before they will agree to review their ideas. Such releases typically state that the individuals assume no liability regarding the receipt or use of such material. Avoid signing any such documents because they defeat the purpose of the strategies discussed in this section.*

■ ■

STRATEGY 8   *Make copies. Keep copies of all materials and letters that you send to others. Some people mail an unopened copy of the package back to themselves for this purpose. The postmark date on the front of the envelope may establish that you were the sender of the package in the event of a dispute.*

■ ■

STRATEGY 9   *Consult a lawyer. If your idea is sufficiently unique or potentially valuable, you may wish to consult an experienced copyright or patent lawyer whom you can trust.*

■ ■

Health and Safety in the Workplace

Numerous changes benefiting workers have occurred in the area of health and safety. Federal and state laws have recently been passed which give employees the right to refuse dangerous work and receive accurate reports concerning toxic substances in their working environment. Increased activity by representatives of the federal Occupational Safety and Health Administration (OSHA) has also played a large role in protecting employees from unsafe working conditions.

What is OSHA?   The 1970 Occupational Safety and Health Act requires employers to provide a safe and healthful workplace. This federal law applies to every private employer who is involved in interstate commerce, regardless of size. Additionally, some states have passed occupational safety and health plans approved by federal OSHA. Some of these laws are even stricter in their compliance and enforcement standards than the federal law. For example, in one recent case, the Supreme Court of Illinois ruled that the federal Occupational Safety and Health Act does not prohibit state officials from enforcing criminal penalties against employers who violate OSHA regulations.

In that case, an Illinois company coated wires with toxic compounds. This practice continued despite knowledge by the company's supervisors that such manufacturing processes were producing harmful effects on workers. The company and several of its officers were indicted on criminal charges of aggravated battery and reckless conduct under state law. When the company appealed, the Supreme Court ruled that the state of Illinois was allowed to proceed with its own prosecution, notwithstanding the existence of the federal OSHA law, since "prosecutions of employers who violate state criminal law by failing to maintain safe working conditions for their employees will surely further OSHA's stated goal of assuring so far as possible every working man and woman in the nation safe and healthful working conditions."

The Occupational Safety and Health Administration is the federal agency created to enforce the law in this area. The agency issues regulations on worker safety that employers must follow. OSHA inspectors visit work sites to be sure that employers adhere to the rules. Penalties are sometimes imposed including fines of up to $10,000 for each violation and/or imprisonment for up to six months for employers and key personnel who willfully or repeatedly violate OSHA laws or fail to correct hazards within fixed time limits.

The law includes an extremely broad general duty clause requiring all employers to furnish a workplace that is free from recognized hazards. This means that employers are required to comply with safety rules, are subject to inspections without notice (with an employee representative present) and that no employee who makes a complaint can be subject to retaliation, loss of work or benefits, or demotion.

What protections are available to workers under OSHA?   Under this law, workers are allowed:

- To refuse to perform work in a dangerous environment (e.g., in the presence of toxic substances, fumes or radioactive materials)
- To strike to protest unsafe conditions
- To initiate an OSHA inspection of dangerous working conditions by filing a safety complaint
- To participate in OSHA inspections, prehearing conferences and review inspection hearings
- To assist the OSHA compliance officer in determining that violations have occurred
- To petition that employers provide adequate emergency exits, environmental control devices (e.g., ventilation, noise elimination devices, radiation detection tags, signs and protective equipment) and the ready availability of medical personnel
- To request time off with pay to seek medical treatment during working hours

- To request eating facilities in areas which have not been exposed to toxic substances
- To request investigations when they are punished for asserting their rights.

One of the most important aspects of the federal OSHA law is that it provides workers with protection against retaliation after asserting their rights. In one recent case, for example, a number of workers walked off the job claiming it was too cold to work. The company fired them, stating they violated established work rules by stopping work without notifying their supervisor. The workers filed a complaint alleging this was an unfair labor practice. The U.S. Supreme Court ruled that since the workers were within their constitutional rights to strike over health and safety conditions, the firing was illegal. As a result, the workers were subsequently given their jobs back together with lost pay.

Note: *It is not necessarily a good idea to suddenly walk off your job when you believe you are working in a dangerous or unhealthy environment unless it is likely that the work is placing you in imminent danger of serious injury. You should first attempt to discuss such conditions with your supervisor, union delegate or OSHA representative. This will make your demands seem more reasonable and minimize potential conflict.*

However, if you feel you have been punished for complaining about your safety and health rights, speak with a representative of your nearest OSHA office *immediately* (i.e., within 30 days of the time you discover the retaliation). Request an attorney, OSHA or union representative to file the complaint for you if you are too sick, since the complaint must be filed in a timely fashion to avoid dismissal under the Statute of Limitations.

Finally, be sure to fully discuss the facts with an OSHA representative *before* talking any action. After OSHA conducts the investigation, it may demand that your employer restore your job, earnings, benefits and seniority if you have been illegally punished. OSHA is also empowered to institute a lawsuit in federal court to protect your rights, so be sure that you speak to a representative from your nearest OSHA office as soon as possible. You may also wish to retain an experienced labor lawyer to protect your interests in this regard. All of these options should be taken immediately to protect your rights in this area.

Warnings before Massive Layoffs

Employees are entitled to be warned of massive layoffs under the federal Worker Adjustment and Retraining Notification Act. This law (P.L. 100-379) became effective February 4, 1989 and was the subject of bitter battles between business and labor interests. The focus of the law requires employers with more than 100 workers to give employees and their communities at least 60 days' notice (or comparable financial benefits) of plant closings and large layoffs that affect 50 or more workers at a job site when this number is more than 33% of all workers. The law is unique in its provisions dealing with retraining of displaced workers. However, it is also extremely technical and must be thoroughly understood before action is contemplated in this area.

The following thumbnail sketch will highlight important aspects of the Act; suggestions will then be offered on the law's possible effects on workers and employers throughout the United States.

What the law says   Section 3(a) of the Worker Adjustment and Retraining Notification Act ("WARN") prohibits employers from ordering a plant closing or mass layoff until 60 days *after* the employer has given written notice of this to:

1. Affected employees or their representatives
2. The state dislocated-worker unit; and
3. The chief elected official of the unit of local government where the closing or layoff is to occur.

Employers are defined as business enterprises that employ more than 100 full-time workers (part-timers are characterized as those working less than 20 hours per week or less than six months in the preceding year) or who employ more than 100 employees who in the aggregate work at least 4,000 hours per week excluding overtime.

The Act calls for covered employers to give notice of a plant closing or mass layoff. A *plant closing* is defined as the "permanent or temporary shutdown of a single site of employment, or one or more facilities or operating units within a single site of employment, if the shutdown results in an employment loss at the single site of employment during any 30 day period for 50 or more employees excluding part-time employees." *Employment loss* is defined under the law as "a termination other than for cause, voluntary departure or retirement, or a layoff for more than 6 months or a reduction in hours of work of more than 50 percent during each month of any 6 month period."

In contrast to a plant closing, a *mass layoff* is a reduction in force resulting in employment loss during any 30-day period of 50 full-time employees who constitute at least 33% of the full-time employees at a single site of employment, or 500 employees.

Who the Law affects.   The law does not appear to affect governmental, non-profit and service organizations. Also, many layoffs of small and very large companies may not be affected by the Act's requirements due to the numbers of persons affected. Additionally, if the plant closing or mass layoff was caused by a natural disaster (for example, a flood, earthquake or severe drought), or was due to the closing of a temporary facility or completion of a project whose employees were hired with the understanding their work was of limited duration, the law will not adversely affect the employer. The same is true for problems caused by strikes, lockouts or permanent replacement of strikers.

There are other exceptions as well. The 60-day rule does not have to be strictly followed if the employer, reasonably and in good faith, was forced to shut down the plant in a shorter time to obtain needed capital or business, or if the closing or mass layoff was caused by business circumstances not reasonably forseeable at the time the required notice was to be given.

Finally, it appears that the law does not protect workers who lose their jobs less than 60 days after the effective date of a sale. This is because the Act was intended to protect workers only from closings or layoffs prior to a sale. The law appears to merely obligate the seller to give notice until the sale is completed; it is still unclear to what extent, if any, the buyer would be liable thereafter.

What are the Penalties for noncompliance?   Any employer who orders a plant closing or mass layoff without furnishing appropriate notice may be liable in a civil action to each affected employee for:

1. One day's back pay for each day of violation up to 60 days. This amount is calculated at the higher of the employee's average regular rate or final regular rate of pay less any wages paid during the layoff period and any voluntary or unconditional payments (e.g. severance) paid to the affected worker which were not legally required
2. The value of medical expenses and other benefits paid directly to the affected employee
3. The value of actual payments made to third parties on behalf of the affected employee

Employers are also subject to fines not to exceed $500 per day to the appropriate unit of local government where the closing or layoff occurs unless the employer continues to pay benefits to affected employees as described above within three weeks of the shutdown or layoff. However, this fine may be reduced by showing that a "complained of wrongful act or ommission" was in good faith and that the employer had reasonable grounds for believing that the act or omission was not a violation of law.

Critics contend that the law is weak since federal courts do not have the authority to *enjoin* (force an employer to reopen or rehire) plant closings and layoffs. The Act only awards the above-cited economic sanctions plus reasonable attorney fees and costs to the prevailing party. Thus, some legislators interested in protecting the rights of employees are arguing that the Act has no teeth and, at best, merely gives workers notice of the firing and possibly some severance pay if a job is eliminated prior to the 60-day notice period.

Employers covered by the law must now carefully orchestrate all moves *before* closing marginally profitable plants. Obviously, affected workers and the community must be notified properly and additional benefits will have to be given to comply with the Act's provisions.

■ ■

STRATEGY   *Now that you have a better understanding of the law, if you believe you are being victimized by a substantial reduction in force and the employer is not applying the law properly, speak to an experienced labor attorney immediately or contact your nearest regional office of the Department of Labor for more information. Companies must be careful when contemplating substantial reductions of their workforce, and a representative from the Department of Labor can advise you quickly if your rights are being violated.*

■ ■

4

ALL ABOUT
DISCRIMINATION

Although employment discrimination is illegal, it is widely practiced throughout the United States. In fact, many hundreds of thousands of claims are filed each year with the various federal, state and local agencies empowered to investigate, enforce and protect the civil rights of workers.

Federal and state laws prohibit employers from discriminating against employees or potential employees on the basis of:

- Age
- Sex or marital status
- Race, color or creed
- Religion or national origin
- Disability or physical handicap

This applies throughout all stages of employment including recruiting, interviewing and hiring; promotion, training, transfer and assignment; and discipline, layoffs and discharge procedures. Also, an illegal act can be committed by any member of an employer's staff, from the president down to the supervisor and receptionist! Typical remedies for illegal conduct include awards by judges, juries and arbitrators of job reinstatement, back pay, payment of retroactive benefits and counsel fees.

When a recently fired employee consults with me in my office, one of the first points I consider is whether the individual has a valid claim of unfair termination based upon age, sex or race discrimination. For example, assuming equal work, did the company pay the same salary and benefits to women as to men? Was a black employee fired justifiably because of excessive absences and lateness? Was an elderly sales employee the first to be fired because of a slipping sales quota?

As you will learn in this chapter, recognizing and fighting back against job discrimination is not always easy. The subtleties of this become apparent with the examples used above. For example, suppose a company fired a

60-year-old salesperson because he wasn't meeting quota. That sounds like a legitimate reason, right? Maybe, but what if the company's sales were down in many of its territories? Were younger salespeople fired as well, or were they merely given a warning and placed on probation?

Using our other examples, were white workers with the same record of absences and lateness merely warned and not fired? Was the female employee fired for complaining that she did not receive the same benefits as her male counterparts? If so, discrimination has occurred which must be redressed.

The information in this chapter will help you recognize when you have been victimized by discrimination. You will learn what practices are illegal and how to file a timely complaint, prove your charges and collect damages for your claim. For example, if you are being forced to work in a hostile and offensive environment and are the victim of sex harassment, you will learn how to send letters to document the exploitation. Recent Supreme Court cases dealing with major discrimination subjects will also be discussed and analyzed to make this chapter as timely as possible.

FEDERAL AND STATE DISCRIMINATION LAWS

The most comprehensive and significant federal legislation dealing with employment discrimination is Title VII of the Civil Rights Act of 1964, as amended by the Equal Employment Opportunity Act of 1972. This law applies to companies employing more than 15 persons and affects private employers, employment agencies and labor organizations.

In addition to federal laws regulating the employment process, most states have also enacted antidiscrimination statutes relating to employment. These state statutes and the agencies that enforce them are highly significant. For example, many small employers not covered by Title VII *do* fall within the jurisdiction of state law, and some local laws are even more strict and inclusive.

Some of these even prohibit discrimination based on marital status, physical handicap or sexual orientation. If you are 40 to 70 years of age, black, a woman, pregnant, disabled or otherwise identifiable as a minority, the EEOC under the federally enacted Civil Rights Act of 1964 will provide protection against unfair dismissal. But many states and municipalities have enacted their own laws that offer even greater protection; for example, age discrimination protection may apply to the young as well as those who are middle-aged and older, and homosexuals may be protected under local sex discrimination laws. If you want to learn whether you have this extra protection, contact an appropriate state or city agency or employment agency for further details, or speak to a knowledgeable labor attorney.

A question frequently asked by employers is: Which law takes precedence? The answer, essentially, is *the law that is the strictest.* Thus, to insure proper protection of your rights, try to be familiar with federal *and* state laws as well as those laws governing employment in your local business community or municipality. If there is a difference in coverage on the same subject, seek to enforce the law which is the most favorable to your situation.

We will now discuss the elements of sex, race, and age discrimination and related subjects in greater detail.

SEX DISCRIMINATION

The law requires similar employment policies, standards, and practices for males and females. Equal treatment applies in a variety of areas, including hiring, placement, job promotion, working conditions, wages and benefits, layoffs and discharge.

The following checklist will familiarize you with the kinds of practices that are illegal. In general, it is discriminatory for an employer to:

- Refuse to hire women with preschool-age children while hiring men with young children
- Require females to resign from jobs upon marriage when there is no similar requirement for males
- Include spouses of male employees in benefit plans while denying the same benefits to spouses of female employees
- Restrict certain jobs to men without offering a reasonable opportunity for women to demonstrate their ability to perform the same job adequately
- Refuse to hire, train, assign or promote pregnant or married women, or women of childbearing age, merely on the basis of sex
- Deny unemployment benefits, seniority, or layoff credit to pregnant women, or deny a leave of absence for pregnancy, irrespective of whether it is granted for illness
- Institute compulsory retirement plans with lower retirement ages for women than for men.

One common form of illegal activity in this area pertains to unequal pay for equal work. For example, one major university was recently ordered to pay 117 women an award of $1.3 million after a Federal Court judge ruled that the university paid less money to women on the faculty than to men in comparable posts.

Another common form of sex discrimination is *harassment*. Unwelcome sexual advances, requests for sexual favors, and verbal or physical conduct of a sexual nature all constitute sexual harassment when:

1. The person must submit to such activity in order to be hired
2. The person's consent or refusal is used in making an employment decision (e.g., to offer a raise or promotion)

3. Such conduct unreasonably interferes with the person's work performance or creates an intimidating, hostile or offensive working environment (e.g., humiliating comments are repeatedly addressed to the complainant).

Sexual harassment cases are dangerous to employers because some courts have ruled that companies are responsible for the acts of their supervisory employees *regardless* of whether the company knew or even should have known of the occurrence. This makes the employer strictly liable for the acts of any supervisor in some states. In cases where the employee is subjected to slur, insult or innuendo, courts are allowing claimants to prevail if they can prove that sexual harassment incidents took place which were neither isolated nor trivial. Some courts have even ruled that companies are liable for incidents which they should have known about (but didn't) when no effective action is taken to end the harassment—even if the company's official policies prohibit sexual harassment.

It is important to understand that sexual harassment cases are on the rise in a variety of nontraditional areas. For example, if you are a worker who was passed over for a promotion or denied benefits in favor of an individual who submitted to sexual advances, you too are considered a victim of sexual harassment under federal guidelines.

Also, the harassment can come from any source, not just fellow employees. For example, sexual harassment was found in one case when female employees were required to wear revealing uniforms and suffer derogatory comments from *passersby*.

Claims of sexual harassment are not limited to women. One recent case received nationwide coverage. A jury awarded $196,500 in damages to a man who claimed his supervisor demoted him because he refused her sexual advances. According to court testimony, the employee and his supervisor met one night in a hotel room, but the man refused to continue the relationship. The man proved he was demoted and passed over for a promotion as a result. In another case, the termination of a male employee for his rejection of advances from his homosexual male supervisor proved costly to a company.

Imaginative lawyers representing claimants in sexual harassment suits are also asserting other nontraditional causes of action in federal and state courts. These include wrongful discharge, infliction of emotional distress, invasion of privacy, assault and battery, and fraud. Awards from these suits can include consideration for mental anguish, back pay, reinstatement and punitive damages.

To avoid these and other potential legal hazards pertaining to sex harassment cases, employers have begun disseminating periodic reminders in policy manuals, journals and letters distributed to employees that the company does not tolerate sexual harassment of any kind on the job, that anyone who experiences or observes such treatment should report this to management (or their immediate supervisor) immediately and that all communications will be held in strict confidence with no direct or indirect reprisals to the informant or complainant.

In addition, companies are taking careful steps to instruct supervisors about sexual harassment and other forms of discrimination, what the adverse effects on the company could be and ways to handle problems if they arise.

How to Prove Sex Harassment

In order to prove sex harassment, you must take steps to document your claim. For example, if you are being teased on the job, it is wise to complain to a supervisor *in writing*. Judges, arbitrators and Equal Employment Opportunity Hearing Officers are more willing to award damages for sex harassment when a formal complaint was made requesting that the offensive conduct stop *and the request was ignored*.

The following true case illustrates this point. A woman was the only female traffic controller stationed at an air traffic center. While working there, she was subjected to substantial sexual slur, insult and innuendo by other employees, including various supervisory personnel. When the woman alerted her supervisors of this in a letter, several suggested that her problems might be solved if she "submitted to one of the controllers."

The court held that the woman proved that sexually harassing actions took place, that such acts were offensive and severe, and that the employer did little to stop them after receiving a warning (through her letter); she was awarded substantial damages as a result. Thus, by sending a letter similar to the one shown on the opposite page, you may be able to prove a repetitive pattern of conduct and demonstrate that the offensive acts were not condoned.

(Note: You may wish to send a copy of this letter to the president or other higher officer of the company. Additionally, always keep a copy of the letter for your files and save the receipt to prove delivery.)

If you feel you are the victim of harassment, discuss the incident with other employees you trust to discover if they have suffered similar abuse. If so, you may strengthen your claim and be less at risk of being fired in retaliation for making a complaint (since there is always safety in numbers).

Finally, speak to an experienced labor lawyer immediately if the matter is not resolved satisfactorily. An experienced lawyer can tell you whether it makes sense to immediately file a claim in court or with an appropriate agency such as the Equal Employment Opportunity Commission or if it is more desirable for him or her to contact the employer and try to settle the matter out of court. In any event, a course of strategy should be implemented and followed *immediately* so you don't suffer more abuse and to protect your rights in this area. If you delay contacting an appropriate agency or lawyer to assert your rights, such delay may be deemed a *waiver* of your rights or an acceptance by you of such illegal acts, which can jeopardize your claim.

Date

Name and Title of Supervisor
Name of Company
Address

Re: Complaint of Sex Harassment

Dear (Name of Supervisor),

I have recently been subjected to a number of offensive, harmful and disruptive acts which I believe constitute sex harassment in violation of my rights.

The acts I am specifically complaining about occurred on (specify date, time and place) and were as follows: (describe the acts committed, by whom, if witnesses were present, etc.).

After being subjected to such acts, I requested of (specify the individual) that they cease and stated that they were unwelcome. However, on (date) they continued (specify new acts, place, what occurred, etc.).

Such acts are intimidating and repugnant and have had a severe emotional (and physical) impact on my working efforts (specify other harm resulting if appropriate). I have not asked for such treatment and will not tolerate such unprofessional conduct in the future.

Therefore, please treat this letter as a formal warning and advise all male employees in my department to cease and desist such activities. Additionally, if such acts continue, be advised that I will take all necessary steps to protect my rights, including contacting a representative from the State Human Rights Commission or the federal Equal Employment Opportunity Commission.

Hopefully, such actions will not be necessary and I thank you for your attention and cooperation in this matter.

Very truly yours,

Name of Complainant

SENT CERTIFIED MAIL, RETURN RECEIPT REQUESTED

Related Rights of Maternity, Pregnancy Leave, Child Care and Disability

Childbirth leave and pregnancy-related disability are protected by numerous federal and state laws. In fact, the rights of pregnant workers have changed dramatically over the past few years. Recently, some states have passed strong laws protecting the rights of pregnant workers. These states include Connecticut, Montana, Massachusetts, California, Minnesota, Oregon and Puerto Rico. The laws in these states give female workers either job security (i.e., the right to have a job back within a certain period of time after giving birth) or the ability to enforce the right to take a maternity leave.

Some states, such as California, New York, New Jersey, Rhode Island and Hawaii, provide paid maternity leave (one-half to one-third of the regular salary) under Worker's Compensation laws for a period of usually up to 26 weeks. Other states (Minnesota, Oregon and Connecticut) are granting workers, both male and female, the right to care for their newborn and adopted children for a period of time after birth. Additionally, Congress is currently considering passing legislation giving all workers unpaid parental and medical leave.

Although it should be a blessing, being pregnant can be a period of great uncertainty for working women. Most know very little about their rights pertaining to maternity, child care, disability practices and job security. But their ignorance is understandable since the laws in this area are quite complex.

The material in this section highlights recent developments and trends in the law affecting parental and maternity leaves and pregnancy rights.

The law   A company cannot treat pregnancy-related disability or maternity leave differently from the way it treats other forms of disability leaves of absence. To do so violates both federal and state discrimination laws. The Pregnancy Discrimination Act, an amendment to Title VII of the Federal Civil Rights Act of 1964, prohibits discrimination on the basis of pregnancy, childbirth and related medical conditions. The law requires companies to review their leave, benefit, reinstatement and seniority policies to ensure that they treat maternity-related absence *the same* as other temporary absences for physical disabilities.

The following specific examples illustrate what employers must do under the law:

- Employees who are on maternity leave (defined as the child-care period commencing after disability from the pregnancy and birth has ended) are entitled to accrue seniority, automatic pay increases and vacation time on the same basis as other employees on medical leave.
- Employers may not require pregnant workers to exhaust vacation benefits before receiving sick pay or disability benefits unless all temporarily disabled workers are required to do the same.
- Employers may require a physical examination and doctor's certification of ability to return to work only if such is required of all temporarily disabled employees.
- Although employers may require workers to give notice of a pregnancy, such a requirement must serve a legitimate business purpose and must not be used to restrict the employee's job opportunities.

- Employers are prohibited from discriminating in hiring, promotion and firing decisions on the basis of pregnancy or because of an abortion.
- After the birth, an employer cannot prohibit a woman from returning to work *sooner* than the company policy dictates.

The law also demands equality for pregnant workers in the area of health-care coverage. Although companies are not required to provide any health-care benefits, pregnancy must be treated the same as any other medical condition. If health care is provided, maternity care must be included, and coverage must be the same for spouses of males and females. Also, limitations on maternity coverage for preexisting conditions must be similar to limits on other disabilities. Finally, if extended benefits for other disabilities are given, so too must extended benefits be given for pregnancies occurring during a covered period.

Job security   Perhaps the biggest concern faced by pregnant workers is the ability to get their jobs back after giving birth. Unfortunately, with the exception of Connecticut and Montana, most states do *not* have laws requiring companies to hold jobs open for pregnant workers. This is particularly true if you take an extended maternity leave (three months, for example) and the company has a stated policy in a manual or handbook that restricts all employees from taking extended or excessive personal leaves.

However, legislation is now pending in 28 states (including Vermont, Ohio, North Dakota, Missouri, New Hampshire, Mississippi, Indiana, Florida, Massachusetts, District of Columbia, New Jersey and Maryland) requiring reinstatement to the same or equivalent position of employment unless it is not possible due to "changed circumstances" (i.e., it is impossible or economically unfeasible to rehire the individual). Additionally, pending legislation in Congress called the Family and Medical Leave Act seeks to provide employees with 10 weeks of unpaid, job-protected leave over a 24-month period for the birth or adoption of a child or to care for a seriously ill child or parent. For personal health reasons, an employee would be guaranteed 15 weeks' leave over a 12-month period.

Hopefully, some of these laws will be passed by the time you read this information. However, for your protection you should know the particular laws in your state; also, before leaving, it is a good idea to discuss whether you can get your old job or a comparable one back when you are able to return to work. If you can prove (i.e., you have witnesses) that a specific promise was made to keep the job open for you, speak to a lawyer when the company reneges on such a promise; you may have a valid cause of action in this area.

Some companies protect themselves from potential liability by giving pregnant workers a job at the same rate of pay when they are able to return to work but with different tasks and diminished job responsibilities. The employer is not generally obligated to reemploy you in the same job capacity, so be aware of this.

Parental leaves   Parental leaves for postnatal care are different from disability leaves since they are typically given without pay and are considered personal leaves of absence, as opposed to money given for an absence from work caused by a physical disability. Minnesota, Oregon and Connecticut have recently passed laws allowing both parents to care for their newborn children. Under the Minnesota law, for example, parents may take up to six weeks of unpaid leave if they are full-time employees. Oregon offers up to 12 weeks of unpaid leave for both parents, while Connecticut grants state employees a minimum of 24 weeks of unpaid leave over a two-year period.

Male employees should be mindful that if an employer permits extended personal child-care leave to mothers, guidelines promulgated by the Equal Employment Opportunity Commission require that male employee-fathers receive the same benefits. You may also be entitled to paid short-term leave (referred to as paternity leave) and should inquire if short-term leave with pay is available. Some companies give fathers paid time off, so don't be afraid to ask for this if applicable.

Common rules to remember   The following strategies should simplify confusing law in this area:

- Employers must provide pregnant workers with paid leave for their actual disability due to pregnancy and related childbirth if leave with pay is provided for workers with other disabilities.
- If unpaid leaves of absence are provided by a company, mothers and fathers of newly-born or adopted children must be given such personal leave as well.
- If your company places a time restriction on the duration of maternity leaves and the same restrictions are *not* applied to leaves for other temporary disabilities, this is illegal.
- If the company refuses to guarantee your job after a personal leave for postnatal care has ended, be sure that such a policy treats all other personal leaves the same way.
- If a company permits extended child-care leave to mothers, male employee-fathers must receive the same benefits.
- Pregnancy is a disability that must be treated the same as any other disability.
- If you are out of work on leave for a pregnancy-related medical disability that actually continues (e.g., complications substantiated by required medical proof) for a period of time not exceeding four months, speak to a lawyer immediately if the company refuses

to reemploy you after you are physically able to return to work and perform your duties. Some states automatically require re-employment under Worker's Compensation laws; be aware of this if applicable.

- The law requires the granting of maternity leave of absence if leaves of absence are granted for other reasons.

- Be suspicious if an employer places time restrictions on the duration of pregnancy-related leaves (e.g., that pregnancy leaves not exceed four months); this may be illegal.

- Be aware that it is illegal to place pregnant workers on involuntary sick leave if the company has no policy of placing employees with other forms of disability on involuntary leave.

- Recognize that you may not get your job back if you are able and willing to return to work after a pregnancy. However, the job of a worker with a pregnancy-related disability must be held open on the same basis as jobs that are held open for employees on sick or disability leaves for other reasons.

Speak to a lawyer immediately or contact your nearest Equal Employment Opportunity Commission district office or state Commission on Human Rights office if you believe you were fired, demoted or denied benefits on the basis of pregnancy. An experienced labor lawyer or agency representative can help you weigh your options to achieve the quickest and most satisfactory results.

Since the laws are rapidly giving pregnant working mothers more rights and allowing fathers time off to help care for newly born children, do not be pressured or intimidated into accepting a decision which appears to be unfair. To avoid misunderstandings, request a full explanation of your benefits and options with a duly authorized representative of the company. Go in with a ballpark proposal and be prepared to *negotiate* certain benefits, because many items are negotiable (no matter what you are told). Then if you are unsatisfied, weigh all your options carefully and be apprised of the law in this area to protect your rights. Remember, all actions taken by the employer must be justified under the law. The burden of proving that decisions are appropriate and necessary falls on the employer, since any practice which excludes employment or denies benefits on the basis of pregnancy is closely scrutinized. In addition, if there is an investigation into such charges, a company faces the risk of having the Equal Employment Opportunity Commission and other agency investigators evaluate treatment accorded other employees returning after nonmaternity leaves of absence.

Thus, never be afraid to assert your rights where applicable. You may discover that the employer will have no choice but to respond favorably to your demands to avoid potential problems and investigations.

Retirement Plans and Fringe Benefits

Besides unequal pay for equal work, retirement, pension plans and fringe benefits are often found to be unequally applied; any program which favors one sex over another violates federal and state discrimination laws.

Be aware that the following practices have been declared illegal in the application of fringe benefits pertaining to vacations, insurance coverage, pensions, profit-sharing plans, bonuses, holidays and disability leaves:

- Conditioning benefits available to employees and their spouses and families on a particular status (e.g., "head of household" or "principal wage earner")
- Making certain benefits available to wives of male employees but denying them to husbands of female employees
- Basing provisions of a pension plan on norms applied differently according to sex
- Denying a job or benefit to pregnant employees or applicants

These are just some of the ways employers commit violations pertaining to benefits. If you have doubts about any current practices, seek competent legal advice at once.

Preemployment Screening

Although common illegal practices in this area were discussed in Chapter 1, it is worthwhile to mention this again. Unfortunately, many employers ask illegal questions of females at job interviews, particularly with respect to their marital status. Federal Equal Employment Opportunity Commission guidelines and state regulations declare that the only lawful question that may be asked of a female applicant is "What is your marital status?"

Familiarize yourself with the kinds of questions that are illegal at job interviews. Then, if you refuse to answer such questions and are denied a job as a result, you may wish to consider filing charges with the Equal Employment Opportunity Commission or appropriate state rights organization alleging sex discrimination on the basis of such illegal inquiries.

Recent Supreme Court Rulings Pertaining to Sex Discrimination

In the spring 1989 term, the Supreme Court decided several cases which commentators suggest will create additional barriers for women trying to use the legal system to redress discrimination in the workplace. For example, in the case of *Price Waterhouse* v. *Hopkins,* the court raised the burden of proof required by a successful female litigant claiming a denial of a promotion due to sex. In that case, the court essentially ruled that employers must prove that their refusal to promote a woman is based on legitimate business reasons, but lowered the business justification required to the weakest possible standard.

Some experts suggest that this ruling essentially may "take the sting out" of various claims made by disgruntled female employees or ex-employees who believe they were denied benefits, promotions, etc., on the basis of gender. However, since each case is determined by its unique facts and circumstances, and because it remains unclear how lower courts will interpret and apply the results of this case, do not be dissuaded from taking action where warranted. *Always* consult an experienced labor lawyer before making any decision or taking action in this area.

AGE DISCRIMINATION

Federal and state discrimination laws are designed to promote employment of older persons based upon their abilities, irrespective of age. They also seek to prohibit arbitrary discrimination and to help employers and workers find ways of addressing problems arising from the impact of age upon employment.

The following thumbnail sketch outlines what employers *can* do under federal and state discrimination laws pertaining to age:

- Fire older workers for inadequate job performance and good cause (e.g., tardiness or intoxication)
- Entice older workers into early retirement by offering additional benefits (e.g., bigger pensions, extended health insurance, substantial bonuses, etc.) which are voluntarily accepted
- Lay off older workers, provided younger employees are similarly treated
- Discriminate against older applicants when successful job performance absolutely requires that a younger person be hired for the job (e.g., in the case of a flight controller)

However, the following actions are *prohibited* by law:

- Denying an older applicant a job on the basis of age
- Imposing compulsory retirement before age 70
- Coercing older employees into retirement by threatening them with termination, loss of benefits, etc.
- Firing older persons because of age
- Denying promotions, transfers, or assignments because of age
- Penalizing older employees with reduced privileges, employment opportunities or compensation because of age

Significant damages are recoverable when an individual receives unfair treatment because of age. These may include job reinstatement in the event of a firing, wage adjustments, back pay and double back pay, promotions, recovery of legal fees and filing costs, and punitive damages. Recourse can also include the institution of an affirmative action program on behalf of fellow employees.

Thus, it is illegal to terminate anyone on the basis of age. Whenever an older employee (over 40) is fired and that individual is claiming discrimination, the issue is basically whether the company's decision was made because of age or was the result of a reasonable, nondiscriminatory, rational business reason. Typically, the older worker must use circumstantial evidence to prove that the employer's motive was improper. This is sometimes done by demonstrating that he or she was between 40 and 70 years of age, was doing satisfactory work, and the position was then filled by a substantially younger employee under 40.

Discrimination may also be proved by age-related statements made to the claimant (such as "You are too old"; "Why don't you retire?") or by statistics (for example, the fact that the company fired five older workers in the past year and replaced them all with employees under 40).

When employers can support firing decisions with documentation of poor work performance or similar factors, an older worker's chances of proving age discrimination diminish. Additionally, if staff avoids making liability-sensitive statements, remarks or threats with respect to age and the employee is unable to obtain statistical proof that the company had a practice of firing older workers and replacing them with younger ones, the chances of success with a claim in this area may also be reduced.

We will now cover areas where age discrimination typically occurs and consider ways to protect your rights.

Preemployment Screening

Employers sometimes set requirements that are too high, or commit violations through illegal ads. Many make statements or ask questions during the hiring interview that are illegal. For example, unintentional discrimination against older applicants occurs when they are told by an interviewer that:

- They are "overqualified"
- They lack formal education credits even though they are highly qualified by previous work experience and a college degree is not necessary for successful job performance
- They must take a preemployment physical which is either unnecessary, not job-related or not requested of all other applicants
- They are required to answer questions such as "How old are you?" or "What is the date of your birth?" or "Why did you decide to seek employment at your age?"

With respect to preemployment questions concerning age, be aware that under federal and state guidelines, employers can *only* ask the applicant if he or she is between 18 and 65, and if not, to state his or her age. Any other type of question concerning age is illegal. If you refuse to answer such a question and you believe you were denied a job as a result, you may consider contacting the Equal Employment Opportunity Commission, a local Human Rights Commission office or a state attorney general's office to pursue your rights.

Physicals

Companies sometimes require potential employees to take preemployment physicals. This is legal provided all applicants are required to take physicals in the screening process. However, review all medical history forms and applications before filling them out; these sometimes contain discriminatory questions. Also, beware of discriminatory questions sometimes asked by company doctors; employment cannot be denied on the basis of such illegal questions.

Advertisements

Pay special attention to the language in advertisements used to attract job candidates. The Age Discrimination in Employment Act of 1967 prohibits all companies from publishing advertisements indicating any preference, limitation, specification or discrimination based on age. For example, the Department of Labor recently published an Interpretive Bulletin stipulating that

> when Help Wanted notices or advertisements contain terms and phrases such as "age 25 to 35," "young," "girl," "boy," "college student," "recent college graduate," or others of a similar nature, such a term or phrase discriminates against the employment of older persons when used in relation to a specific job and will be considered a violation of the Act.

Thus, targeted advertisements containing the following language are illegal:

- "Industrial management trainee, recent college graduate"
- "Sales trainee, any recent degree"
- "Prefer recent college grad"
- "Corporate attorney, 2–4 years out of college"

(Note: Help Wanted notices or advertisements which include a term or phrase such as "college graduate" or other education criterion, or specify a minimum age less than 40, such as "not under 18," or "not under 21," are not prohibited by federal statute.) Employers must be sure that advertisements are worded properly to comply with the law, since discriminatory advertising will be used as evidence against an employer should a related complaint be filed.

Job Requirements

When preparing criteria for a particular job, companies sometimes set a higher requirement than necessary to attract a higher caliber of applicant, which may tend to discriminate between classes of applicants. For example, in the case of *United States* v. *Georgia Power Company*, the requirements of a high school diploma and aptitude test scores raised a question as to whether they really were related to successful job performance. The diploma requirement was found to be unlawful because any requirement must measure the person for the job, and not the person "in abstract." In this case it was ruled that the qualification of a high school diploma did not measure the individual's ability to do the job.

If you are an older applicant and believe a potential employer has established unwarranted requirements which are not job-related, you may have a valid cause of action for age discrimination; be aware of this.

Progressive Discipline and Warnings

A second major area where age discrimination frequently occurs relates to on-the-job discipline and warnings. The practice of progressive discipline (in which notice is given to the employee of a company's dissatisfaction with his or her work performance) is used in reducing the risk of wrongful termination lawsuits. By documenting the incidence of employee disciplinary measures through precise records of conferences, warnings, probation notices, remedial efforts and other steps, companies sometimes demonstrate that an eventual termination was not done out of a discriminatory motive but stemmed from a good-faith business decision.

Many companies, however, apply their system of discipline and warnings in a haphazard fashion and fail to use the same punishment for similar infractions. That could invite a lawsuit based on age discrimination if there are several employees with a chronic problem (such as absenteeism) and the older employee is the first to be fired for that reason while workers under 40 are only given warnings.

If you are an older employee who believes an employer is treating you more harshly than younger workers for identical infractions, you may be a victim of age discrimination; speak with experienced labor counsel immediately.

Discharge

The law states that it is illegal to fire anyone on the basis of age. Thus, whenever an older employee is fired, the issue basically is whether the employer's decision was made because of age or was the result of a reasonable, nondiscriminatory business factor. Usually, the older worker must use circumstantial evidence to prove that the employer's motive was improper. This is sometimes done by demonstrating that he or she was between 40 and 70 years of age, was doing satisfactory work, was fired, and the position was then filled by a substantially younger employee. It can also be proved by direct evidence, such as statements made to the claimant, and with statistics.

Forced Retirement

Another related area of age discrimination involves forced retirement. This occurs when companies exert pressure on older workers to opt for early retirement or face firing, demotion or a cut in pay. Some also threaten workers with poor recommendations unless they accept an offer of early retirement.

Companies contemplating a large layoff or seeking to reduce payroll through early retirement incentives must do so carefully to avoid charges of age discrimination. Under the Age Discrimination in Employment Act (ADEA) enacted in 1967, it is illegal to impose compulsory retirement before age 70 unless the employee is a "bona fide executive" receiving an annual company-paid retirement benefit of at least $27,000 per year after reaching 65, or is in a "high policy-making position" during a two-year period prior to reaching age 65.

Some states have passed similar laws which protect older employees from being victimized by forced retirement and mandatory retirement plans. For example, under a recent law enacted in New York, most public employees cannot be forced to retire no matter how old they get. Private sector employees (with limited exceptions for some executives, tenured college faculty members, firefighters, police officers and other law enforcement positions) are also protected.

Ask yourself the following questions if you believe you were fired because of age:

- Did you request a transfer to another position before you were fired? Was it refused? If so, were similar requests granted to younger workers?
- How were you terminated? Were you given false reasons for the termination? Did you consent to such action or did you send a certified letter protesting the discharge?
- Were you replaced by a younger worker? Were younger workers merely laid off, and not fired?

Positive answers to these questions may prove you were fired as a result of age discrimination. And your case will be strengthened when fellow employees are also victimized. For example, 143 persons were recently forced to retire prematurely from an insurance company at the age of 62. The large number of employees made it difficult for the company to overcome charges of age discrimination, and the workers collectively received more than $6 million in back wages.

In another case, a company denied job training to two older employees and then fired them. The company claimed the men were unskilled and not qualified to continue employment. The workers filed timely claims and recovered $79,200 in lost wages, benefits and legal fees.

RACIAL DISCRIMINATION

Statistics indicate that more than 29 million blacks, 17 million Hispanic Americans, 6 million Jews, 2.5 million people of Arab descent and 1.1 million Native Americans will enter the U.S. workplace during the next 20 years. Although such minorities were discriminated against in the past, the enactment of various federal laws, including Title VII of the Civil Rights Act and 42 USC Sections 1981 and 1982, prohibits intentional discrimination based upon ancestry or ethnicity.

These federal laws prohibit employers of 15 or more from discriminating on the basis of race or color. They do *not* apply to employers with 14 or fewer employees, private membership clubs, religious organizations and Indian tribes, but the vast majority of states have even stronger laws directed to fighting job-related race and minority discrimination. In many states, for example, companies with less than eight workers can be found guilty of discrimination.

The problem is that although employment discrimination is illegal, it is commonly practiced throughout the United States in direct and subtle ways, and most minority workers know little about how to recognize race discrimination and how to fight back. Some companies practice blatant forms of minority discrimination by paying less salary and other compensation to blacks, Hispanics, Asians, Pacific Islanders, American Indian and Alaskan natives (i.e., Native Americans), and other persons having origins in Europe, North Africa and the Middle East. Others engage in quota systems by denying promotions and jobs to individuals on the basis of race and color. Still other employers utilize more sophisticated and subtle forms of race discrimination. For example, black and other minority applicants are frequently denied jobs after answering illegal questions pertaining to their credit and financial history—areas where companies have no legal basis to inquire.

This section will help you recognize if and when you are being victimized by race discrimination and what to do about it. If you are a new worker, you will learn how to go about resolving problems and avoiding confrontations when possible. You will also gain a better understanding of what types of conduct are allowed and the proper steps to take to make a formal complaint and seek redress (i.e., through a private attorney or by utilizing the free services of offices including the federal Equal Employment Opportunity Commission (EEOC) or state agencies such as the Division of Human Rights or attorney general's office).

The Law

The law generally forbids private employers, labor unions, state and local government agencies, and employment agencies from:

- Denying an applicant a job on the basis of race or color
- Denying promotions, transfers or assignments on the basis of race or color
- Penalizing workers with reduced privileges, reduced employment opportunities and reduced compensation on the basis of race or color
- Firing a worker on the basis of race or color

Recognize that discrimination can occur during any number of the following employment stages: recruiting, interviewing and hiring, promotion, training, transfer and assignment, discipline, layoffs, and discharge procedures.

Also, an illegal act can be committed by any member of the employer's staff, from the president down to the supervisor, interviewer or receptionist. It can even occur through outside independent contractors (such as surveillance teams hired by the company). In the event violations are proven, you may be entitled to receive benefits including job reinstatement, back pay, payment of retroactive benefits (lost seniority, additional pension and profit-sharing monies, etc.), counsel fees, and money as compensation for pain and mental anguish (if this can be proved).

For example, I recently represented a black supervisor who was confined to an office and interrogated by private investigators hired by a company to obtain a confession regarding warehouse stock that was missing. Despite his claims of innocence, my client was questioned for two hours; later, he was fired by the company. I learned that the reason for the firing was pretextural—i.e., that the company was out to discharge him because he was black. Although the company claimed it was not responsible for the incident since it had hired an outside service to investigate and make recommendations regarding the matter, I negotiated a generous settlement (which included sums for mental anguish), even though my client obtained a better-paying job within one month after his discharge.

Common Areas of Exploitation

Although it is legal for employers to pose questions at the hiring interview which test your motivation, maturity, willingness to accept instruction, interest in the job and ability to communicate, inquiries made to further discriminatory purposes are illegal. Common areas of exploitation encompass questions pertaining to color, national origin, citizenship, language and relatives. For example, it is illegal to ask the following questions under federal Equal Employment Opportunity Commission guidelines and state regulations:

Color	What is your skin color?
National Origin	What is your ancestry? What is your mother's native language? What is your spouse's nationality? What is your maiden name?
Citizenship	Of what country are you a citizen? Are your parents or spouse naturalized or native-born citizens? When did they acquire citizenship? Are you a native-born citizen?
Language	What is your native tongue? How did you acquire the ability to read, write and speak a foreign language?
Relatives	Names, addresses, age and other pertinent information concerning your spouse, children or relatives not employed by the company. What type of work does your mother or father do?

Recognize that you have the right to refuse to answer any of the above questions at the hiring interview. If you choose not to answer them, you can politely inform the interviewer that you believe such question(s) are illegal and refuse to answer them on that basis. Then, if you are denied the job, you may have a strong case for damages after speaking with a representative of the Equal Employment Opportunity Commission, the Human Rights Commission or a knowledgeable attorney if you can prove the denial stemmed from your refusal to answer the questions.

Another common area of race or minority discrimination occurs when companies deliberately impose higher hiring standards than necessary, which tends to exclude minorities. Remember that all employment criterion-requirements must be directly related to the job and minorities cannot be excluded unnecessarily.

Proving you were individually excluded from a job based on your race or color may be more difficult. Here, it is helpful to obtain statistical data to show that the employer's practices are illegal. For example, if ten positions for an engineering job were filled and none of the jobs was offered to a minority, that may be sufficient to infer that the company violated the law. However, you would need assistance from a competent attorney or discrimination specialist to prove this because the rules necessary to prove statistical disparities are complex.

You may have an easier time of demonstrating race discrimination when you are *directly* treated unfairly on the job. For example, if you are repeatedly harassed and called names on the job, or are treated differently from nonminorities (for example, if you are absent several days from work and you are suspended or placed on formal probation, while white workers with the same or a greater number of absences are only given an informal warning), then it is best to gather this factual information for discussion with an executive or officer in your company's personnel department. (Note: Do not complain to the supervisor who made the decision since you may be tipping your hand and end up getting nothing for your troubles.)

In the light of the recent Supreme Court decision *Wards Cove* v. *Antonio*, you may have an easier time proving race discrimination on an *individual* basis as opposed to relying on statistical disparities. In *Wards Cove*, the court ruled that those alleging race bias collectively must prove that the employer had no business reason for imposing the job requirement they are contesting. This case overruled an earlier decision requiring employers to justify employment policies that were shown by statistics to have an unfair impact on minorities. Thus, in certain cases, employers now only have to supply a business justification for their action (not prove validity) and the complainant has the burden of demonstrating that the business justification was not legitimate.

How to Fight Back

Once you recognize you have been treated unfairly, you must react quickly and correctly to protect your rights. This includes *immediately* speaking with a competent lawyer or representative from an agency empowered to investigate your claim. Time is of the essence, since in most situations complaints must be filed with an EEOC office within 180 days of the alleged illegal act to avoid the expiration of the Statute of Limitations. If you are protesting illegal activity but have not been fired, no one can stop you from filing a complaint. The law forbids employers from threatening reprisals or retaliation.

It is not necessary for the complaint to be lengthy or complicated. The main purpose is to allege sufficient facts to trigger an agency investigation. If you file charges with the EEOC or other agency, the advantage is that the charges are investigated and processed at no cost to you. The disadvantage is that the matter will probably drag on far longer than if a private lawyer takes your case and files a formal lawsuit on your behalf.

In one recent case I reviewed, the complainant alleged sufficient race discrimination in the following complaint:

> I am black. On (date), I was notified by (name), my supervisor at (name of employer) that I was fired. I asked him to tell me why I was fired; he said it was because I called in sick six times in the past year. I know of several white employees who called in sick more than six times in the past year and were not fired.

Once you sign and notarize the complaint, the company will then be notified and sent a copy and requested to submit a detailed written response within a short period of time (typically no longer than 30 days). Investigators will then commence formal investigations where warranted, which often include field visits and interviews with company personnel and witnesses. No-fault settlement conferences are sometimes convened to explore amicable resolutions and more than 40% of all cases are settled informally this way.

However if the case cannot be settled, you will eventually obtain a hearing before a magistrate or judge.

Strategies to Win Your Case

Always speak to other minority employees to determine if they have received similar discriminatory treatment. Additionally, discuss your problem with friendly witnesses who are willing to testify on your behalf if necessary. Corroborative testimony is often crucial in helping minority claimants win their cases and should never be overlooked.

If you receive an unfavorable performance evaluation or warning which you believe is subjectively tainted because of your minority status, consider submitting a written response which documents why the appraisal or warning is incorrect. This way, you can document your protest and demonstrate that you did not acquiesce (through silence or inaction) in the employer's version of the facts.

Finally, it is recommended that you receive an opinion from an experienced labor lawyer *before* taking any form of action. After the consultation, you may learn, for example, that your grounds regarding the alleged discrimination are baseless or cannot be proved. If this occurs, it would be unwise to speak to management and complain about an incident which had no legal basis since you could be alienating interested parties and jeopardizing your job or future opportunities in the process.

Unfortunately, of the hundreds of individuals who consult with me each year alleging various discriminatory violations, fewer than one in three have viable, provable claims which I am willing to accept and act on in their behalf. Thus, it is important to obtain sound legal advice *before* embarking on any action in this area.

▌ RELIGIOUS DISCRIMINATION

The Civil Rights Act of 1964 prohibits religious discrimination and requires employers to reasonably accommodate the religious practices of employees and prospective employees. This law covers employers of 15 or more persons. Various state laws also prohibit discrimination on the basis of creed—for example, due to a person's observance of a certain day as a Sabbath or holy day. In New York, for example, employers may not require attendance at work on such a day except in emergencies or in situations in which the employee's presence is indispensable. Absences for these observations must be made up at some mutually agreeable time, or can be charged against accumulated leave time.

In one recent case, the Supreme Court decided that the Civil Rights Act requires companies to try to accommodate the religious beliefs of employees, even if it means weekends off, and can be held liable if they don't try. In the case in question, an auto manufacturer hired a woman to work on an assembly line. The woman was a member of the Worldwide Church of God. At first, the job did not conflict with her religious beliefs (which specifically prohibited her from working from sunset Friday to sunset Saturday) because the assembly line operated only from Monday through Friday. However, when the company required mandatory overtime on Saturdays, the worker refused based on religious grounds and was fired after missing a series of Saturday work shifts.

The employee brought suit in federal court alleging the company violated Title VII of the 1964 Civil Rights Act that makes it unlawful to fire or discriminate against an employee on the basis of "race, color, *religion*, sex or national origin" and that a 1972 amendment to the law requires employers to prove they are unable to accommodate an employee's religious practice without "undue hardship."

The primary issue before the trial court was whether the company had made a bona fide attempt to accommodate the needs of the employee, and the court ruled that the woman's absence did not injure the company because it was not unreasonable to grant her request. The worker was awarded $73,911 in back pay and benefits despite the employer's argument that it could not properly run its business because of: (1) high absenteeism rates on Saturday; (2) numerous complaints from co-workers that she should not receive special privileges; and (3) waiting lists of more senior employees requesting transfers to departments with no Saturday work.

The Supreme Court let the lower court ruling stand. In its decision, the Supreme Court commented that the company could have acted on the employee's request without undue hardship through the use of people employed specifically for absentee relief.

If you are a true religious observer whose beliefs conflict with your work schedule, remember that you have certain rights, including the following:

- Employers have an obligation to make reasonable accommodations to the religious needs of employees and prospective employees.
- Employers must give time off for the Sabbath or holy day except in an emergency.
- In such an event, the employer may give the leave without pay, may require equivalent time to be made up or may allow the employee to charge the time against any other leave with pay except sick pay.

However, be aware that:

- Employers may *not* be required to give time off to employees who work in key health and safety occupations or to any employee whose presence is critical to the company on any given day.
- Employers are *not* required to take steps inconsistent with a valid seniority system to accommodate an employee's religious practices.
- Employers are *not* required to incur overtime costs to replace an employee who will not work on Saturday.
- Employers have *no* responsibility to appease fellow employees who complain they are suffering undue hardship when a co-worker is allowed not to work on a Saturday Sabbath due to a religious belief while they are required to do so.
- Employers are *not* required to choose the option the employee prefers, as long as the accommodation offered is reasonable.
- Penalizing an employee for missing a workday because of refusing to work on Christmas or Good Friday most likely constitutes religious discrimination, depending on the facts.

If you are a religious observer experiencing difficulties from an employer (making it impossible to practice your religion on a Saturday Sabbath) you now know what your rights are. Also, be aware that a bona fide objection to union membership must be accommodated. One method of accommodation is to allow an employee whose religious beliefs preclude union membership to donate a sum of money equivalent to union dues to a nonlabor, nonreligious charitable organization.

Speak to a lawyer immediately if you are being victimized or if the employer denies accommodating your religious beliefs on the basis of "undue hardship." This is an exception that companies try to use in some situations to circumvent current law in this area.

HANDICAP DISCRIMINATION

The past decade has seen a tremendous increase in litigation and legislative activity at the state and federal level structured to protect handicapped individuals from job discrimination. There is good reason for this: the number of Americans having disabilities has been estimated to be from 37 million to 43 million people, half of whom fall within the prime working ages of 16 and 64. Additionally, although more than two-thirds of Americans who have disabilities would like to be gainfully employed if given the chance, their unemployment rate as a group is 66%.

Until recently, the main federal law protecting handicapped individuals against discrimination was the Rehabilitation Act of 1973, which applied to government contractors and employers who receive federal assistance.

This law prohibits denying an otherwise qualified applicant or employee a job or opportunity, including fringe benefits, promotion opportunities and special training, solely on the basis of a handicap. And employers who have government contracts or subcontracts worth over $2,500 must take affirmative steps to employ and promote handicapped workers and must not discriminate against them.

Due to the limited applicability of the Rehabilitation Act of 1973, on July 26, 1990 Congress enacted the Americans with Disabilities Act (ADA) [P.L. 101-336]. The Equal Employment Opportunity Commission has jurisdiction and enforcement authority over Title I of the ADA, prohibiting employment discrimination against anyone with a disability.

Experts suggest that this federal law will go a long way towards making existing facilities accessible to handicapped employees, restructuring some jobs to provide for reasonable accommodation of persons with handicaps, and offering more part-time or modified work schedules for persons with disabilities.

The law protects any person with a physical or mental impairment that substantially limits "one or more major life activities." This covers a broad range of disabilities, including deafness, heart disease, cancer, AIDS and emotional problems; it even covers alcohol or drug abusers who rehabilitate themselves. Once the law takes effect (in July 1992 for employers with 25 or more workers, and in July 1994 for employers with 15 or more workers), companies will be bound to:

- Eliminate any inquiries on medical examinations or forms designed to identify an applicant's disabilities
- Avoid adverse classifications of job applicants or employees because of disability
- Avoid participating in a contractual relationship, including a collective bargaining agreement, that has the effect of discriminating against job applicants or employees with disabilities
- Avoid discriminating against an applicant or employee because of that individual's relationship or association with another who has a disability
- Make reasonable accommodations to the known physical or mental limitations of an applicant or employee, unless doing so would impose an undue hardship on the employer
- Avoid denying employment opportunities to an applicant or employee if the denial is because of the need to make reasonable accommodation to a disability
- Avoid employment tests or selection criteria that have a disparate impact on individuals with disabilities unless the test or criterion is shown to be job-related and supported by business necessity

■ Administer employment tests in the manner most likely to accurately reflect the job-related skills of an applicant or employee who is disabled

Although critics complain that businesses will be forced to spend millions of dollars to comply with the new law, proponents of the bill argue that such costs will be more than offset by bringing millions of unemployed individuals into the taxpaying workforce.

In addition to federal law, most states prohibit discrimination as a result of physical handicaps, and in those states it is illegal to deny employment if a handicapped person is capable of performing the job in question. Decisions not to hire an applicant because of physical defects or a mental condition are scrutinized closely; you cannot be denied employment merely because you have a history of physical or mental impairment that has been cured or because being hired would increase the employer's insurance costs.

The following general rules are applicable under the laws of many states. *Always* consult with an attorney or research the laws of your particular state where applicable.

1. **When applying for a job,** it is illegal to be asked questions such as "Do you have a disability?" or "Have you ever been treated for any of the following diseases?" (Note: It is legal to be asked a question such as "Do you have any impairments, physical, mental, or medical, which would prevent you from performing in a reasonable manner the activities involved in the job or occupation for which you have applied?")

2. **Preemployment physicals** are illegal if they are not uniformly requested of all applicants for a particular job or are not reasonably necessary to test minimum physical standards for the work to be performed.

3. **Denial of a job or dismissal from a job** due to a disability which does not prevent you from performing in a reasonable manner the activities involved in the job or the occupation sought or held is illegal.

4. **AIDS is a handicap** which you may seek protection for under various state and federal discrimination laws.

However:

5. **Generally, employers are permitted to terminate** workers who are physically unable to perform their duties due to a physical or mental impairment. But the employer must demonstrate present inability to do the work required, not future or past inability.

6. **Employers may deny jobs** to handicapped workers if they can demonstrate that the position poses a danger to the individual's health and welfare.
7. **Employers may deny jobs** to handicapped workers if they can demonstrate that the job generally cannot be performed by such a class of individual (for example, the job of airline pilot or firefighter).
8. **Employers may deny jobs** to handicapped workers if they can demonstrate that the hiring would interfere with productivity or create dangers in the workplace.
9. **Obesity and drug and alcohol addiction** may be considered a disability under various state laws; be aware of this and act accordingly to protect your rights if necessary.

STRATEGIES TO ENFORCE YOUR RIGHTS

Recognizing discrimination is only part of the battle; proper steps must also be taken to enforce your rights. As stated previously, the law entitles victims of discrimination to recover a variety of damages. This may include reinstatement, job hiring, receiving wage adjustments, back pay and double back pay, receiving promotions, recovering legal fees, filing costs and punitive damages, or instituting an affirmative action program on behalf of fellow employees, depending on the particular facts of your case.

In seeking to enforce your rights, you will not be alone. More than 60,000 formal complaints are filed each year with the Equal Employment Opportunity Commission (EEOC) and approximately 10,000 discrimination lawsuits are tried in court annually. This does not include the many hundreds of thousands of complaints brought to state and local agencies and other institutions.

To start the ball rolling, it is necessary to file a formal complaint. No one can stop you from filing a complaint; the law forbids employers from threatening reprisals or retaliation (such as loss of a promotion) when action is taken. The following facts must be included in the complaint:

1. Your name.
2. The names, business addresses and business telephone numbers of all persons who committed and/or participated in the discriminatory act(s).
3. Specific events, dates and facts to support why the act(s) were discriminatory (e.g., statistics, whether other employees or individuals were discriminated against, and if so, the person(s) victimized, and by whom).

The complaint must be signed and sworn to by the complainant However, it is not necessary for the complaint to be lengthy or elaborate.

The main purpose is to allege sufficient facts to trigger an investigation. That is the advantage of filing charges with an appropriate agency; charges of discrimination are initiated and investigated at no cost to you. If the complaint seems plausible, the EEOC or other agency will develop the claim on your behalf. Once a formal complaint is received, the agency assigns it a number. A copy of the complaint, together with a request for a written response, is then sent to the employer. The employer must respond to the charges within several weeks. This is done either by a general denial of the claim or by the filing of specific countercharges against you.

After charges and countercharges have been examined by an investigator, the employer and the complainant are invited to attend a no-fault conference for the purposes of exploring an amicable settlement and discussing the case generally. At that time, the investigator may also make arrangements to visit the employer's premises, examine documents and other pertinent records, and talk to witnesses and other employees. Approximately 40% of all complaints are disposed of at the settlement conference.

The conference is conducted by an experienced investigator. Pressure is typically placed on the employer to offer a monetary settlement (for example, back pay) or some other form of restitution to avoid the large legal expenses that would be incurred in the course of the investigation and eventual hearing, and because the investigator may commence examining the employer's business records, including employment applications, inter-office memos and pay records if a settlement is not reached.

If your case cannot be settled at the conference, many options are available, including:

- Your hiring a lawyer privately and suing the employer in a civil lawsuit, typically in federal court
- Representing yourself *pro se* (without a lawyer) and suing the employer in federal court
- The agency acting on your behalf to protect your rights and proceeding to a fact-finding hearing and determination
- The Equal Employment Opportunity Commission or Department of Justice commencing a lawsuit for you and/or others similarly situated in a class action lawsuit
- Your hiring a private attorney and commencing a private lawsuit in state court and, if applicable, alleging other causes of action as well as violations of discrimination laws

The advantage of suing an employer privately is that you may receive a quicker settlement. The EEOC and other agencies have many thousands of claims to process and follow; your case could take years before it is acted upon. With a private attorney working for you, he or she will be able to move the matter along more expeditiously. However, private lawsuits can be very expensive. That is why it is best to contact the nearest district office of the EEOC and speak with an intake person or investigator, or contact a private lawyer and discuss your options *before taking action*. Appendix II at the end of this book lists the nearest EEOC office in your region.

No matter what course of action is considered, do not delay needlessly. In many situations, you must file a formal complaint within six months of the time the alleged acts occurred to avoid the expiration of the Statute of Limitations. Some complainants take their time and unfortunately discover their cases are dismissed because they waited too long to file.

Finally, there are many other local and state agencies that can handle your complaint. Often, state and local laws are more favorable than federal law and it may be advantageous to file charges with these agencies. Do *not* automatically assume your case must be filed with the EEOC.

That is another reason why a competent lawyer should be retained—to advise you of all your options to maximize your claim.

PART III

██ █

HOW TO AVOID BEING FIRED UNFAIRLY AND WHAT TO DO IF YOU ARE

S tatistics indicate that 3.8 of every 100 employees are fired or resign from their jobs each month. Experts suggest that more than 250,000 workers each year are terminated unjustly. The vast majority of these individuals work without written contracts or basic job security. Unlike unionized employees, who work under collective bargaining agreements (which often establish grievance procedures and protect members from unfair dismissals), the average worker must fend for himself.

Until recently, employees had few options when they received a "pink slip." This was because of a legal principal called the employment-at-will doctrine, which was generally applied throughout the United States. Under this rule of law, employers hired workers at will and were free to fire them at any time with or without cause and with or without notice. From the nineteenth- to the mid-twentieth century, employers could discharge individuals with impunity for a good reason, a bad reason or no reason at all with little fear of legal reprisal.

However, some state legislatures began scrutinizing the fairness of this doctrine beginning in the 1960's. Courts began handing down rulings to safeguard the rights of non-unionized employees. Congress passed specific laws pertaining to occupational health and safety, civil rights and freedom to complain about unsafe working conditions.

Twenty years later, there has been a gradual erosion of the employment-at-will doctrine in many areas. For example, some states have enacted public policy exceptions that make it illegal to fire workers who take time off for jury duty or military service. Some courts have ruled that statements in company manuals, handbooks and employment applications constitute implied contracts which employers are bound to follow. Other states now recognize the obligation of companies to deal in fairness and good faith with long-time workers. This means, for example, that they are prohibited from terminating workers in retaliation when they tattle on abuses of authority (i.e., whistle blowing), or denying individuals an economic benefit (a pension that is vested or about to vest, commission, bonus, etc.) that has been earned or is about to become due.

A few states are even allowing wrongfully terminated workers to sue in tort (as opposed to asserting claims based in contract) and recover punitive damages and money for pain and suffering arising from the firing. Employees who have sued under tort theories for wrongful discharge have recovered large jury verdicts (sometimes in the six figures) as a result. Innovative lawyers are asserting federal racketeering (RICO) claims, seeking criminal sanctions and treble (triple) damages against companies. This is in addition to fraud and misrepresentation claims against individuals responsible for making wrongful termination decisions.

Given the changing legal climate, it is understandable that more people are seeking information about their rights and are fighting back after being fired. For example, they are requesting and *receiving* benefits which include severance pay greater than the company's last offer, accrued bonuses, continued medical, dental and life insurance coverage, office space, telephones, secretarial help, resumé preparation and out-placement guidance while looking for a new job.

This section of the book deals with important considerations to remember and follow when you are fired.

In Chapter 5, you will learn how to recognize when you are fired illegally. This is the first step in understanding when you have been exploited and collecting what you are due.

Chapter 6 stresses correct negotiating strategies to assist you in maximizing severance and other termination benefits. You will learn the right questions to ask and points to clarify at the termination session to increase what can be obtained. Actual letter agreements are included to illustrate how to confirm the deal in writing after it is accepted. Additionally, you will learn what to look out for when requested to sign a release or settlement agreement prepared by your employer.

Although it is unlikely that you will succeed in getting your job back after reading this chapter, you can discover how to enforce your rights without hiring a lawyer. You will also learn the steps to take when a satisfactory settlement is not achieved through informal means. If you are victimized but cannot obtain benefits with your ex-employer and cannot afford a lawyer, you will learn where to obtain assistance through various federal, state and local agencies. In addition, you will discover ways to collect evidence and strengthen a claim before a lawyer is retained.

Since many people do not know how to resign from a job properly, and frequently lose valuable benefits as a result, Chapter 7 was written to help you avoid problems in this area.

In Chapter 8, you will become familiar with a variety of post-termination problems that are frequently encountered by terminated individuals. These include protecting your good name and reputation when the employer gives you a poor reference, and learning how to stop employers from enforcing covenants not to compete and other restrictive barriers to future employment.

In addition, information in the chapter discusses helpful strategies which can increase the chances that you will obtain unemployment benefits and prevail at unemployment hearings.

5

||||||||||||||||||||||||||||||||||||||||||||||||

RECOGNIZING WHEN
YOU HAVE BEEN FIRED
ILLEGALLY

Not every firing is illegal. If you are fired in a state which still recognizes the employment-at-will doctrine, you may have little bargaining power in getting your job back. (See the state-by-state chart at the end of this chapter.) However, you are still entitled to monies earned and due *before* the firing, such as commissions, profit sharing, and perhaps bonuses, even in states which follow this doctrine.

And notwithstanding this law, you may still have a statutory right to fight the discharge. This is because all states have laws protecting workers who are fired due to discrimination, whistleblowing and other acts; these laws operate independently of the employment-at-will principal.

The first step in determining when action should be taken is to know the particular laws in your state. This can be done by consulting an experienced labor attorney or investigating the law yourself in order to determine whether you have been fired illegally.

STATUTORY RESTRICTIONS

A variety of federal and state statutes restrict an employer's freedom to discharge employees. These form the legal basis for many challenges to firings. The most comprehensive and significant federal legislation is Title VII of the Civil Rights Act of 1964, as amended by the Equal Employment Opportunity Act of 1972. Under this law, employers cannot fire workers based upon personal characteristics of sex, age, race, color, religion, national origin, and nondisqualifying physical handicaps or mental impairments unrelated to job qualifications. If you believe that your termination from a job was due to discrimination, see Chapter 4 for information on discrimination and the law. The law also protects from reprisals workers who exercise their first amendment and other rights. If you have lost your job because you spoke up about health and safety conditions, or because you refused to take a lie detector test, see relevant portions of Chapter 3. Other factors may enter into the legality of a firing, and a discussion of these follows.

Credit Problems

The Consumer Credit Protection Act of 1973 forbids employers from firing workers whose earnings have been subjected to a wage garnishment arising from a single debt. However, employees may presumably be fired after other garnishments. Some states have enacted laws which give workers additional protection; check the applicable law in your state if appropriate.

Severance and Retirement Benefits

The Employee Retirement Income Security Act of 1974 (ERISA) prohibits the discharge of any employee who is prevented thereby from attaining immediate vested pension rights or who was exercising rights under ERISA and was fired as a result.

You are also entitled to certain rights as a participant in an employer's pension and/or profit sharing plans. ERISA provides that plan participants are entitled to examine without charge all plan documents, including insurance contracts, annual reports, plan descriptions and copies of documents filed by the plan with the U.S. Department of Labor. If you request materials from a plan (including summaries of each plan's annual financial report) and do not receive them within 30 days, you may file a suit in federal court. In such a case, the court may require the plan administrator to provide the materials and pay you up to $100 a day until you receive them (unless the materials were not sent for reasons beyond the control of the administrator). See Chapter 6 for more about your rights under ERISA.

Asserting Union Rights

The National Labor Relations Act prohibits the firing of any employee because of his or her involvement in union activity, because of filing charges, or because of testifying pursuant to the act. Contact the closest regional office of the National Labor Relations Board if you believe you have been fired for one of these reasons.

The law also protects employees who band together to protest about wages, hours or other working conditions. For example, if a group of non-union employees complain about contaminated drinking water, or about failure to receive minimum wages or overtime pay, their employer could be prohibited from firing them as a result of this law if their charges are proven.

Attending Jury Duty

The Jury System Improvements Act of 1978 forbids employers from firing employees who are empaneled to serve on federal grand juries or petit juries. Most states have enacted similar laws.

Reporting Railroad Accidents

Two federal laws govern here. The Federal Railroad Safety Act prohibits companies from firing workers who file complaints or testify about railroad accidents; the Federal Employer's Liability Act makes it a crime to fire an employee who furnishes facts regarding a railroad accident.

PUBLIC POLICY EXCEPTIONS

The information contained in the previous section gives you a better understanding about the numerous federal laws protecting workers from being fired unfairly. But many courts and state legislatures have carved out other exceptions to the employment-at-will doctrine based on public policy considerations.

For example, workers are protected from discharge who:

- Refuse to violate criminal laws by committing perjury on the employer's behalf, participating in illegal schemes (e.g., price-fixing or other antitrust violations), mislabeling packaged goods, giving false testimony before a legislative committee, altering pollution control reports, or engaging in practices abroad which violate foreign, federal and state laws
- Perform a public obligation, exercise a public duty (e.g., attend jury duty, vote, supply information to the police about a fellow employee, file Worker's Compensation claims) or observe the general public policy of the state (e.g., refuse to perform unethical research)

These public policy exceptions to the employment-at-will doctrine are widely recognized and are followed in most states.

For example, tattling on abuses of authority, or "whistleblowing," is now protected conduct in many states. The state of Michigan has enacted a "Whistleblower's Protection Act" which typifies the laws in such states. This law protects employees from retaliation after they report suspected violations of laws or regulations, and provides specific remedies, including reinstatement with back pay, restoration of seniority and lost fringe benefits, litigation costs, attorney fees and a $500 fine.

People who work for federal agencies are also protected from being fired for whistleblowing. In one recent case, a nurse was dismissed after reporting abuses of patients at a Veterans Administration Medical Center. She sought reinstatement and damages before a federal review panel. The panel ordered that she be reinstated and awarded her $7,500 in back pay.

The following true cases illustrate examples of firings that were found to be illegal in this area:

- A quality control director was fired for his efforts to correct false and misleading food labeling by his employer.
- A bank discharged a consumer credit manager who notified his supervisors that the employer's loan practices violated state law.
- A financial vice president was fired after reporting to the company's president his suspicions regarding the embezzlement of corporate funds.

However, be aware that not all whistleblowing conduct is protected under this public policy exception. Some companies have successfully fired workers who questioned internal management systems, "blew the whistle" without properly investigating the facts, bypassed management or tattled in bad faith.

■ ■

STRATEGY   *All individuals wishing to protect their jobs should seek competent legal advice before engaging in whistleblowing activity, since the law is often unclear and each case is decided upon its own particular merits.*

■ ■

IMPLIED CONTRACT EXCEPTIONS

In addition to federal and state statutory restrictions on an employer's freedom to discharge employees and the public policy exceptions outlined above, there are newer protections that may restrict the at-will authority of employers to terminate employment without having to state a reason for the termination. This protection is in the form of "implied contract" terms created by representations and promises published by employers in their employee handbooks.

During the first half of the twentieth century, a number of state courts ruled that company retirement, sick leave, and fringe-benefit plans described in their employee manuals were enforceable promises of compensation. Today, your rights to your employer's retirement and benefit plans are protected by federal law under ERISA (Employee Retirement Income Security Act), discussed earlier.

But ERISA did not affect the right of an employer to terminate your job "at will" without having to give the reason for firing you. Then, in the

1960's and 1970's, employers began to use their employee handbooks to dress up their images as good places to work by promising job termination only for "good cause" or under specified procedures. A number of state courts began to view these promises as enforceable "implied contracts," even though they may not have been read by the employee until after accepting employment and they were not signed by either party as is customarily required to enhance contract enforceability.

By 1990, more than 30 state courts, as listed in the table beginning on page 113, have ruled that the promises in employee handbooks may be legally enforceable as implied contracts. In spite of this progress, many questions still exist. What if the employer promises, then makes a disclaimer, equivalent to taking back the promise? What if after you are hired your employer changes the employee handbook, taking back some of the promises contained in the version in effect when you were hired and upon which you relied? For how long are the promises effective? And there are more questions.

Basically, the first step to protecting your rights in this area is to investigate whether the company has enunciated its firing policies in writing. If such statements exist in work rules, policy manuals, periodic memos or handbooks, these must be analyzed to determine if the words are sufficiently definite to constitute promises you can rely upon. Courts are sometimes ruling that statements in employee handbooks are not legal promises but merely sales puffery aimed at enhancing morale. Also, the existence of disclaimers may be legally sufficient to void the enforceability of such promises. So too may the same result occur if the company reserves the right to print revisions to the manual after you are working which eliminates promises which were previously contained in earlier editions of the manual which you were given, and relied upon, when being hired.

Since each case must be analyzed on its particular facts, to put it simply, if you believe that you are being deprived of your rights as stated in your employer's employee manual, see an attorney experienced in employment rights. The lawyer may find that an implied contract exists.

The following actual case illustrates this: A man worked as a copywriter for a major publishing company. The man did not sign an employment contract when he was hired. However, during negotiations, he was assured that the job was secure because the company never terminated employees without just cause, and his employment application stated that employment was subject to the provisions of the company manual on personnel policies and procedures.

The manual stipulated that "employees will be fired for just and sufficient cause only" after internal steps toward rehabilitation have been taken, and after those steps have failed.

For eight years the employee received periodic raises and job promotions, and he turned down offers from other companies. Despite that, the employee was fired suddenly without warning. He sued the company, claiming he had been wrongfully discharged. The company claimed that since he had been hired at will, he could be terminated at any time with or without cause and without notice.

However, the court ruled in the employee's favor. It stated that the facts created a company obligation not to deviate from termination procedures in its policy manual.

The implied contract exception to the employment-at-will doctrine may extend to oral promises made at the hiring interview. For example, if you are told by the company president at the hiring interview, "Don't worry, we never fire anyone around here except for a good reason," a legitimate case might be made to fight the firing provided you could prove that the words were spoken and that it was reasonable to rely on them (i.e., that they were spoken seriously and not in jest).

This recently occurred in a case decided in Alaska. At the hiring, an employer stated that an applicant could have the job until reaching retirement age so long as he performed his duties properly. When the employee was fired suddenly, he argued that his job performance was excellent and that he had relied upon this promise of job security in deciding to accept the job. He won the case after proving the words were spoken. (Note: several witnesses overheard the promise at the job interview and testified to this fact at the trial.)

A New Jersey employee complained that he relied on an employer's oral promise that he could only be fired for cause and so turned down a position offered by a competitor. Several months later he was summarily fired. The court, noting that promises were made inducing him to remain in the company's employ, ruled that the employer had made representations which transformed the employment-at-will relationship into employment with termination for cause only. After finding that the employee's decision not to accept the competitor's offer was significant, binding the employer, the court ruled in the employee's favor.

However, be aware that not all oral promises are enforceable against an employer, particularly when you are promised "a job for life." Promises of lifetime employment are rarely upheld due to a legal principal referred to as the Statute of Frauds. Under this law, all contracts with a job length exceeding one year must be in writing to be enforceable. As a result, courts are generally reluctant to view oral contracts as creating permanent or lifetime employment. Usually such contracts are viewed as being terminatable at will by either party. Thus, a "lifetime contract" may theoretically be terminated after one day!

Some states have laws that limit the duration of an employment contract to a specified number of years (e.g., seven). Thus, if you currently have a contract that you believe is for lifetime employment, it may not be enforceable. Consult an experienced labor attorney if you hope to obtain such a contract in the future.

IMPLIED COVENANTS OF GOOD FAITH AND FAIR DEALING

Courts in California, Montana, New Hampshire and Massachusetts, among other states, have further eroded the "at-will" doctrine by imposing a duty of good faith and fair dealing on long-term employment relationships. For example, one man with 40 years of service claimed he was fired so his company could avoid paying commissions otherwise due on a $5 million sale. A Massachusetts court found this to be true and awarded him substantial money even though he had been hired at will. Another employee was fired after working 14 years without a written contract or job security. However, the court ruled that the company fired him merely to deprive him of the vesting of valuable pension benefits in his fifteenth year of service. The employee was awarded $75,000 in damages.

Typically, the duty of employers to act in good faith and fair dealing only applies to cases where an employee has been working for the company for many years or where a person is fired just before he or she is supposed to receive anticipated financial benefits (commissions, bonuses, accrued pension, profit-sharing, etc.).

In one recent case, however, the Montana Supreme Court reasoned that the covenant of good faith and fair dealing is a duty imposed by law. The court upheld a $50,000 jury award of punitive damages (more than 25 times the compensatory damage award) because the employer had promised to write a favorable letter of recommendation in exchange for an employee's resignation. Despite this promise, the employer delivered a letter of recommendation merely stating the complainant's dates of employment. Additionally, the employer only returned a copy of the original letter of resignation despite the employee's request for the original. These actions, the court found, justified the jury's finding of "fraud, oppression or malice."

But not all long-time workers are entitled to such protection. Remember that if an employer fires you for a lawful reason (i.e., for cause), the fact that you have been with the company for a substantial time or are eligible for a substantial benefit may *not* make the firing illegal under a covenant of good faith and fair dealing theory.

The above legal theories are exceptions to the traditional employment-at-will rule and may be useful in recovering greater benefits or damages when you are fired. The law varies greatly from state to state, and each case warrants attention based upon its particular facts and circumstances. However, this information should help you determine if you have been fired illegally or unfairly. For example, you should now understand many of the instances when firings become *suspect*. These include:

- When you are about to receive a large commission or vested stock option rights

- If the company fails to act in a manner specified in its employment applications, promotional literature, policy statements, "welcome aboard" letters, handbooks, manuals, written contracts, correspondence or memos, benefit statements or disciplinary rules
- If you are fired right after returning from an illness, pregnancy or jury duty
- If you are fired after complaining about a safety violation or other wrongdoing
- If you are over 40, belong to a minority, or are a female and believe you were fired primarily because of such personal characteristics
- If you are a long-time worker and believe the firing was unjustified
- If you received a verbal promise of job security or other rights which the company failed to fulfill

In many situations, the company may still have a right to fire based on the traditional employment-at-will rule. But even in those states which adhere to the rule, you can obtain *additional* benefits by demonstrating your knowledge of the above exceptions and appealing to the company's sense of decency and fair play.

The next chapter provides strategies on the correct steps to take to obtain greater benefits when you are fired. This can be done with or without a lawyer. However, if negotiations are unsuccessful, if the employer refuses to consider post-termination benefits or if you desire to sue your former employer in court, it will be necessary to hire an experienced labor attorney to protect your rights.

The following chart lists current exceptions to the employment-at-will doctrine on a state-by-state basis. However, the law is constantly changing; this list was compiled after an exhaustive investigation of reported cases throughout the United States only through the mid-1980's. Thus, it is necessary to consult an attorney to get up-to-date information on state law.

COMPENDIUM OF STATES RECOGNIZING EXCEPTIONS TO THE EMPLOYMENT-AT-WILL DOCTRINE		
STATE	EMPLOYMENT-AT-WILL EXCEPTIONS	COMMENTS
Alabama	Implied contract	Recognizes language in personnel manuals as implied contract
Alaska	Good faith	Employer obligation recognized; Alaska Supreme Court yet to rule on effect of personnel manuals

Arizona	Implied contract	May require employers to follow implied contract terms in employee manuals in limited instances
Arkansas	Public policy Implied contract	Exceptions recognized where employee is discharged for refusing to violate a criminal statute or duty; recognizes language in personnel manuals as implied contract
California	Public policy Good faith Implied contract	May require employers to follow oral assurances to terminate only for good cause, or to employ as long as work remains satisfactory; requires employers to follow implied contract terms in employee manuals in broad instances; recognizes obligation of employers to discharge in good faith
Colorado	Implied contract	Strong at-will employment state; recognizes language in personnel manuals as implied contract
Connecticut	Public policy Good faith Fair dealing Implied contract	Public policy exceptions are recognized in limited instances; recognizes covenant of good faith and fair dealing when employer engages in fraud, deceit or misrepresentation; recognizes language in personnel manuals as implied contract
Delaware	———	Strong at-will employment state
District of Columbia	Implied contract	Strong at-will employment jurisdiction; recognizes language in personnel manuals as implied contract
Florida	———	Strong at-will employment state; state supreme court yet to rule on personnel manuals
Georgia	———	Strong at-will employment state; state supreme court yet to rule on personnel manuals
Hawaii	Public policy Implied contract	Recognizes public policy exceptions in limited instances; recognizes language in personnel manuals as implied contract
Idaho	Implied contract	Strong at-will employment state; recognizes language in personnel manuals as implied contract

Illinois	Public policy Good faith Fair dealing Implied contract	Recognizes public policy exceptions in many instances; recognizes employer duty of good faith and fair dealing in limited situations; recognizes language in personnel manuals as implied contract
Indiana	Public policy	Recognizes public policy exceptions in many instances
Iowa	———	Strong at-will employment state; state supreme court yet to rule on personnel manuals
Kansas	Public policy Implied contract	Recognizes public policy exceptions in limited situations; recognizes language in personnel manuals as implied contract
Kentucky	Implied contract	Strong at-will employment state; recognizes language in personnel manuals as implied contract
Louisiana	———	Strong at-will employment state; state supreme court yet to rule on personnel manuals
Maine	Oral assurances	May require employers to follow oral assurances in limited situations; state supreme court yet to rule on personnel manuals
Maryland	Public policy Implied contract	Recognizes public policy exceptions in limited situations; recognizes language in personnel manuals as implied contract
Massachusetts	Good faith Fair dealing	Recognizes implied duty of good faith and fair dealing in employment contract, particularly where employee is fired to be deprived of expected financial benefits
Michigan	Public policy Implied contract	Recognizes public policy exceptions in many situations; recognizes language in personnel manuals as implied contract
Minnesota	Implied contract	Recognizes language in personnel manuals as implied contract in limited situations
Mississippi	——	Strong at-will employment state; state supreme court yet to rule on personnel manuals
Missouri	———	Strong at-will employment state

Montana	Public policy Good faith Fair dealing Implied contract	Recognizes public policy exceptions in limited situations; recognizes implied duty of good faith and fair dealing in limited situations; recognizes language in personnel manuals as implied contract
Nebraska	Implied contract	Strong at-will employment state; recognizes language in personnel manuals as implied contract
Nevada	Public policy Implied contract	Recognizes public policy exceptions in many situations; recognizes language in personnel manuals as implied contract
New Hampshire	Public policy Implied contract	Recognizes public policy exceptions in many situations; recognizes language in personnel manuals as implied contract in limited situations
New Jersey	Public policy Oral assurances Implied contract	Recognizes public policy exceptions in many situations; may require employers to follow oral assurances; recognizes language in personnel manuals as implied contract
New Mexico	Public policy Implied contract	Recognizes public policy exceptions in many situations; recognizes language in personnel manuals as implied contracts in limited situations
New York	Public policy Implied contract	Strong at-will employment state, but does recognize public policy exceptions in many situations; recognizes language in personnel manuals as implied contracts in limited situations
North Carolina	———	Strong at-will employment state; state supreme court yet to rule on personnel manuals
North Dakota	Implied contract	Strong at-will employment state; recognizes language in personnel manuals as implied contract
Ohio	Implied contract	Strong at-will employment state; recognizes language in personnel manuals as implied contract
Oklahoma	Implied contract	Recognizes language in personnel manuals as implied contracts in limited situations

Oregon	Public policy Implied contract	Recognizes many public policy exceptions; recognizes language in personnel manuals as implied contracts in many situations
Pennsylvania	Public policy	Recognizes many public policy exceptions; state supreme court yet to rule on personnel manuals
Rhode Island	———	Strong at-will employment state; state supreme court yet to rule on personnel manuals
South Carolina	Implied contract	Strong at-will employment state; recognizes language in personnel manuals as implied contract
South Dakota	Valid proof Implied contract	Not an employment-at-will state; employee is presumed to be hired for such length of time as the parties adopt for the estimation of wages; employer must prove valid termination based on habitual neglect of duty, continued incapacity to perform or willful breach of duty; recognizes language in personnel manuals as implied contract
Tennessee	Public policy	Strong at-will employment state; recognizes public policy exceptions in limited situations; state supreme court yet to rule on personnel manuals
Texas	Public policy	Strong at-will employment state; recognizes public policy exceptions in limited situations; state supreme court yet to rule on personnel manuals
Utah	———	Strong at-will employment state; state supreme court yet to rule on personnel manuals
Vermont	Implied contract	Strong at-will employment state; recognizes language in personnel manuals as implied contract
Virginia	Public policy Implied contract	Strong at-will employment state; recognizes public policy exceptions in limited situations; recognizes language in personnel manuals as implied contract

Washington	Public policy Oral assurances Implied contract	Recognizes public policy exceptions in many situations; may require employers to follow oral assurances in many situations; recognizes language in employee manuals as implied contract in certain situations
West Virginia	Public policy Implied contract	Recognizes public policy exceptions in many situations; recognizes language in personnel manuals as implied contract
Wisconsin	Public policy Implied contract	Recognizes public policy exceptions in many situations; recognizes language in personnel manuals as implied contract
Wyoming	Implied contract	Strong at-will employment state; recognizes language in personnel manuals as implied contract

Author's Note: Since laws change rapidly, the above information may not be entirely accurate by the time you read this compendium. Thus, be sure to consult with an experienced labor attorney or research current case decisions and statutory developments in your state to be sure you know your rights in this area.

6

||||||||||||||||||||||||||||||||||||||||||||||||||

PROTECTING YOURSELF
WHEN YOU ARE FIRED

Many employers fire workers without warning—for obvious reasons. By firing workers suddenly, employers believe they will keep workers off-balance, without sufficient time to anticipate the discharge and plan ahead.

No matter how you learn the news, it is important to remain calm so you can carefully consider your options. The fact that you are fired suddenly (as opposed to being given a warning) does *not* mean you should accept fewer benefits than you deserve. The following strategies will help you increase severance benefits and/or damages in the event you are fired.

The first question to ask yourself when you are fired is whether the employer had a valid legal basis for doing so. The preceding chapter mentioned various instances where employers are prohibited from discharging workers, even those employed at will. However, these are not the only prohibited kinds of actions. For example, do you have a written contract? If so, what does it say? Employers cannot fire you in a manner inconsistent with the terms of the written contract. Thus, if you are hired for a definite term (for example, one year) you cannot be fired prior to the expiration of the contract term except for cause. This is just one example of the many points we will now consider.

▌ REVIEWING YOUR CONTRACT

If you signed a written contract, reread it. Review what it says about termination. For example, can you be fired at any time without cause, or must the employer send you written notice before the effective termination date? Look to see if notice of termination (for example, 30 days before the last day of employment) is required. Remember that the failure to give you timely notice, or any notice at all, may place the company in breach of contract if notification is required. Even better, it may cause the agreement to be extended for an additional period of time.

119

For example, many companies have written contracts with their executives. Some of these agreements run for a period of one year and state that if timely notice of termination is not given at least 30 days prior to the expiration of the one-year term, the contract will automatically be extended and renewed under the same terms and conditions for an additional year. If the company fires the executive two weeks before the end of the year, or forgets to send timely notice, the employee could have a legal basis to insist on working for an additional year. Or he or she would then have a strong claim to negotiate for additional compensation rather than filing a lawsuit.

So be sure you know what the contract says in order to map out an effective action plan. If you signed an employment contract, you should also consider the following:

Were you hired for a definite term? (e.g., your contract states "This agreement is effective for a period of one year commencing on February 1, 1991 and terminating on January 31, 1992.") If so, then the employer can only terminate you prior to the effective termination date, i.e., January 31, 1992, *for cause*.

The following are examples of cause which justify contract terminations:

- Theft or dishonesty
- Falsifying records or information
- Punching another employee's time card
- Leaving the job or company premises without prior approval from a supervisor
- Insubordination or disrespect of company work rules and policies
- Willful refusal to follow the directions of a supervisor (unless doing so would endanger health or safety)
- Assault, unprovoked attack or threats of bodily harm against others
- Use of drugs or possession of alcoholic beverages on company premises or during company-paid time while away from the premises
- Reporting to work under the influence of drugs or alcohol
- Disclosing confidential and proprietary information to unauthorized third parties
- Unauthorized possession of weapons and firearms on company property
- Intentionally making errors in work, negligently performing duties, or willfully hindering or limiting production
- Sleeping on the job
- Excessive lateness or irregular attendance at work
- Failing to report absences
- Sexually harassing or abusing others
- Making secret profits
- Misusing trade secrets, customer lists and other confidential information

■ ■

STRATEGY   *You are increasing your chances of recovering damages in a lawsuit when you are hired for a fixed term of employment. This is because the burden of proof falls on the employer to demonstrate the specific actions constituting a legitimate reason to fire before the expiration of the fixed term. Often, it is difficult to prove this. Thus, always try to negotiate for a* fixed *term of employment before being hired.*

■ ■

Does the contract prohibit additional benefits upon termination? Some agreements specify that employees have no additional claims for damages after discharge. Others place a limit on benefits (for example "Upon termination for any reason, the employee will be limited to receiving severance equivalent to one week's pay for each full year of service.") By signing a written contract containing such a clause, you may be minimizing post-termination negotiating power.

Does the contract restrict you from working for a competitor or establishing a competing business after termination? This is referred to as a restrictive covenant or covenant not to compete, which may or may not be enforceable depending on the particular facts and circumstances. (Note: restrictive covenants are discussed in detail in Chapter 8.) If so, be sure you receive a detailed opinion concerning your rights.

Thus, remember that your rights may be enhanced or diminished depending upon the type of contract in existence. That is why it is important to always negotiate a fair agreement before accepting a job.

ORAL PROMISES OF JOB SECURITY

As previously discussed, courts in some states are ruling that employees have the right to rely on oral representations made before hiring or during the working relationship. Interviewers, recruiters and other intake personnel are often careless and make statements which can be construed as promises of job security. They sometimes use words such as "permanent employment," "job for life," or "just cause termination" as well as make broad statements concerning job longevity and assurances of continued employment (such as "Don't worry—no one around here ever gets fired except for a good reason") or specific promises regarding career opportunities.

When such statements are sufficient to be characterized as promises of job security, when you can prove the actual words were spoken and when you can demonstrate that you relied on such statements to your detriment, you may be able to contest the firing if you work in a state which recognizes this exception to the employment-at-will doctrine. The following actual case is a good illustration.

An executive worked for a company for 32 years without a written contract. The man was suddenly fired. He sued his company and argued that he had done nothing wrong to justify the firing. At the trial the executive proved that:

- The company's president told him several times that he would continue to be employed if he did a good job;
- The company had a policy of not firing executives except for cause;
- The man was never criticized or warned that his job was in jeopardy; and
- He had a commendable track record, his employment history was excellent, and he had received periodic merit bonuses, raises and promotions.

The executive won the case because the facts created an implied promise that the company could not arbitrarily terminate him.

■ ■

STRATEGY   *Try to remember and document what was said, when, where, who said it and the names of any witness(es) who were present whenever such promises were made. This may help your case at a later date if you are fired in a manner inconsistent with such promises.*

■ ■

A word of caution: Some employers design employment applications or contracts which specify that employment is at will, that no one has made additional promises regarding job security and that you acknowledge not receiving such promises. You may have a difficult time arguing this point (regardless of verbal promises) when you sign such a document.

WRITTEN PROMISES OF JOB SECURITY IN COMPANY MANUALS

If company manuals promise job security, has the employer followed stated policy? It is important to review all manuals, handbooks, memos, correspondence, benefit statements, "welcome aboard" letters, employment applications, policy statements and disciplinary rules. Know what they say regarding firings. For example:

- Can you appeal the decision?
- Must the employer give you a warning before firing?
- Are there specific rules regarding severance?
- Can you be fired at will or only for cause?
- Is there a system of progressive discipline or can you be fired immediately without notice?
- Are there internal grievance policies?

- Can you arbitrate the dispute rather than litigate?
- Do you have the right to receive a written reason for the firing?
- Do you have the right to review your personnel file after the firing?

You may be able to contest the firing and sue for damages if the employer has favorable policies in writing which aren't followed. Thus, review all company policies as soon as possible to determine if promises have been broken.

▪ ▪

STRATEGY   *Sometimes it is difficult to review these materials after a discharge because you may not be on the premises and may be unable to obtain such documents because many employers insist that ex-employees return all company property upon being fired. If this is the case, ask friendly co-workers to lend you their materials for review. Photocopy relevant text as soon as possible. Better still, if you have suspicions you may be fired, plan ahead by gathering copies of these materials before you are asked to leave. Bring this information to your lawyer at the initial consultation. This will enable him or her to give you a more accurate opinion as to whether the employer has violated an implied contract term. For example, if the employer has a written policy allowing terminated employees to appeal the firing to a grievance committee, you may wish to do so. If the employer refuses to allow you to file such an appeal despite its stated policy, you might be able to contest the firing as a result.*

▪ ▪

Whenever an individual is fired, I try to gain an advantage for my client by scrutinizing all company policies regarding firings to see if they were followed. If not, this is used as leverage in negotiating for additional severance and other benefits.

PERSONNEL RECORDS

Some states permit workers to review and copy the contents of their personnel files. For example, California law provides that an employee is to be given access to personnel files used to determine his or her qualifications, promotions, pay raises, discipline and discharge. Other states which allow both employees and terminated employees to inspect personnel files maintained by employers include Connecticut, Delaware, Illinois, Maine, Michigan, Nevada, New Hampshire, Ohio, Oregon, Pennsylvania, Washington and Wisconsin. Some of these states also permit inspection by a representative designated by the employee.

Additionally, most states give employees the right to review information supplied to the employer by a credit reporting agency under the Fair Credit Reporting Act of 1971, as well as to review all medical and insurance information in the file. However, confidential items such as letters of reference, records of internal investigations regarding theft, misconduct or crimes not pertaining to the employee, and confidential information about other employees are generally prohibited from being viewed.

Sometimes, these files do not support firing decisions because they contain favorable performance appraisals, recommendations and memos. If you can only be fired for cause and the employer gives you specific reasons why you were fired, your file may demonstrate that such reasons are factually incorrect and/or legally insufficient. If this occurs, you may have a strong case against the employer for breach of contract.

■ ■

STRATEGY   *Try to make copies of all pertinent documents in your file while working for the employer (particularly favorable records). If you have received excellent performance reviews and appraisals and the file indicates you received large merit salary increases and other benefits, you may be able to contest the firing and be rehired. Or, you may use this information to successfully negotiate more severance than the company is offering.*

■ ■

Several years ago, I represented a man who worked for a prestigious financial institution. The client was part of a four-member team responsible for devising and selling tax shelters on behalf of the employer.

The man had worked approximately 9 ½ years for the company and was earning an annual base salary of $125,000. Each year he had consistently received large year-end bonuses (the previous year's bonus had been $50,000).

The man was suddenly fired in late November. The company claimed his work performance was not satisfactory and that he did "not fit the image of an investment banker." The client hired me because he believed his job performance was excellent. He also felt cheated since the company offered no severance benefits, would not allow him to receive a pension which was due to vest within six months, and refused to pay him a bonus for the substantial portion of the current year he had worked.

After thoroughly investigating the matter, I asked the client if he had collected copies of pertinent information from his personnel file. Fortunately, he produced a number of excellent performance reviews. In addition, he was able to locate a memo which had been circulated throughout the company and delivered to the company's president. The memo congratulated each member of his group by name for placing a large tax shelter that year and each member (including my client) was cited for outstanding work.

During negotiations, I informed management of the existence of this memo. I argued that in view of my client's history of receiving large raises and year-end bonuses, excellent performance evaluations and the favorable memo, the firing of my client was unjustified and was probably done to save the company a large sum of money. I also advised the company that a jury would probably take a dim view of what had transpired.

After extensive meetings, I was able to obtain an out-of-court settlement that included a year-end bonus, severance pay representing one month's payment of salary for every year of employment, the company's agreement to qualify my client for a substantial pension, continuation of employer-paid medical insurance for six months, substantial payment for an outplacement employment search (up to $7,500) by a reputable firm and a favorable recommendation in writing.

In reflection, it is highly doubtful that I would have been able to negotiate such a favorable settlement without a copy of the "kudo" memo collected by my client. Thus, never underestimate the importance of collecting *all* favorable documents while working for a company.

Even if you did not keep copies of such material, don't despair entirely. An employee may have access to his or her personnel file as part of the discovery process during a lawsuit even in those states which do not ordinarily allow access. And, in many instances, employment data which was not subject to employee inspection cannot be introduced and used against you in a lawsuit without your permission.

Additionally, in some states (such as Illinois and Michigan), you can bring legal proceedings to expunge false information which is contained in your file and is known by the employer to be false. These states even allow you to collect attorney fees, fines, court costs and damages in the event you discover false information or records of off-premises activities (political, associational, etc.) which do not interfere with your work duties.

(Note: In Chapter 8 you will learn how to protect yourself when false or defamatory information is communicated to prospective employers or third persons. The chapter will also discuss the concept of Service Letter laws; i.e., the requirement in some states that workers must be given truthful written reasons for their discharge and what damages may ensue when it is discovered that such reasons are inaccurate. You will also discover how to prevent private and confidential information from being communicated by a current employer to others.)

REFUSALS TO PAY EXPECTED FINANCIAL BENEFITS

Many companies fire workers to deprive them of the fruits of their labors. This includes a year-end bonus, commissions, wages, accrued vacation or pension benefits that are about to vest. In some states, if an employer fires someone just before he or she is supposed to receive anticipated benefits, the firing may be illegal.

Even if the firing is legal, you may be entitled to collect this money in negotiations or during a lawsuit. For example, the Department of Labor in most states requires employers to pay accrued vacation and earned wages to terminated workers. Additionally, you may be able to receive a pension if you are about to qualify for a vested pension but are fired. This is because employers are forbidden in most states and under the federal Employment Retirement Income Security Act from firing long-time workers who are close to receiving such benefits. Consult an experienced labor lawyer immediately if you believe you have been victimized in this area.

Salespeople who earn commissions are now receiving additional statutory protections in this area. Many states now require that companies promptly pay commissions to their independent sales representatives (or agents) who are fired. When prompt payment is not made, companies may be liable for penalties up to *three times the commission amount* plus reasonable attorney fees and court costs if the case is eventually litigated. Some of the states which have enacted laws protecting sales representatives and their commissions include Alabama, Arizona, California, Florida, Georgia, Illinois, Indiana, Iowa, Kansas, Kentucky, Louisiana, Maryland, Massachusetts, Minnesota, Mississippi, Missouri, New Hampshire, New Jersey, North Carolina, Oklahoma, New York, Ohio, South Carolina, Tennessee, Texas, and Washington and more states are bound to enact similar legislation.

Additionally, you may have a valid claim if you are fired right before the payment of a year-end bonus. Some employers require workers to be employed on the day bonus checks are issued as a condition of payment. However, workers are sometimes fired unfairly and are denied bonuses which have been earned. As noted, I recently represented a man who had worked a full year and was expecting a bonus of $7,500 to be paid on February 15 of the following year. The company's policy required workers to be employed on the date of payment in order to receive the bonus. My client was fired on February 10 for alleged misconduct due to an unauthorized absence taken the day before. The employer refused to pay severance or the bonus.

I proved that my client had a justifiable excuse for missing work on the day in question. Further, I argued that the employer's policy of paying earned bonuses only if the worker was still employed the following year was unfair. Although I was unable to obtain his reemployment, I did manage to obtain severance pay equivalent to two weeks for every year of employment, as well as the expected bonus.

■ ■

STRATEGY   *Always request a bonus if you are fired close to the end of the year and are entitled to a bonus by contract or job history (i.e., you consistently received bonuses in prior years). If the employer tells you that bonuses are only paid if you are still working on the day the check is issued and that you were fired before then, argue that you would have received said bonus but for the firing. And argue that you are entitled to a pro rata share of the bonus if you are fired close to but before the end of the year. For example, if you are fired on December 1, negotiate to receive eleven-twelfths of the bonus you were expecting.*

■ ■

▎OFFERS OF SEVERANCE PAY

Although there is generally no legal obligation to pay severance monies, most employers in the United States *do* offer such payments when a firing is due to a group layoff, business conditions outside the employee's control (such as reorganization) or for reasons other than employee misconduct.

However, there may be a legal obligation to pay severance when:

- You have a written contract stating that severance will be paid
- Oral promises are given regarding severance pay
- The employer voluntarily promises to pay severance
- The employer has a policy of paying severance and this is documented in a company manual or employee handbook
- The employer has paid severance to other employees in similar firings and thereby has created a precedent

If you are fired and are not offered severance, it is advisable to request a meeting with a qualified representative of the employer to discuss clarification regarding severance and available wage equivalents.

Many employers are fearful of the increasing amount of employee-related litigation and are flexible in easing the departure of terminated individuals. Thus, you should begin the discussion by appealing to corporate decency and fair play. For example, it might be stated that severance pay is necessary to carry you over while you look for a new job, or that more severance is needed since you anticipate it will take longer to find a suitable job than the amount of severance currently offered. Always be polite and act professionally; being vindictive or making threats won't solve anything.

Most employers have different policies regarding severance depending on the industry and company. However, it is recommended that you attempt to receive *one month* of severance for every year worked as a starting point. If this can be achieved, you can leave the company knowing that you have received a fair severance offer.

Although severance pay is a common problem for individual employees whose employment has been terminated, the extensive merger and acquisition activity in recent years has caused the issue of severance pay to become one of large-scale financial and legal significance. For example, if your company is sold and you continue to work for the new employer, you may be able to assert rights under the federal Employee Retirement Income Security Act and welfare benefit plans in the event the new employer denies severance to a group of workers at a later date.

Additionally, you may have grounds for a valid lawsuit in the event you have a vested pension but are fired just weeks short of becoming entitled to greater severance, larger monthly pension payments and improved medical and insurance benefits. This happened to an executive recently who sued his former employer in federal court.

The case involved the termination of a former vice president of a large manufacturing company after 32 years of service. At the time of the firing, the man earned $132,500. Although the executive was fully vested before he was terminated, he was approximately one month short of becoming entitled to substantially higher pension payments and additional severance. He sued his former employer under Section 510 of ERISA that makes it illegal for employers to discharge anyone for the purpose of cutting off their employee benefits or stopping them from collecting vested pension rights.

After the employee persuaded the jury that the reasons advanced for his discharge were unworthy of credence and were motivated by a discriminatory purpose—to deny him additional benefits (which the employer could not rebut)—he won the case and recovered damages of $650,000 representing additional pension and severance payments.

Cases such as this demonstrate the responsibility of employers to comply with all pension laws and ERISA regarding severance when a business is sold or when company policy has created an expectation that the purchasing company will continue an established severance policy crediting employees with prior years of service from the selling company.

Also, if you begin working for a new employer who ceases business operations (i.e., declares bankruptcy) within a relatively short period of time after the hiring, you may have a valid claim of severance from the selling company under certain conditions.

Courts are beginning to recognize the rights of employees to severance in many situations, particularly when there is a massive layoff or group sale of assets due to a merger and acquisition.

■ ■

STRATEGY   *You should not automatically acquiesce to a denial of benefits if you are fired and not offered severance, whatever your particular situation. Recognize that most workers are now receiving severance when they are fired; others are negotiating and receiving greater severance than the company's first offer. Statistics from my own practice support this. The vast majority of all clients who hire me to negotiate firings obtain more severance and other benefits than the amount first offered directly to them by the employer. Remember this and guide yourself accordingly.*

■ ■

▎ RELIANCE ON HIRING PROMISES

What if you resign a current job because you are offered a position with a new employer, but the job offer is then withdrawn? What happens if you are fired immediately after starting the new job? Unfortunately, this is a common problem which happens to thousands of workers each year in the United States.

Fortunately, you may be protected by a legal principal called *promissory estoppel*. In a recent Minnesota case, for example, the court rejected the company's argument that employers should be permitted to change their minds regarding job offers when they hire at will.

I recently represented a man who flew to Texas and was offered a prestigious sales position. He resigned from a lucrative job to begin working for the new employer. Two weeks later, he was fired when the company stated he "didn't fit in." The man attempted to get his old job back but was unsuccessful. He hired me to collect damages resulting from this unfair treatment. The case was settled satisfactorily out of court after I instituted a lawsuit on his behalf.

■ ■

STRATEGY   *Always obtain a written contract with a new employer before you resign from a current employer. The contract should guarantee employment for a minimum period of time (such as 3 months) to avoid the kind of exploitation described above. Other strategies regarding how to resign properly are discussed in the next chapter.*

■ ■

Recognize that you may have rights if you are offered a job and rely on this promise of employment to your detriment. Consult an experienced labor lawyer immediately if this happens to you.

ISSUES FOR OLDER WORKERS

The Age Discrimination in Employment Act (ADEA) was enacted in 1967 prohibiting employers from firing workers between the ages of 40 and 70 because of their age. A number of similar discrimination laws have also been enacted in most states.

If you are an older worker and are being pressured to retire voluntarily by accepting an early-retirement option or face the risk of being fired, demoted or given a cut in pay, you may have grounds for an age discrimination complaint with the Equal Employment Opportunity Commission (EEOC) or a state agency such as the Division of Human Rights. See Chapter 4 for information on age discrimination and the law.

Early retirement programs in and of themselves *are* legal and do not violate federal age discrimination laws so long as participation is voluntary. However, if you are offered a financial package containing early retirement inducements, be sure that it really contains worthwhile incentives such as additional pension benefits (i.e., extra years of age and service for pension calculations), lump sum severance payments (e.g., an extra year's pay), cash inducements and retirement health programs.

Avoid accepting early retirement packages which penalize you if you return to the workplace with a new job. Some companies, for example, permanently discontinue health coverage when the employee takes another job where coverage is provided. The problem here is that you could wind up working for the new employer for a short period of time (say, six months) and find yourself out of a job. Accepting this condition would cause you to forfeit valuable health benefits which are essential during your older years.

Also, if the employer offers decreasing benefits with increasing age, this may penalize you unfairly. Before accepting an early retirement package, accept the fact that you may have a difficult time finding a new job or starting your own business because of your age. You should also recognize that inflation may eat away at your pension if you don't have a secure financial nest egg. Finally, if you are an older worker being asked to sign a waiver or release in exchange for more severance or early retirement inducements, be aware that the newly enacted federal law called the Older Workers Benefit Protection Act may give you added protection and should be reviewed with your attorney.

DETERMINING IF THE DECISION WAS FAIR

When a terminated worker consults with me regarding his or her discharge, I consider the following to determine whether the firing was justified and/or legal.

- Are there mitigating factors that excuse or explain the employee's poor performance or misconduct?
- Was the employee victimized by a supervisor's bias or subjective evaluations rather than objective criteria?
- How long has the employee worked for the company? What kind of overall record does the employee have?
- Is termination appropriate under all of the circumstances? Does the punishment fit the crime?
- Has the employer followed a consistent policy of terminating workers with similar infractions?
- Is the employer retaliating against the employee because of a refusal to commit illegal or unethical acts, obey a subpoena, falsifying records, or serving on extended jury duty or in the military rather than a bona fide business reason, disciplinary problem or poor performance?
- Has the employee been fired because she filed a sex harassment complaint, is pregnant or refused to submit to sexual favors?
- Is the fired employee being deprived of severance or other financial benefits that are due? Is this contrary to the employee's contract, letter agreement, company handbook or employee manual?
- Is the firing contrary to a written contract?

If any of the above considerations apply to you, consult an experienced labor attorney immediately if appropriate.

MASSIVE LAYOFFS AND PLANT CLOSINGS

You may be entitled to receive benefits including salary and/or severance for an additional period up to 60 days if you weren't given ample notice before losing your job. This is because of the recently enacted Worker Adjustment and Retraining Notification Act (P.L. 100-379). This law and its applications are detailed at the end of Chapter 3.

Speak to an experienced labor attorney immediately if you believe that the law is not being properly followed in your case. Additionally, you may be entitled to receive free training in your local community where the plant closing or discharge en masse occurs. Thus, contact the nearest Department of Labor Office for further details if you are victimized in this area.

NEGOTIATING STRATEGIES TO RECOVER MAXIMUM COMPENSATION AND OTHER BENEFITS

The first rule of thumb to remember when you are fired is to try and stall for time. Certainly, you should request additional time to think things over when informed of the firing decision. Stalling for time can help you learn important facts. This includes many of the points discussed in a previous section of this chapter (requesting to see your personnel file to review and collect favorable documents; learning who made the decision to fire you to see if there is a possibility of appealing that decision or whether that person had proper authority to terminate you; reconstructing promises of job security that were made; reviewing employment manuals, etc.). This information can help you in negotiations for additional severance and other benefits.

Thus, if possible, do not accept the employer's first offer regarding severance. Always request a negotiating session to obtain more benefits. The following negotiation points are the actual strategies I give my clients; they can help you obtain a better severance arrangement, whatever your situation.

Wages (also referred to as salary continuation)

1. Try to stay on the payroll as long as possible.
2. Negotiate for the employer to continue to provide medical, dental and hospitalization coverage (paid for by the employer) while you are receiving severance wages.
3. Avoid arrangements where you are offered severance for a specified period (e.g., six months) which automatically *cease* when you obtain a new job. Rather, make the offer noncontingent on new employment, or arrange that differential severance will be paid in a *lump sum* if you obtain a new job prior to the expiration of the

severance period. (For example, arrange that three months' worth of severance will be paid in a lump sum if a new job is obtained three months before the six months of salary continuation expires.)

4. If severance pay is to be paid in a lump sum, ask for it immediately, not in installments over time.

5. Recognize that if you receive salary continuation rather than a lump sum payment you may be ineligible for unemployment benefits until the salary continuation payments cease; thus, consider the benefits of a lump sum payment rather than extended salary continuation.

6. Avoid accepting the employer's first offer; *negotiate, negotiate, negotiate.*

7. Attempt to receive at least four weeks' severance for every year of employment.

Other Compensation

1. If you have relocated recently at the request of the employer, try to obtain additional relocation allowances.

2. Discuss accrued vacation pay, overtime and unused sick pay. Be sure you are paid for these items.

3. If you were fired without notice, ask for two additional weeks of salary in lieu of the employer's lack of notice.

4. If commissions are due or about to become due, insist that you be paid immediately; do not waive these expected benefits.

Bonus

1. Understand how your bonus is computed.

2. If you were entitled to receive a bonus at the end of the year, ask for it now.

3. Argue that the firing deprived you of the right to receive the bonus if the employer refuses to pay; or

4. Insist that your bonus be prorated accordingly to the amount of time you worked during the year if the above argument is rejected.

Pension and Profit-Sharing Benefits

1. Ask for details regarding the nature of your benefits. You are entitled to an accurate, written description of all benefits under federal law.

2. Be aware of all plans, funds and programs that may have been established on your behalf. These may include the following:

- **Defined contribution plans** (e.g., profit-sharing plans, thrift plans, money purchase pension plans, and cash or deferred profit-sharing plans). All of these plans are characterized by the fact that each participant has an individual bookkeeping account under the plan which records the participant's total interest in the plan assets. Monies are contributed or credited in accordance with the rules of the plan contained in the plan document.
- **Defined benefit plans** These are characterized as pension plans which base the benefits payable to participants upon a formula contained in the plan. Such plans are not funded individually as in defined contribution plans. Rather, they are typically funded on a group basis.
- **Employee welfare benefit plans** These are often funded through insurance and typically provide participants with medical, health, accident, disability, death, unemployment or vacation benefits.
- **ERISA (Employee Retirement Income Security Act) plans** These may not be as definite as the above. Rather, if the employer communicates that certain benefits are available, whom the intended beneficiaries are and how the plan is funded, the employer may be liable to pay such benefits even in the absence of a formal, written plan.

3. If you are fired just before the vesting of a pension (e.g., two months before the vesting date), argue that the timing of the firing is suspect and that public policy requires the employer to grant your pension. If the employer refuses, consult an experienced labor lawyer immediately.

4. Demand a copy of the employer's pension and/or profit-sharing plans from the plan administrator if the employer refuses to furnish you with accurate details. Note: You may have to pay for the cost of photocopying said plan(s) when requesting them. As a participant in the company's pension and/or profit sharing plans, you are entitled to certain rights and protections under the Employee Retirement Income Security Act of 1974 (ERISA). ERISA provides that all plan participants are entitled to examine without charge all plan documents, such as insurance contracts and copies of all documents filed by the plan with the U.S. Department of Labor including detailed annual reports and plan descriptions.

   Under ERISA, if you request materials from a plan (including summaries of each plan's annual financial report) and do not receive them within 30 days, you may file suit in federal court. In such a case, the court may require the plan administrator to provide the materials and pay up to $100 a day until you receive the materials, unless the materials were not sent for reasons beyond the control of the administrator.

5. Contact the plan administrator immediately to protect your rights if your claim is denied. Under federal law, every employee, participant or beneficiary covered under a benefit plan covered by ERISA has the right to receive written notification stating specific reasons for the denial of a claim. Additionally, you have the right to a full and fair review by the plan administrator if you are denied benefits.

If you have a claim for benefits which is denied or ignored in whole or in part after making such a request, you may file suit in a state or federal court. If it should happen that plan fiduciaries misuse a plan's money, or if you are discriminated against for asserting your rights, you may seek assistance from the U.S. Department of Labor, or you may file suit in a federal court. The court will decide who should pay court costs and legal fees. If you are successful, the court may order the person you have sued to pay these costs and fees. If you lose, (i.e., if it finds your claim to be frivolous) the court may order you to pay these costs and fees.

Other Benefits

1. Request continued use of an office, secretary, telephone or mail facilities to assist you in your job search, if appropriate.
2. Consider requesting a loan to tide you over while looking for a new job, if appropriate.
3. Consider requesting continued use of your company car or ask to buy the car or take over the lease at a reduced rate, if appropriate.
4. Request that the employer pay for outplacement guidance, career counseling and resumé preparation services including typing and incidental expenses, if appropriate.

Medical, Dental and Hospitalization Coverage

1. Does coverage stop the day you are fired or is there a grace period? Ask for a copy of the applicable policy.
2. Can you extend coverage beyond the grace period?
3. Be sure to have your benefits explained to you if you do not understand them.
4. Can you assume the policy at a reduced personal cost? This is sometimes referred to as a *conversion policy.*
5. If you are married and your spouse is working, you may be covered under your spouse's policy. If so, do you want to continue paying for your own policy?
6. Be sure the employer has notified you regarding your rights under COBRA (the Consolidated Omnibus Budget Reconciliation Act of 1985). The following will explain COBRA rights in greater detail.

The COBRA Law and Post-termination Health Benefits   On April 7, 1986, the Consolidated Omnibus Budget Reconciliation Act of 1985 ("COBRA") was enacted. The most important provisions of this law require many private employers (who employ more than 20 workers on a typical business day) to continue to make group health insurance available to workers who are discharged from employment. Most people benefit since the cost of maintaining such insurance is cheaper; the individual pays for coverage at the employer's group rate rather than the cost of an individual policy.

All employees who are discharged as a result of a voluntary or involuntary termination (with the exception of those who are fired for *gross misconduct*) may elect to continue plan benefits currently in effect *at their own cost* provided the employee or beneficiary makes an initial payment within 30 days of notification and is not covered under Medicare or any other group health plan. The law also applies to qualified beneficiaries who were covered by the employer's group health plan the day before the discharge. Thus, for example, if the employee chooses not to continue such coverage, his or her spouse and dependent children may elect continued coverage at their own expense.

The extended coverage period is 18 months upon the termination of the covered employee; upon the death, divorce or legal separation of the covered employee, the benefit coverage period is 36 months to spouses and dependents.

The law requires that employers or plan administrators separately notify all employees and covered spouses and dependents of their rights to continued coverage. After receiving such notification, the individual then has sixty days to elect to continue coverage. Additionally, employees and dependents whose insurance is protected under COBRA must also be provided with any conversion privilege otherwise available in the plan (if such coverage exists) within a six-month period preceding the date that coverage would terminate at the end of the continuation period.

In the event the employer fails to offer such coverage, the law imposes penalties ranging from $100 to $200 per day for each day the employee is not covered.

■ ■

STRATEGY   *Be sure you know your rights under COBRA in the event you are fired. This is especially true if you or a spouse or dependent is sick and needs the insurance benefits to pay necessary medical bills. You are entitled to such protection even if you only have worked for the employer for a short period of time. In fact, under the law as it presently exists, most short-term employees can generally enjoy COBRA protection for periods exceeding the length of their employment. The only requirement is that you must have been included in the employer's group plan at the time of the firing.*

■ ■

Remember, however, that you cannot obtain benefits if you are fired for gross misconduct. This term is relatively ambiguous; the burden of proof is on the employer to prove that the discharge was for a compelling reason (fighting on the job, stealing, working while intoxicated, etc.). Also, be aware that some employers reduce a person's working hours to a point which makes them ineligible for group health coverage. However, COBRA is still available to workers in these situations.

If an employer refuses to negotiate continued health benefits as part of a severance package or fails to notify you of the existence of such benefits, contact the personnel office immediately to protect your rights. If the employer refuses to offer continued COBRA benefits after a discharge for any reason, consult an experienced labor lawyer immediately.

Life Insurance

1. Can you convert the policy to your benefit at your own cost? Don't forget to inquire about this.
2. Is there any equity in the employer's life insurance plan which accrues to you upon termination? Inquire about this and ask for a copy of all policies presently in effect.

Date

To whom it may concern:

I am pleased to submit this letter of recommendation on behalf of (Name of Employee).

(Name of Employee) worked for the company from (date) through (date). During this period (Name of Employee) was promoted from (specify title) to (specify title).

During the past (specify) years, I have had the opportunity to work closely with (Name of Employee). At all times I found him/her to be diligent and dependable and (Name of Employee) rendered competent and satisfactory services on the company's behalf.

I heartily recommend (Name of Employee) as a candidate for employment of his/her choosing.

Very truly yours,

Name of Officer
Title

Your Cover Story

1. Clarify how the news of your departure will be announced. Discuss and agree with management on the story to be told to outsiders.

2. Consider whether you want it to be known that you resigned for personal reasons or that you were terminated due to a "business reorganization." These are neutral explanations which are preferable to firings for misconduct or poor performance.

3. *Recognize that if you resign you may be forfeiting unemployment benefits.* Thus, avoid resigning wherever possible. Although you may prefer that outsiders be told you resigned for personal reasons, confirm with the employer that you will be able to apply for unemployment benefits. That way your local Department of Labor Board will be advised that there was a termination (as opposed to a resignation, since this is what really happened) and you can still tell outsiders you resigned if appropriate.

4. Request that a copy of a favorable letter of recommendation be given to you *before* you leave the company. The letter should state the dates of your employment, the positions held and that you performed all of your job duties in a diligent and satisfactory fashion. If possible, the letter should be signed by a qualified officer or supervisor who worked with you and knows you well. Do not rely on promises that the employer will furnish prospective employers with a favorable recommendation, since many fail to do this after employees leave the company. Thus, *always* attempt to have such a letter *in hand* before you leave, for obvious reasons.

The letter shown on the opposite page is an example of the kind of recommendation you may find acceptable.

Note: It is best not to include the specific reason for the parting in such a letter. This will enable you to offer whatever reasons you feel appropriate under the circumstances.

5. Request that key members of the company be notified of your departure in writing. If possible, approve the contents of such a memo before distribution. Written memos can dispel false rumors about your termination. A positive memo may assist you in obtaining a new job. Remember, news of a firing usually spreads rapidly; you don't want to be the subject of false rumors or innuendo.

An example is shown below.

MEMORANDUM

To: Employees of (Name of Company or pertinent division)

From: (Name of Officer or Supervisor)

Subject: Resignation of (Name of Employee)

I wish to inform you that (Name of Employee) has decided to pursue other interests and has elected to resign effective (specify when) from the company.

(Name of Employee) has contributed greatly to the growth of the (specify) division and he/she will indeed be missed.

We all wish (Name of Employee) the best of continued good health and success.

A memo similar to the one shown may enable you to leave in a positive manner. Additionally, it may minimize the effects of the circumstances surrounding the termination. Don't forget to ask for this when appropriate.

Golden Parachutes

1. Determine if you are entitled to receive additional benefits under a severance contract or golden parachute. Generally, golden parachutes are arrangements between an executive and a corporation that are contingent upon a change in control of the corporation. Typically, additional cash and other economic benefits are paid to the terminated individual following the discharge (provided the employee is not fired for cause). Although most companies cover only a limited group of key employees, some companies have determined that it is appropriate to cover a much larger group.
2. Speak to an experienced labor attorney immediately to protect your rights if the employer refuses to provide all the benefits specified in your contract.

PROTECTING THE SEVERANCE ARRANGEMENT

After you have negotiated your severance package and are satisfied that you have adequately covered all of your options and benefits, you must decide whether to accept the company's final offer or retain a lawyer in the attempt to obtain additional compensation.

Before retaining a lawyer, be sure that you feel comfortable with him or her and that the lawyer will be able to render competent services on your behalf. This can be accomplished by following many of the strategies contained in the chapter entitled "How to Hire and Get the Most from Your Lawyer."

SAMPLE LETTER ON BEHALF OF EMPLOYEE
FOR SEVERANCE OWED

Date

Name of Company Officer
Title
Name of Company
Address
Address

Dear (Name of Company Officer),

Please be advised that this office represents (Name of Employee), a long-time employee of your firm.

In this regard, I suggest that you or your representative contact this office immediately so that we may attempt to discuss a variety of issues regarding my client's severance and other benefits in an amicable fashion to avoid protracted and expensive litigation.

Thank you for your prompt cooperation in this matter.

Very truly yours,

Name of Attorney

SENT CERTIFIED MAIL, RETURN RECEIPT REQUESTED

Whomever you retain, it is important that the lawyer get started on your matter immediately. Time is crucial in all termination cases; action must be taken immediately to demonstrate the seriousness of your resolve. In fact, the longer a lawyer waits before contacting the employer, the weaker the case becomes. That is why I prefer to contact the employer within one week after the individual has been fired.

When I am retained to represent a terminated individual, a letter is sent to the employer by messenger or certified mail, return receipt requested, usually the day I am hired. This insures that the employer is notified quickly that I have been hired to discuss and negotiate the circumstances surrounding the person's termination, the inadequacy of the severance offer, the amount of money in commissions or other benefits still due and other considerations. The initial demand letter is kept brief because I do not want to "tip my hand" and state my case to someone I have never spoken with. Of course, it is always desired that the employer contact me as soon as possible. *This helps my negotiating position.*

A variety of techniques are used during negotiations; I typically stress that the employer should offer more to settle the matter amicably and avoid time-consuming and expensive legal action.

The above is an example of an actual demand letter sent by my office when I represent a terminated employee seeking severance.

An officer of the employer or a company attorney usually contacts me after receiving such a letter. Negotiations then ensue to determine if the matter can be settled out of court. Usually the matter is settled. I believe this is due to a number of factors. First, most employers want to avoid the poor publicity that can arise from a protracted court battle. Additionally, when companies are contacted by attorneys representing terminated employees, they must weigh whether it is wise to offer additional compensation to settle out of court versus spending thousands of dollars in legal expenses and lost work hours resulting from defending the charges in formal litigation. Additionally, if the firing is illegal, company exposure can amount to hundreds of thousands of dollars in actual damages (which doesn't include interest, attorney fees and costs that are sometimes awarded).

A pragmatic approach is often taken and most matters are settled. The employee receives additional severance and other benefits and the employer avoids a lawsuit. Remember that the mark of a good settlement is that no side is truly happy with the result. The employer believes too much money was paid to settle; conversely, the employee sometimes feels that he or she received too little. However, given the confines of the legal system (the long delays before the case is actually tried, the tremendous expenses involved, etc.) most terminated employees can achieve a fair out-of-court settlement for their troubles.

If you decide that contacting a lawyer is not necessary when you have obtained a fair and equitable settlement on your own, request that the employer confirm the deal in writing. Such a letter will clarify the points which were agreed upon and document the severance arrangement that has been made. Additionally, if the employer fails to abide by an important term (such as a promise of salary continuation for six months), the letter can increase your chances of success if you decide to sue for breach of contract.

The following letter was given to a former client of mine who recently negotiated to receive an additional one year's severance arrangement and other benefits with my assistance. Note the protections insisted on by the employer in the latter part of the agreement.

                                                    Date

Name of Employee
Address
Address

Dear (Name of Employee),

  This will confirm our agreement regarding your employment status with (Name of Employer).

  We agreed as follows:

  1. Your services as Vice President of (specify division) will terminate by mutual agreement effective (date).

2. Although your services as Vice President will not be required beyond (specify date), you agree to be available to (Name of Employer) through (specify termination date) to render advice, answer any questions and provide information regarding company business.

3. Through (specify termination date) except as provided in paragraph 4 below, you will continue to receive your regular bi-weekly salary of (specify) and you may continue to participate in those company benefit plans in which you are currently enrolled. In addition to your final paycheck, you will receive from the company on or about (specify termination date) or given as provided for in Paragraph 4 hereunder, the sum of (specify) less applicable deductions for local, state and federal taxes, as a bonus for the present year.

4. If you obtain other regular, full-time employment prior to (specify termination date), then, upon commencement of such employment (date of new employment), your regular bi-weekly salary payments and your participation in company benefit plans, as described in Paragraph 3 above, shall cease; however, medical and dental coverage previously provided you shall be continued for an additional period of three months at a cost to be borne by (Name of Employer). In such event, you will receive in a lump sum (less applicable deductions for taxes) the remaining amount you would have received on a bi-weekly basis from the date of new employment through (specify termination date) plus the (specify sum) bonus (less taxes) payment referred to in Paragraph 3 within two weeks of your date of new employment. You agree to notify the company immediately of the date on which such regular full-time employment will commence.

5. You acknowledge that the sums referred to in Paragraphs 3 and 4 above include any and all monies due you from the company, contractual or otherwise, to which you may be entitled, except for any vested benefit you may have in the (Name of Employer) Savings and Investment Plan and the Pension Plan.

6. (Name of Employer) will provide you with available office space, telephone service and clerical help on an as-needed basis at (address) until you obtain other regular full-time employment or (date), whichever occurs first.

7. You agree to cooperate fully with (Name of Employer) in their defense of or other participation in any administrative, judicial or collective bargaining proceeding arising from any charge, complaint, grievance or action which has been or may be filed.

8. You, on behalf of yourself and your heirs, representatives and assigns, hereby release (Name of Employer), its parents, their subsidiaries and divisions, and all of their respective current and former directors, officers, shareholders, successors, agents, representatives and employees, from any and all claims you ever had, now have, or may in the future assert regarding any matter that predates this agreement, including, without limitation, all claims regarding your employment at or termination of employment from (Name of Employer), any contract, express or implied, any tort, or any breach of a fair employment practice law, including Title VII, the Age Discrimination in Employment Act and any other local, state or federal equal opportunity law.

9. You acknowledge that you have had the opportunity to review this agreement with counsel of your own choosing, that you are fully aware of the agreement's contents and of its legal effects, and that you are voluntarily entering into this agreement.

10. You agree that any confidential information you acquired while an employee of the company shall not be disclosed to any other person or used in a manner detrimental to the company's interests.

11. Neither you nor anyone acting on your behalf shall publicize, disseminate or otherwise make known the terms of this agreement to any other person, except to those rendering financial or legal advice, or unless required to do so by court order or other compulsory process of law.

12. The provisions of this agreement are severable and if any provision is held to be invalid or unenforceable it shall not affect the validity or enforceability of any other provision.

13. This agreement sets forth the entire agreement between you and the company and supersedes any and all prior oral or written agreements or understandings between you and the company concerning this subject matter. This agreement may not be altered, amended or modified except by a further writing signed by you and (Name of Employer).

14. In the event (Name of Employer) becomes insolvent, bankrupt, is sold, or is unable in any way to pay the amounts due you under the terms of this agreement, then such obligations shall be undertaken and assumed by (specify Parent Company) and all such sums shall be guaranteed by (Name of Parent Company).

15. In the event that any monies due under this agreement are not paid for any reason, then the release referred to in paragraph 8 shall be null and void and of no effect.

If the foregoing correctly and fully recites the substance of our agreement, please so signify by signing in the space below.

Dated:

                     Very truly yours,

                     Name of Employer

               By:

                     Name of Officer, Title

Accepted and agreed:

_____
Name of Employee

In the event the employer refuses to provide such a letter, it is advisable to send a letter to the company by certified mail, return receipt requested, confirming the arrangement that has been made. The letter should state that if any terms are ambiguous or incorrect a written reply will be sent to you immediately. If no response is received, you will able to rely on the terms of the letter in most situations. The following is a good example:

Date

Name of Corporate Officer
Title
Name of Employer
Address
Address

Re: **Our Severance Agreement**

Dear (Name of Corporate Officer),

This will confirm our discussion and agreement regarding my termination:

1. I will be kept on the payroll through (specify date) and will receive (specify) weeks' vacation pay, which shall be included with my last check on that date.

2. (Name of Company) shall pay me a bonus of (specify) within (specify) days from the date of this letter.

3. (Name of Company) will purchase both my nonvested and vested company stock, totaling (specify) shares at the buy-in price of (specify) per share, or at the market rate if it is higher at the time of repurchase, on or before (specify date).

4. (Name of Company) will continue to maintain in effect all medical, dental, hospitalization and life insurance policies presently in effect through (specify date). After that date, I have been advised that I may convert said policies at my sole cost and expense and that coverage for these policies will not lapse.

5. I will be permitted to use the company's premises at (specify location) from the hours of 9:00 a.m. until 5:00 p.m. This shall include the use of a secretary, telephone, stationery, and other amenities at the company's sole cost and expense to assist me in obtaining another position.

6. I will be permitted to continue using the automobile previously supplied to me through (specify date) under the same terms and conditions presently in effect. On that date, I will return all sets of keys in my possession together with all other papers and documents belonging to the company.

7. (Name of Company) will reimburse me for all reasonable and necessary expenses related to the completion of company business after I submit appropriate vouchers and records within (specify) days of presentment thereto.

8. (Name of Company) agrees to provide me with a favorable letter of recommendation and reference(s), and will announce to the trade that I am resigning for "personal reasons." I am enclosing a letter for that purpose which will be reviewed and signed by (Specify Person) and returned to me immediately.

9. Although unanticipated, (Name of Company) will not contest my filing for unemployment insurance benefits after (specify date), and will assist me in promptly executing all documents necessary for that purpose.

10. If a position is procured by me prior to (specify date), a lump sum payment for my remaining severance will be paid within (specify) days after my notification of same. Additionally, the stock referred to in Paragraph 3 above will be purchased as of the date of my employment with another company if prior to (specify date) and will be paid to me within (specify) days of my notification.

If any of the terms of this letter are ambiguous or incorrect, please advise me immediately in writing specifying the item(s) that are incorrect. Otherwise, this letter shall set forth our entire understanding in this matter, which cannot be changed orally.

(Name of Corporate Officer), I want to personally thank you for your assistance and cooperation in this matter and wish you all the best in the future.

Very truly yours,

Your Name

SENT CERTIFIED MAIL, RETURN RECEIPT REQUESTED

Be sure to draft the agreement accurately since all ambiguities are usually construed against the person who writes such a letter. In addition, be prepared to send follow-up letters if warranted by your particular situation. Using the preceding case as an example, it would be wise to notify the company in writing if you obtained another job prior to the severance cut-off date. This is confirmed as shown in the sample on the opposite page.

RELEASES

Always be cautious if the employer asks you to sign a release. Generally, releases extinguish potential claims. Employees sometimes voluntarily sign such documents when they are fired, without fully understanding the ramifications of such an act. Later they regret taking such action after consulting a lawyer and learning they forfeited valuable rights without receiving much in return.

Since you may be out of luck if you sign such a document, consider the following strategies *whenever* you are asked to sign a release; the following can make you more knowledgeable in this area.

▪ ▪

STRATEGY 1   *Never sign a release unless you are satisfied with the company's offer. This is understandable since you should never relinquish a potentially valuable right without obtaining something of value in return.*

▪ ▪

Date

Name of Corporate Officer
Title
Name of Company
Address
Address

RE: Subsequent development to our agreement dated (specify)

Dear (Name of Corporate Officer),

I hope all is well with you and yours.

As a follow-up to our letter of agreement dated (specify), I am informing you that I have accepted employment with another company effective (specify date).

Therefore, I expect to receive a lump sum payment representing all unpaid severance through (specify date) plus (specify) weeks of vacation pay on or before (specify date).

Furthermore, I believe I am entitled to compensation for my stock totaling (specify amount) within (specify date).

As of this date, I am returning all keys to the office by messenger together with keys to the company car. I have also included the last voucher for company-related expenses.

Thank you for your prompt cooperation in these matters.

Very truly yours,

Your Name

Enc.

VIA MESSENGER

■ ■

STRATEGY 2   *Read the release carefully before signing it. Most releases are complicated documents. Many have settlement agreements, releases, waivers and nondisclosure provisions all contained in one document.*

For example, what does the release say? Are you prohibited from telling others about the terms of your settlement? This is referred to as a "gag order" provision. Many employers insert gag order clauses in the release which require all settlement monies to be forfeited and returned in the event you reveal the terms of the settlement to others. Obviously, you should question this provision and avoid signing it if possible.

Does the release prohibit you from working for a competitor or starting a competing business? Without such a clause you are free to work for the employer of your choosing. This is a valuable right which should never be given up easily.

■ ■

STRATEGY 3   *Negotiate additional clauses for your protection. Typical clauses add to the client's protection. First, make sure the release will be null and void if any monies due under the agreement are not paid. Second, a guarantee might be included which obligates the parent company to pay all remaining sums due under the agreement in the event a subsidiary corporation becomes bankrupt, insolvent or fails for any reason to pay the amount due. These are examples of the kinds of points to consider and implement in your agreement.*

■ ■

STRATEGY 4   *Obtain mutual releases where appropriate. Try to get the employer to give you a release whenever you are giving one to the employer. This is because you want to be sure that the employer can never sue you at a later time for something you did.*

■ ■

STRATEGY 5   *Speak to a lawyer immediately whenever the employer requests that a release be signed. Not understanding the consequences of their actions, people often waive valuable rights by signing such agreements. For example, you may be waiving valuable claims based on discrimination, breach of contract, unfair discharge, additional commissions or other monies owed. Never sign such a release until you are knowledgeable of all potential rights that you are giving up.*

■ ■

A competent lawyer can also take other practical steps for your protection. For example, he or she can insist that the release be held in *escrow* until all sums due under the agreement have been paid. This means that the employer could not rely on the signed release until it had fully performed all of the obligations required by the release. This is important and should never be overlooked.

If you believe the release was signed under conditions of fraud, duress or mistake, it can be rescinded provided you act promptly. Thus, it is essential to consult a lawyer immediately.

Finally, as previously stated, the federal Older Workers Benefit Protection Act was signed into law by the president on October 16, 1990. The act codifies existing law by providing that an older worker may not waive rights or claims of discrimination under the Age Discrimination in Employment Act (ADEA) unless the waiver is clear, voluntarily signed, part of an agreement where additional severance pay, early-retirement benefits or other monies is given, and the individual is given at least 21 days to consider the agreement containing such a waiver. Speak to a lawyer to advise you of your rights if you are asked to sign a complicated waiver which you believe does not comply with the requirements of this new law.

III

RESIGNING PROPERLY

Most people do not know how to resign properly. The slightest mistake can expose you to a lawsuit or cause the forfeiture of valuable benefits. Some people resign without receiving a firm job offer from a new employer. Later, after learning the new job did not materialize, they are unable to be rehired by their former employers and spend months out of work unnecessarily.

It doesn't have to happen this way. Problems such as these can avoided by thinking ahead. A proper resignation occurs when you are able to step into a new job with increased benefits without missing a day's pay, have no legal exposure and collect what you are owed from the former employer.

The following rules should be considered whenever you are thinking about resigning from a present job.

1. **Sign a written contract with a new employer before resigning**. This is essential. A written contract with a definite term of employment (for example, six months or one year) may protect you from situations in which the new employer changes his or her mind and decides not to hire you, or fires you after a short period of time. Since this often happens with devastating consequences, you should *never* leave a job without first obtaining a signed, written contract or letter agreement from a new employer. If the new employer is hesitant about putting the deal in writing, think twice before making the move to "greener pastures."

2. **Review your current contract or letter of agreement**. What does it say regarding termination? For example, if the contract states that written notice is required to be sent by registered mail 30 days prior to the effective termination date, be sure to comply with those terms. Otherwise, your failure to do so could cause the employer to sue you for breach of contract.

   Does your contract or letter of agreement contain provisions restricting you from working for a competitor, disseminating confidential or proprietary information learned on the job, or calling on accounts previously served by you during your current employment? Such clauses are called restrictive covenants or covenants not to compete, and may or may not be enforceable depending upon the particular circumstances and facts. These are explained in greater detail in Chapter 8.

3. **Is it necessary to give notice?** In many jobs, notice is not required if you are hired at will. However, the employer will usually benefit when you offer notice because it will then have the time to seek and train a replacement. It may also enable you to bargain for additional severance benefits before walking out the door.

▪ ▪

STRATEGY   *Two weeks' notice is probably more than adequate; avoid giving more notice than necessary. Do not offer notice if you believe this will jeopardize your new position. However, if you are entitled to a large bonus or commission in the near future, avoid resigning before you have received such a benefit.*

▪ ▪

4. **Should you resign by letter?** Most people think it is proper to resign by letter. However, it is not always in your best interest to do so. A letter can clarify resignation benefits, request prompt payment of monies previously due or put you on record that the resignation will not be effective until some later date. If this is important, then a letter should be sent. However, you should keep the letter brief and avoid giving specific reasons for the resignation, because this can preclude you from offering other reasons or tipping your hand in the event of a lawsuit.

The example on the following page is the kind of resignation letter you may wish to draft. Notice that it is hand-delivered or sent by certified mail, return receipt requested. These methods will prove delivery and should be followed whenever practical.

5. **Should you resign if given the choice?** Many people mistakenly believe that it is better to resign rather than be fired. *This is not always true.* By resigning, you may waive valuable benefits including severance pay, bonuses and other monies. This is because many employers have written policies which state that no severance or other post-termination benefits will be paid to workers who resign. Additionally, you are not entitled to unemployment insurance benefits after voluntarily resigning from a job in many states. If you are a commission salesperson, it is more difficult to argue that you are entitled to commissions due on orders shipped after a resignation (as opposed to after a firing).

Thus, always think twice about resigning if the employer gives you the option of resignation or discharge. In fact, I usually prefer

Date

Name of Officer
Title
Name of Employer
Address

Re: My Resignation

Dear (Name of Officer)

Please be advised that I am resigning from my job as (title) effective (date).

As of this date, I believe that (describe what salary, commissions, other benefits) are due and I look forward to discussing my termination benefits with you.

I shall be returning all property belonging to the company (specify) by (date) and will be available to assist you in a smooth transition if requested.

Thank you for your cooperation in these matters.

Very truly yours,

Your Name

HAND DELIVERED or SENT CERTIFIED MAIL,
RETURN RECEIPT REQUESTED

my clients to be fired rather than resign whenever possible, since in this way potential damage claims and severance benefits may remain intact.

If you are worried about what outsiders may think, you can always negotiate that the employer will tell outsiders you "resigned for personal reasons" even if you were fired. In conclusion, always speak to an experienced labor lawyer *before* resigning from any significant job since you may be forfeiting valuable rights unnecessarily.

6. **Keep your lips sealed**. Never tell friends and business associates of your decision to resign before telling your current employer. The expression "loose lips sink ships" is certainly true in this area.

7. **Avoid badmouthing**. It is not a good idea to tell others about the circumstances surrounding the resignation, particularly if you are leaving on less-than-pleasant terms. Many employers have sued former employees for defamation, product disparagement and unfair competition upon discovering that slanderous comments were made. Additionally, when the statement disparages

the quality of a company's product and at the same time implies that an officer or principal of the employer is dishonest, fraudulent or incompetent (thus affecting the individual's personal reputation), a private lawsuit for personal defamation may also be brought. Some companies withhold severance pay and other benefits as a way of getting even. Thus, avoid discussing your employer in a negative way with anyone.

8. **Return property belonging to the employer**. Disputes sometimes occur when property belonging to the employer is not returned. You must return such property (automobile keys, confidential customer lists, samples, etc.) immediately upon resignation to avoid claims of conversion, fraud and breach of contract.

■ ■

STRATEGY   *If returning items by mail, get a receipt to prove delivery. Additionally, recognize that some states permit you to retain company property as a lien in the event you are owed money which the employer refuses to pay. However, since many states do not recognize this, speak to an experienced lawyer before taking such action.*

■ ■

8

■ ■

HANDLING OTHER POST-TERMINATION PROBLEMS

The average worker has many concerns after leaving a job. For example, he or she must worry about whether or not the former employer will give a favorable reference. But what steps can be taken if the employer gives a bad reference to prospective employers? Additionally, what should be done if your former employer contests unemployment insurance benefits while you are out of work? Can your former employer enforce confidentiality and restrictive covenants prohibiting you from working for a competitor? What is the quickest and cheapest way to collect commissions and other monies that may be due?

This chapter discusses a variety of post-termination problems which commonly affect workers. The following strategies will identify common problems and offer practical solutions to such concerns.

RESTRICTIVE COVENANTS AND RELATED PROBLEMS

As explained in detail in Chapter 2, restrictive covenants are agreements that prohibit a person from directly competing with, or working for the competitor of one's employer. Historically, promises by employees not to compete with employers after termination of a job were enforceable provided a bona fide business interest existed which required protection, there was no undue hardship on the employee, the restriction was not unreasonable in terms of time and/or geographic scope, did not violate public policy and was not considered a restraint of trade. Utilized by companies to protect hard-won business and retain prized employees, such agreements were generally protected by the courts.

However, many courts are now viewing such covenants as unfair because they limit a person's ability to earn a living. As a result, executive mobility is becoming harder to contain. When judges decide that such contracts go too far in restraining employees, they either modify the terms (making them less restrictive) or declare such covenants to be totally unenforceable and of no legal effect.

There are no set rules regarding the enforcement of restrictive covenants. *Each case must be analyzed on its own particular merits.* For example, some kinds of non-compete pacts stand a better chance of being upheld than others. These include situations where the seller of a business agrees not to start a competing business which could injure the buyer's interests, where trade secrets are involved or where the employer paid additional consideration (for example, a bonus of $10,000 was given to the employee as inducement to sign a contract containing a restrictive covenant).

The relevant factors typically considered by a judge are:

- Any unfairness in length of time or geographic limitations (e.g., greater than one year; the entire United States)
- The degree of hardship on the employee if the covenant is enforced
- Any additional compensation given to the individual as inducement to sign a contract containing such a clause
- The degree to which the individual has access to confidential information such as customer lists, trade secrets, specific business methods, established needs of customers and related information
- Special skills or training of the employee
- The bargaining power of the parties
- The status of the individual: whether he or she is an employee or an independent contractor. (Note: In a number of states, a company cannot legally restrain independent contractors from working for a competitor even after signing an agreement with a restrictive covenant.)
- Possible breaches by the employer of any of its own obligations under the contract (e.g., a failure to pay salary or other compensation). When employers violate agreements this may release the individual from any liability arising from obligations contained in a restrictive covenant.

When restrictive covenants do seem to be a threat, however, there are a number of ways to possibly arm yourself from being aggrieved.

1. **Understand what constitutes a trade secret.** A trade secret consists of any formula, pattern, device or compilation of information used in business that gives a company an opportunity to obtain an advantage over competitors who do not know or use it.

    In determining whether a trade secret is involved, a court generally looks at three basic elements:

- Whether the employer took precautions to guard the secrecy of the information;
- Whether the employer spent considerable time and money developing the information; and
- Whether the employer informed employees that trade secrets were involved and that they were obligated to act in a confidential manner.

The most frequently disputed issue concerning trade secrets involves customer lists. A "secret" list is not a list of companies or individuals that can be compiled from a telephone directory or other source that anyone can examine. A list becomes confidential when the names of customers can be learned only by someone through his employment (for example, when an employee secretly copies a list of customers that the employer spent considerable time, effort and money compiling and keeps under lock and key).

When an employee has become friendly with customers in the course of his previous employment, he is allowed to call on them for new employers. However, the law generally states that employees are prohibited from using their knowledge of customer buying habits, requirements or other special information when soliciting their former employer's accounts. For example, if the individual knows that a particular customer will be in short supply of a product, it may be illegal to solicit that account for the new employer.

Special information about a customer constitutes secret or confidential information when:

- The information is not readily accessible to competitors;
- The employee solicited the customer with intent to injure the former employer;
- The former employee sought out preferred customers whose trade is particularly profitable and whose identities are not generally known;
- The employer's business is such that customers ordinarily patronize only one firm; and
- The established business relationship between customers and the former employer would normally continue unless interfered with.

2. **Avoid taking confidential information with you when you leave.** Many states have passed laws making it a crime to steal trade secrets. In some states it is a misdemeanor or felony for anyone to steal company property consisting of valuable or secret scientific material.

   Additionally, assuming that valuable written material is stolen and transported to another state, the FBI and the Justice Department may become involved. That's because it is a federal crime to sell or receive stolen property worth more than $5,000 that has been transported across state lines.

3. **Consult an experienced labor lawyer immediately if an ex-employer threatens to sue to enforce a restrictive covenant.** You may be surprised to learn that the employer will be unsuccessful in the event of a lawsuit. Thus, don't be intimidated by such threats. Remember, courts in many states are now ruling that non-compete agreements are not enforceable when they restrict a person's right to work (particularly if the trade you are involved in is your only means of support), when they are merely being used to guard the employer's turf, when trade secrets are not involved or when a person needs to work to support a family member with special needs (such as a spouse who is ill).

    Thus, never take action detrimental to your interests (i.e., sign a document admitting wrongdoing) until you have spoken to an experienced labor attorney. Many people are pressured by ex-employers to do things they later regret; avoid this.

4. **Is the employer in breach of any obligations or duties owed to you?** When companies are in breach of important contract terms, the law presumes they have "unclean hands"; sometimes in such situations restrictive covenants will not be applied against you. For example, I recently defended several sales employees who had gone into business in competition with an ex-employer. Previously, the individuals contacted me to review an employment agreement that had been signed with the ex-employer. The agreement contained a restrictive covenant. During the consultation I learned that the employer had reduced their salary despite their protests to save the company money. I advised them that since the employer was obligated to pay a predetermined salary specified by contract, the failure to do so might release them from the covenant in the agreement.

    The employees were sued after commencing business operations. At the trial, the judge heard testimony regarding this unilateral cut of pay. The judge agreed that the employer had unfairly reduced their compensation without consent and ruled that the restrictive covenant could *not* be enforced against them.

DEFAMATORY JOB REFERENCES

Defamation can occur in the workplace whenever an employer communicates information about an employee. For example, defamatory statements are often made to outsiders and prospective employers regarding an employee's job performance or problems on the job. Third parties are sometimes shown an employee's personnel file or performance evaluations. Such records often contain derogatory comments which are later proved to be untrue. In other situations, inaccurate memoranda are circulated within a company. This causes serious consequences when the employer does not take adequate precautions to determine whether derogatory information in the memoranda is accurate.

One terminated employee sued his former employer for defamation when letters describing the employee's poor job performance were distributed and read by several executives. The employee was awarded $90,000 after proving the information contained in the letters was false.

In another case, I recently represented a man who was fired after being accused of drinking excessively at lunch. The client obtained a copy of a memo confirming this which was read by several employees. I recovered $15,000 for the client in an out-of-court settlement after proving the accusation to be untrue.

Cases such as these illustrate how common employee defamation lawsuits have become. More employees are suing former employers for defamation; in fact, such suits now account for approximately one-third of all defamation actions, and the average winning verdict has reached $112,000, according to a company that monitors litigation in this field.

Failure to recommend a former employee for a new position can give rise to a potential cause of action for libel or slander even when the employee has sustained no actual economic harm. This is because all states generally recognize a valid defamation lawsuit when false written or spoken words are communicated to a third party which disparage a person in his trade, office or profession and when the employer (or former employer) negligently failed to check the accuracy of such statements.

The following forms of wrongs fall under the larger heading of defamation:

1. **Slander**—Arises when an unfair and untrue oral statement is communicated to a third party which damages the individual's reputation. The spoken words must pertain to a person's poor moral character, unreliability, dishonesty, financial instability (e.g., a statement that the person is filing for bankruptcy or is always being sued when this is false, or failure to live up to contractual obligations or business responsibilities).

2. **Libel**—Arises when an unfair and untrue statement is made about a person in writing. The statement becomes actionable when it is read by a third party and damages the person's business or personal reputation. Such comments are frequently made in a letter or memo.

Mere statements that an employee was discharged from employment, or truthful statements pertaining to that employee's work habits, are not defamatory. Truth is a total defense against claims of libel or slander. Charging a worker with bad manners, being careless or a troublemaker, not having sufficient skills, or not adequately performing a job will not qualify as defamation. However, statements that the individual was discharged for cause or unsatisfactory performance, incompetence or insubordination coupled with the employer's refusal to give a recommendation may be potentially damaging, and thus actionable as defamation.

In some states the law protects employees fired on false charges of bad conduct who themselves reveal the charges (as opposed to a false communication or reference made by the employer). The following true case illustrates this legal principle.

The Minnesota Supreme Court recently awarded four employees $570,000 when they revealed in job applications that their former employer fired them. The workers had been fired unfairly for gross insubordination for failing to obey a manager's request to falsify expenditure reports. The employees sought other jobs following the termination. In response to inquiries about their previous positions, the employees gave the reason stated by the employer.

The court ruled that a defamation had occurred since the terminated employees were forced when asked to truthfully reply that they had been fired for insubordination. The court determined that any explanations provided by the individuals to prospective employers could not compensate for the negative impression caused by the words "gross insubordination," and the former company's policy of withholding information after a job referral only added to the innuendoes.

Thus, recognize that if you are forced to disclose in a job interview the reason you were let go, such "compelled self-publication" may constitute defamation.

As previously indicated, defamation does not only arise from the dissemination of damaging information to prospective employers. It can also occur on-site. Harshly criticizing an employee can make an employer vulnerable in a defamation lawsuit. For example, if you are accused of stealing company property in front of others and slanderous remarks are made (such as, "You are a crook"), your employer may be guilty of defamation if the remarks are proven false.

Defamation may also arise through acts impugning a person's reputation from the firing itself. In one recent case, a man was discharged after he failed a lie detector test. The employee proved the company defamed him by firing him under circumstances strongly implying he was guilty of theft. After demonstrating that the test results were improperly evaluated by an unqualified and unlicensed polygraph examiner and that he was not guilty of the theft, the man was awarded $150,000.

To avoid exposure in this area, many employers are now advising staff to merely confirm an individual's former employment, the dates of employment and the last position held. They are being advised that it is wise never to offer an opinion about an employee's work performance unless it is conclusively positive.

Most states have ruled that employers have a qualified privilege when discussing an ex-employee's job performance with a prospective employer. This means that the employer may be excused for disseminating information about an individual which later turns out to be false if the person responsible for disseminating such information did so in the course of his or her normal duties (such as a personnel supervisor who writes performance appraisals about individuals).

However, a qualified privilege can be lost or abused and an employer can be liable if an executive or personnel supervisor knowingly makes false defamatory comments about a former employee due to reckless disregard for the truth, ill will or spite.

The first thing to remember in any defamation lawsuit is that you must prove that false statements were made. This is often hard to do. For example, if you are told by an employment recruiter he or she heard slanderous comments from your former employer, the recruiter would have to testify in court in order for you to prevail, and many people are reluctant to do this.

In addition, truth is an absolute defense in any defamation lawsuit. This means that if your employer disseminates harmful information which is true, or you are fired for a legitimate reason which is properly documented and can be proven by the company, you may lose your case.

Finally, many cases are lost when employers assert a qualified privilege defense.

However, even if a lawyer determines that commencing a lawsuit in this area is not in your best interest, you can compel an employer to stop disclosing harmful information to others. That is why it is critical to consult an experienced labor lawyer immediately to analyze and protect your rights.

Strategies for Protection

The following is a summary of key points to remember in this area:

1. **Act promptly if you discover that an ex-employer is making defamatory remarks which inhibit your chances of obtaining new employment.** This includes sending letters by certified mail, return receipt requested, to protect your rights. The letter can document what you have learned and put the former employer on notice of your desire to take prompt legal action if the problem persists. The sample on the opposite page illustrates this.
2. **Take immediate action if you believe you are being blacklisted or willfully prevented from obtaining new employment.** Many states have enacted antiblacklisting statutes that punish employers for maliciously or willfully attempting to prevent former employees from finding work. In fact, many state legislatures have passed laws requiring that employers only give truthful oral and written job references when an employee resigns or is fired.

In other states, "service letter" statutes have been passed giving fired workers additional legal protection. These states include Florida, Indiana, Kansas, Maine, Missouri and Montana. Under the laws in these states, employers are required to give a terminated worker a true written statement regarding the cause of his or her dismissal. Once such an explanation is received, the employer cannot furnish prospective employers with reasons which deviate from those given in the service letter.

In those states, an employer can be sued for damages for refusing to tell you why you were fired, for providing you with false reasons, or for changing its story and offering additional reasons to outsiders or during legal proceedings (i.e., at a trial or arbitration).

Thus, it is a good idea to discover the reasons why you were fired, particularly in those states which have passed service letter

---

Date

Name of Officer of Employer
Title
Name of Employer
Address

Dear (Name of Officer),

On (date) I applied for a job with (Name of Potential Employer). At the interview, I learned that you had submitted an inaccurate, unfavorable reference about me.

You supposedly said the reason I was fired was that I was excessively late on the job. We both know this is incorrect. I had the opportunity to review the entire contents of my personnel file after I was dismissed. Not one reference was made anywhere in the file to lateness.

Kindly cease and desist from making any such unfavorable remarks about my job performance, particularly to potential employers. If I learn that you disregard this request, be assured that my lawyer will take immediate legal action to protect my rights.

Thank you for your prompt cooperation in this matter.

Very truly yours,

Your Name

(cc: To Potential Employer)

SENT CERTIFIED MAIL, RETURN RECEIPT REQUESTED

Date

Name of Officer of Employer
Title
Name of Employer
Address

Re: My termination

Dear (Name of Officer),

On (date) I was fired suddenly by your company without notice, warning or cause. All that I was told by (Name of Person) was that my services were no longer required and that my termination was effective immediately.

To date, I have not received any explanation documenting the reason(s) for my discharge. In accordance with the laws of this state I hereby demand such information immediately.

Thank you for your prompt cooperation in this matter.

Very truly yours,

Your Name

SENT CERTIFIED MAIL, RETURN RECEIPT REQUESTED

---

statutes. This can be done by sending the employer a letter similar to the above.

If you do not receive an answer to such a letter within a reasonable period of time (such as 30 days), or if the employer furnishes you with reasons which are untrue, consult an experienced labor lawyer *immediately* to explore your options.

3. **Recognize that some states treat untruthful job references as crimes.** Such states include Arkansas, Maine, Nebraska, New Mexico and Utah. Missouri permits civil actions against employers for compensatory damages for untruthful statements. Additionally, the following states provide for criminal penalties and civil damage lawsuits against former employers: California, Florida, Iowa, Kansas, Montana, North Carolina and Texas. You should also be aware that in California and Kansas, triple damages are awarded in certain situations; Montana and North Carolina statutes provide for additional punitive damages as well.

Thus, use this information to take prompt legal action when appropriate.

4. **Recognize that you have similar rights while working.** It is not necessary to be fired to receive protection in this area. For example,

you may have a valid claim for defamation when harmful records such as memos in personnel files, poor performance evaluations, false offhand remarks, improper theft investigations or false accusations in front of workers are made and/or distributed to third parties. Many states, including Connecticut, Illinois and Michigan, have passed strict laws prohibiting employers from divulging disciplinary information unless the individual in question receives a copy of such a statement.

Protection may also extend to physical acts. For example, an employee working for a large automobile manufacturer was recently suspected of theft when leaving the premises. Hundreds of workers observed him being forcibly searched and interrogated. After proving the charges were unfounded, the man sued the company. He argued that the rough treatment observed by other workers defamed his reputation and held him up to ridicule and scorn (since the treatment implied that he was guilty of theft). After a trial, the man was awarded $25,000 in damages.

5. **Take immediate action if you discover that important employment data and personnel records were released to outsiders without your consent.** In many states, including Connecticut, any dissemination of employment data to prospective employers (other than the dates of employment, position held and latest salary figures) is illegal. Many states prohibit the dissemination of confidential medical information as well. Since the laws in each state vary it is best to consult an experienced labor lawyer immediately upon learning about any of the above.

6. **Demand to inspect the contents of your personnel file if appropriate.** There has been a recent trend allowing terminated workers access to and inspection of their personnel files. In California, Connecticut, Delaware, Illinois, Maine, Michigan, Nevada, New Hampshire, Ohio, Oregon, Pennsylvania, Washington and Wisconsin, for example, people now have the right to inspect their files. Some states even allow people to place written rebuttals in their files. Such rebuttals can refute company action or comments and may be read by prospective employers. In some states, people are even authorized to bring private lawsuits to expunge false information contained in such files.

All of these strategies should be carefully considered whenever you believe false information or poor references have been given to prospective employers after a discharge. Be aware that employers frequently face greater exposure and potential damages in lawsuits from leaking harmful or confidential information after a firing than from the firing itself! Fortunately, many states have passed laws protecting workers in this area and other states are following this trend.

HOW TO INCREASE YOUR CHANCES OF SUCCESS AT UNEMPLOYMENT HEARINGS

Many people who are fired forfeit valuable unemployment insurance benefits. This is because they do not know how to act or represent themselves properly at unemployment hearings. Many are told by unemployment personnel that a lawyer or other representative is not required and that preparation for the hearing is unnecessary. They then attend the hearing and are surprised to learn that the employer is represented by experienced counsel who has brought witnesses to testify against their version of the facts. Additionally, some are unprepared for the grueling, humiliating cross-examination lasting several hours which they are frequently subjected to. Other people lose at the hearing because they do not know the purpose of their testimony or what they must prove to receive benefits.

This section will offer strategies to increase your chances of obtaining benefits at unemployment hearings when your case is contested by a former employer.

Know the Law

Each state imposes different eligibility requirements for collecting unemployment benefits (e.g., the maximum amount of money that may be collected weekly, the normal waiting period required before payments begin, the length of such benefits, and the maximum period you can wait before filing and collecting). States also differ on standards of proof required to receive such benefits. You must know such essential details before filing. This can be done by contacting your nearest unemployment office for pertinent information.

The following questions are some of the points to consider asking:

- How quickly can I file?
- When will I begin receiving payments?
- How long will the payments last?
- What must I do (i.e., must I actively look for employment?) in order to qualify and continue receiving benefits?
- How long did I have to work for my former employer in order to qualify?
- What must I prove in order to collect if my ex-employer contests my claim?
- When will the hearing be held?
- Will I have an opportunity to review the employer's defense and other documentation submitted in opposition before the hearing?
- How can I learn whether witnesses will appear on the company's behalf to testify against me?
- How can I obtain competent legal counsel to represent me?

- How much will this cost?
- Is a record made of the hearing? If so, in what form?
- Is the hearing examiner's decision final and binding or can the decision be appealed?
- Can I recover benefits if I was forced to resign?
- Is the burden on the employer to demonstrate that I was fired for a good reason (such as misconduct) or is the burden on me to prove that I did not act improperly?
- Can I subpoena witnesses if they refuse to appear voluntarily on my behalf? Will the hearing examiner assist me in this regard?
- Are formal rules of evidence followed at the hearing?

As you can see, collecting benefits may not be a simple matter, especially if your claim is contested by an ex-employer.

When a terminated worker comes into my office, one of the first points I consider is whether the employee was discharged for a valid reason. In most states, you *can* collect unemployment benefits if you were fired due to a business reorganization, massive layoff, job elimination or for other reasons that were not your fault. In many situations you can even collect if you were fired for being unsuited or unskilled for the job or for overall poor work performance.

However, you generally *cannot* collect if you resign voluntarily (unless you were forced to resign for a good reason) or if you were fired for *misconduct*.

The following are common examples of acts that often justify the denial of unemployment benefits based on misconduct:

- Insubordination or fighting on the job
- Habitual lateness or excessive absence
- Intoxication or drug abuse on the job
- Disobedience of company work rules or policies
- Gross negligence or neglect of duty
- Dishonesty or unfaithfulness

Although these examples appear to be relatively straightforward, employers often have difficulty proving that such acts reached the level of misconduct. This is because hearing examiners typically seek to determine whether a legitimate company rule was violated and whether or not that rule was justified.

When representing terminated individuals, I am mindful of the standards that hearing examiners, judges and arbitrators use in making decisions at unemployment hearings and arbitrations. Many of these guidelines are relevant to successfully asserting one's claim for unemployment benefits and are repeated here for your benefit:

- Did the employer have a clear rule against the kind of behavior which resulted in the firing?
- Is the rule reasonably related to the orderly, efficient and safe operation of the employer's business?
- Did the employer provide all employees with a reasonable opportunity to learn the company's rules?
- Did the employer provide all employees with reasonable notice regarding the consequences of violating such rules?
- Has the employer administered and enforced the rules consistently and without discrimination among all employees?
- Did the employer take steps to fairly investigate the circumstances involved in the alleged offense?
- Did the employer obtain substantial evidence of the alleged act through this investigation?
- Did such acts meet the standard of law required to prove misconduct?
- Are there mitigating factors which reasonably explain the employee's conduct?
- Was the firing fair under all of the circumstances?
- Were the employer's witnesses credible in proving the action taken?

These considerations demonstrate the degree of sophistication that is often required to prevail at unemployment hearings. That is why you should carefully consider whether you require representation by experienced counsel at the hearing. For example, if you are anticipating receiving the maximum benefits allowed (note: in some states this may exceed $250 per week) and expect to be unable to find gainful employment for a long period of time (e.g., six months), it may be advantageous to hire counsel when the amount of money being contested is significant.

The following information will help you prepare and win your case if you decide that representation is not necessary.

Preparing for the Hearing

Once you file for unemployment insurance and learn that the employer is contesting your claim, it is your responsibility to follow the progress of the case carefully. Plan on being able to attend the hearing on the date in question. If you cannot be present, speak to an employee responsible for scheduling, explain your reasons and ask for another convenient date. This should preferably be done in person. Include future dates when you know you can appear. Call that individual the day before the old hearing date to confirm that your request has been granted.

An unemployment hearing is no different from a trial. Witnesses must testify under oath. Documents, including personnel information, warnings, performance appraisals, and so on, are submitted as exhibits. The atmosphere is rarely friendly. Thus, you must prepare in advance what you will say, how you will handle tough questions from the employer and what you will try to prove to win the case.

When preparing for the hearing, be certain that all your friendly witnesses (if any) will attend and testify on your behalf. If necessary, ask a representative from the unemployment office to issue a subpoena compelling the attendance of key disinterested witnesses (such as co-workers) who refuse to voluntarily attend and testify. Unfortunately, people who tell you they will appear do not always do so, and it may be necessary to subpoena them. If the unemployment representative has no authority to do this, wait until the first day of the hearing. Explain to the judge or hearing examiner the necessity of compelling the appearance and testimony of key witnesses. The judge may grant your request depending on the relevance and reasonableness of the request.

Organize your case before the day of the hearing to maximize your chances of success. Collect all evidence so it can be produced easily at the hearing. Practice what you will say at the hearing. This will relax you and help organize the important facts. You can even prepare an outline of key points to be discussed and questions to ask each witness and employees of the ex-employer.

The Hearing

Arrive early on the hearing day and advise a scheduling clerk of your appearance. Bring your evidence and come properly attired (preferably in business clothes).

■ ■

STRATEGY   *In some states you can review the entire contents of your unemployment file before the hearing; don't forget to ask for this if appropriate.*

■ ■

When your case is called, all relevant witnesses will be sworn in. Stay calm. The judge or hearing examiner will conduct the hearing and ask you questions. Speak directly and with authority. Show the judge your evidence. Talk directly to the judge and respond to his or her questions. Show respect. Always refer to him or her as "Your Honor" or "Judge" and never argue with the judge. If you are asked a question while speaking, stop immediately and answer it. Make your answer direct and to the point.

Avoid being emotional. Avoid arguing with your opponent at the hearing and avoid interrupting his or her presentation.

After your opponent finishes testifying, you will have the opportunity to cross-examine such testimony and refute what was said. In addition, do not be afraid if the employer is represented by an attorney. If you feel intimidated, tell the judge that you are not represented by counsel and are not familiar with unemployment hearing procedures. Ask the judge to intercede on your behalf when you feel your opponent's attorney is treating you unfairly. Most judges are sympathetic since unemployment hearings are specifically designed for you to present your case without an attorney.

Obtaining a decision   Decisions are not usually obtained immediately after the hearing. You will probably be notified by mail (sometimes two to six weeks later). Be sure to continue filing for benefits while waiting for the decision. Many people forget to do this and lose valuable benefits in the process.

Should you appeal?   You should begin collecting weekly or biweekly benefits immediately after receiving a favorable decision. Additionally, you should receive a lump sum check representing benefits previously due.

If you are notified that you lost the decision, read the notice carefully. Most judges and hearing examiners give specific, lengthy reasons for their rulings. If you feel that the ruling was incorrect or you disagree with the judge's opinion, you may wish to file an appeal and have the case reheard. However, it is best to speak with an experienced attorney to get his or her opinion before doing so. You may discover that your chances of success with the appeal are not as good as you think. Appeals are not granted automatically as a matter of right in many states. If a group of judges on the Appeals Board believe that the hearing judge's decision was correct factually or as a matter of law, the decision will go undisturbed.

Recognize that the odds of winning the appeal are not in your favor if you lose at the initial hearing. Often, the amount of time needed to review the transcript or tape of the proceeding(s), prepare an appeal brief, and reargue the case makes it too expensive and time-consuming. Thus, depending on the particular facts of your case, appealing the hearing may not be worth it. However, if new material facts come to light or relevant witnesses are willing to come forward and testify at the appeal hearing, this could make the difference. That is why you should always consult with an experienced labor lawyer before making such a decision.

HOW TO COLLECT BACK WAGES AND BENEFITS DUE TO YOU AFTER TERMINATION

After you have left your job, willingly or otherwise, how do you collect what your employer owes you if it has not been paid to you freely and promptly? Much depends on why you left the job, and under what conditions. If you left voluntarily with prior notice and under favorable circumstances from a reputable employer, you should have no problem. But what if you were fired? What if you were fired on charges of misconduct or poor performance? What are your defenses?

If you have a discrimination claim under Title VII of the Civil Rights Act of 1964, you have recourse in federal court with the Equal Employment

Opportunity Commission. If you win, you may be awarded back pay, reinstatement in your job and payment of your attorney fees. Often, however, one is better advised to sue in state courts based on state statutes where awards can be larger than possible from Title VII, and where, in contrast to federal court, you may be able to demand a jury trial.

State statutes vary widely, but in general they tell when wages must be paid following job termination. Many states provide for penalties and payment of attorney fees if you are not paid in timely fashion. The definition of back wages normally includes everything of dollar value owed to you, including bonuses, deferred compensation, accrued vacation, sick leave and pension rights. Note that most courts will consider only wages due to you up to the time of the court award, not projected or future losses.

In any event, when seeking back wages, you can enforce your rights either by suing directly, or through the assistance of your state labor department. (Note, however, that you are not protected by the federal Fair Labor Standards Act or state wages statutes if you are a non-employee independent contractor.) You should always consider and follow through on your options as quickly as possible when seeking back wages and other benefits.

Small Claims Court

If your claim is small, you may choose to represent yourself in Small Claims Court. You will be spared the expense of a lawyer's fees, as lawyers are not permitted to practice in most Small Claims Courts. Also, many such courts have night sessions as a convenience to those who must work during business hours. You can sue only for money in Small Claims Court. The maximum amount you can sue for will vary according to the laws of your state, but generally will be $1,500, sometimes more. Look for the Small Claims Court in your telephone directory, possibly listed as Justice Court, District Court, Municipal Court or Peace Court. Call your city or state bar association, city hall, or county courthouse to learn the location of the nearest Small Claims Court.

Small Claims Court procedures will vary between cities and states. Your first step is to call the clerk of the court and ask for a written copy and explanation of the specific procedures and rules. Small Claims Courts may be used to sue any person, business, partnership, corporation or government body which owes money to you. But remember, if the maximum limit for which you can sue in Small Claims is less than what you feel is owed you, you will be giving up the amount in excess of the Small Claims Court maximum figure; once you sue in Small Claims Court, you are prohibited from suing again to recover the difference.

Before you can sue successfully in Small Claims Court, you must have a valid claim. This means that you must have clear identification of the person or business you feel has wronged you, you must be able to show how you calculated the value of the damages you suffered and you must determine if there is a legal basis for your claim. In addition, you must make sure that your own actions have not barred you from a successful suit, which would be the case if you waited too long to start action, you were the cause of your own harm or you signed a written release precluding you from taking further legal action.

To begin your Small Claims Court lawsuit, you start by paying a small fee, usually less than $10. Next you present a written complaint, either in person or by mail, stating your name and address, the complete name and address of the person or company you are suing, the amount of money you believe is owed to you and the reasons why you (the plaintiff) are suing. Be sure that your information is both complete and accurate. In some states, you may be required to send a demand letter to the defendant before suing in Small Claims Court and can only sue in the county where the company is located.

The following is an example of a simple complaint. Note the specificity of the facts and dates in the complaint, and note also the statement of efforts made to settle the claim prior to filing the complaint.

> I worked full-time for XYZ Company from February 1, 1989, through July 31, 1991, with a salary of $1,000 monthly. On July 31, 1991, I was dismissed from my job with no warning. I was given no reason for my dismissal. At the time I was dismissed, I was not paid for the month of July 1991. The XYZ Company employee handbook says that employees will be given two weeks' notice before being terminated. I am seeking the $1,000 owed to me for the month of July, 1991, and $500 for the two weeks' notice I should have received. I have demanded both of these amounts in person on August 7 and 15, 1991, by telephone on August 21 and September 11, 1991, and in writing on September 30, 1991. My in-person and telephone requests for payment were ignored, and my written request was refused in a letter dated October 18, 1991.

Someone must prepare and serve a summons to notify your opponent that you are suing him. In some jurisdictions, the court clerk will do this. In others, the preparation and serving of the summons will be your duty. To be sure of who does what, check with the court clerk. If it is your duty, either mail the summons by first-class mail (preferably by registered mail), deliver it in person or hire a professional process server. First, however, ask the court clerk what you will need to prove that the summons was actually served.

Your opponent (the defendant) has several possible responses to your summons. The defendant (or his attorney) can mail a written denial of your claim to the court, or can deny the claim in person by appearing in court on the day the court has set for the hearing. The defendant may even sue you (called a counterclaim) for money you supposedly owe him, such as for tools, materials, supplies, failure to perform your duties and so on. Or, if you are fortunate, you may be offered a settlement.

If the defendant offers to make some payment to you, be sure to include all filing and service charges in your demand. If you are satisfied with the offer, be sure that you receive it before the day set for the hearing. If the payment is by check, wait until the check clears before you consider yourself to have been paid. Whatever you do, don't delay the trial waiting for payment. If you accept the settlement in advance of the hearing, and if you actually have payment in hand, immediately notify the court clerk that you are dismissing the action.

As with any important action or decision you make, prepare yourself in advance of the hearing. Line up your witnesses—friendly, of course, but also believable. If there are witnesses who are important to your case and they refuse to attend your hearing to testify, ask the court clerk to issue subpoenas to compel their attendance. There may be documents and records, such as your personnel records and company payroll records, that are important to your case. You can subpoena these also. If, on the day of the hearing, the court clerk has not received documents or records you have subpoenaed, you can ask for an adjournment.

When you come to the hearing, arrive early to locate the proper courtroom, find your case listed on the court calendar and check in with the clerk. Dress properly, preferably in business clothes. Be sure that you bring everything that is important as evidence for your case, such as canceled paychecks, a copy of the company's employee manual, letters you have sent concerning your claim and written responses from the company, and anything you have to refute counterclaims made against you by the company.

When your case is called, you and your opponent will be sworn in. The judge or a court-appointed arbitrator will then ask you questions. Be relaxed. State your position; be brief and to the point, but don't leave out any important points in your favor. Unless you are accustomed to speaking before groups, it is wise to prepare a short written summary of your case in advance, and read it to the court.

Talk directly to the judge. Answer all questions. Address the judge as "Your Honor" or "Judge." Listen to the judge's instructions, and never argue with or interrupt the judge. Try to be factual and diplomatic, not emotional. Don't argue with your opponent in court, and never interrupt his presentation. After you have both presented your cases, you will have a chance to refute your opponent's case.

If your opponent is represented by an attorney (this is discouraged in many Small Claims Courts), you can politely inform the judge that you are not represented by legal counsel and that you are not familiar with Small Claims Court procedures. Ask the judge to intercede on your behalf any time you feel that your opponent's attorney is treating you unfairly. Most judges will be sympathetic to you in such a situation.

Usually you will have to wait several days for the court to notify you by mail of the decision. If the decision is in your favor, check to be sure that interest and all of your disbursements, including court costs, filing fees and process service fees are added to the amount of your judgment, and make sure you know how and when payment is to be made. Send a copy of the decision to your opponent by certified mail, together with a letter requesting payment.

If you are not paid within a reasonable period of time, contact the court clerk and file a *Petition for Notice to Show Cause*, which will be sent to your opponent, ordering him to come to court and explain why you have not been paid. Also, you should file an *Order of Execution* with the sheriff's, constable's or clerk's office in the county where the opponent is located. With such an order, you can discover where the defendant-debtor has assets which can be seized to satisfy payment of your claim.

The judge or court-appointed arbitrator makes the decision in Small Claims Courts. There are no juries. But some states allow defendants to move the case from Small Claims Court to a higher court and/or obtain trial by jury. If this happens, don't try to represent yourself. You will need the services of a good labor lawyer.

Can you appeal if you lose? Some states do not allow a losing plaintiff to appeal. Also, in all courts, an appeals court will not overturn the decision of a Small Claims Court judge without strong proof that the judge was dishonest or unfairly biased, both of which are difficult to prove. The best course is to do your homework and prepare your case properly the first time and let the chips fall where they may.

9
IIIIIIIIIIIIIIIIIIIIIIIIIIIIIIIIIIIIIIIIIIII
LEGAL PROBLEMS OF
SALES REPRESENTATIVES

S ales representatives (most often called "sales reps," "reps," "agents" or "brokers") are persons or organizations that contract to sell the products of other organizations (called "principals"). When the sales rep is an independent contractor instead of an employee, there are a number of unique legal problems that must be faced. Unlike most workers, sales reps risk income fluctuation because of factors often removed from their control. For example, after orders are procured, reps frequently suffer losses of earnings when principals fail to ship merchandise, fail to provide a proper and accurate accounting of commissions owed, or terminate the relationship (in the absence of a written contract with a definite term) at their whim with little or no notice, without cause.

There are currently millions of salespeople in the United States who earn their livelihood in a variety of selling areas including furniture, apparel, gifts, mass marketing, industrial goods and a multitude of others. However, reps are often exploited, most without knowing it. They sign contracts prepared by the legal staffs of their principals which are typically slanted for the benefit of the company. Others do nothing when their commissions are unjustifiably withheld.

Fortunately, the legal position of sales reps is growing stronger with each passing year. Until several years ago there were no federal or state laws to protect the plight of the independent salesperson. Now, many states have passed legislation *insuring* the prompt payment of commissions after the working relationship ends. Some state laws even require written contracts which specify how commissions are earned, when they must be paid and the penalties that ensue when these procedures are not followed.

No matter what industry they sell in, reps must be knowledgeable about the pitfalls of their business and know how to protect themselves before, during and after their relationship with a principal terminates. This chapter summarizes many of the strategies I offer clients to help them protect their business. You will learn how to investigate a principal before accepting a line, and many of the important points to negotiate and confirm in writing before starting work. If you receive a contract from a company, you will learn what clauses favor the principal and how these clauses can be modified to better your interests. If you have an oral contract with a principal, you will learn how your status can be substantially improved and protected.

For example, this chapter will explain why it is important to save all correspondence and sales records while working to receive an accurate accounting, and how to act properly, enforce your rights and receive all commissions due after the relationship has ended. Also covered are current state laws protecting sales reps and strategies to remember when using these laws to your advantage. (Note: A compendium of all laws and their important features is included for easy reference.)

Additionally, you will understand when it is advantageous to proceed with arbitration to collect what is owed (as opposed to litigation) plus tips to help win your case regardless of the forum used to settle the dispute. In short, whether you are a novice salesperson or an experienced pro, you will become more informed and less vulnerable to being subjected to the injustices of your trade.

CONSIDERATIONS BEFORE TAKING ON A NEW LINE

The first step in reducing the chances of being exploited is to take the time to investigate the principal and the line you are considering representing. For example, some reps are hired as a result of telephone conversations with company officials. Agreements made via the telephone should be entered into with *great caution*. By meeting the principal, inspecting the manufacturing facilities and talking in person with key personnel you will be working with (such as the sales manager) you can avoid future problems. Many times, after agreeing to a specified commission rate and other key terms and investing time and money selling goods for the company, reps are told that the person who offered the package did not have the authority to bind the company or is no longer working there! On other occasions, salespeople have been told over the telephone to "show us what you can do and write your own ticket" only to find stiff opposition from the company once their orders have been placed. These abuses need not occur and can be prevented by taking the following simple steps:

1. Always find out with whom you are talking, his or her position, and the extent of his or her authority to bind the company.
2. Do *not* rely on promises that terms will be worked out at a later date.

3. If you are unfamiliar with a principal or the track record of the manufacturer, ask for the names of a few customers who are currently being shipped products or receive services. Call them to obtain information about the company.

4. Learn who previously represented the company and why he or she is no longer in that position. Then talk to the former salesperson. You may learn that the person resigned because she wasn't being paid on time, or had her commissions unfairly reduced or her territory cut without her consent when the principal unilaterally designated certain accounts as house accounts.

5. Try to investigate the principal's financial history by asking such questions as:

- What is its financial status and credit rating?
- Does it ship damaged goods with a high rate of return?
- Does the firm have a high rate of sales turnover?

Once you are satisfied with the firm's reputation, financial picture and track record, you must carefully negotiate your working arrangement. Too many reps begin working without clearly defining their contract, which often leads to future misunderstandings and problems. The following is a comprehensive checklist which describes numerous points to request, including fall-back points, during the negotiating session:

Territory

- Specify the precise territory you will represent.
- Try to obtain a status as the exclusive rep in that territory (i.e., that the principal cannot appoint another rep to sell goods in your territory).
- Obtain the principal's consent to sell *all* of its products, including those introduced in the future, if possible.
- Specify that you will receive commissions for all sales made in your territory regardless of whether the order is procured by you or received directly by the company without your assistance.
- Specify that there will be no house accounts (i.e., non-commissionable accounts in your territory).
- Define split commission policies in advance. For example, what commission will you receive on orders accepted by customers in your territory but shipped into another salesperson's territory?

Commissions

- Be sure to specify when your commissions will be earned—i.e., will they be earned when the order is accepted? When the order is accepted and shipped? When the order is accepted, shipped and invoiced? Or when the order is accepted, shipped, invoiced and paid for? Some principals will only pay commissions after the order is shipped and *paid for* by the customer. Avoid this arrangement if possible. Try to receive commissions after shipment rather than when the customer pays for the product. If you cannot obtain this, try to get a portion of the commission upon acceptance of the order (such as 50% within one week of acceptance) and the balance when shipment is made and payment is received.

- Consider negotiating guaranteed shipping arrangements where applicable. This can provide you with payment in lieu of shipment if the company fails to deliver its merchandise. Under this scenario, the company guarantees it will ship X% of all accepted orders. If the company fails to ship this percentage, you will be paid on the difference.

- Be sure you understand whether the commission is a gross or net amount. If a net amount, understand how and when deductions are computed. For example, principals often deduct unfair amounts as a result of returns, freight charges, billing and advertising discounts, collection charges, large orders, special customers, off-price goods and reorders. Avoid such deductions if possible.

- What about taxes and tooling expenses? Are these excluded from your earnings?

- Discuss the amount of commissions to be paid if monies are received after a collection agency or law firm collects delinquent arrears.

- Ask to receive credit and payment for reorders (i.e. repeats of merchandise previously purchased by the customer).

- Discuss commission rates for large orders, special customers, off-price goods and reorders.

- Establish an arithmetic formula for determining commission rates on off-price goods. *Never* leave this to the company's sole discretion. For example, on goods sold at 75% of the regular selling price, commissions normally due the rep at 8% should only be reduced to 6%.

- If no arithmetic formula is agreed upon, insist that the parties will discuss and agree on every off-price order but in no event will the rep receive less than x%.

- Discuss and agree on split commission policies (i.e., sales in your territory that are shipped into another rep's territory or vice versa).

- If additional services are contemplated for warehousing, detailed forecasting, collections, etc., be sure to request additional payment for such services which are separate and apart from commissions due.
- Define your status as an independent contractor and determine who pays for expenses and taxes if applicable.
- Ask for a stipulation that commission rates cannot be changed suddenly without your written approval. Many employees and independent sales agents are exploited in this fashion. Also, watch out for house accounts and related problems. House accounts are customers that are neither nonsolicitable or noncommissionable; if the employer insists on this, be sure you understand in advance what customers and accounts will not earn commissions so you don't waste valuable time and effort on them.
- Be sure you negotiate to receive accurate commission reports *together* with copies of all accepted orders and invoices. Proper accounting is vital for all people earning commissions, and employers frequently exploit people in this area. Many people rely on the honesty and integrity of their companies as to the accuracy of the figures presented to them. Although most employers are generally honest, mistakes frequently occur.
- By negotiating to receive complete documentation in addition to the commission statement, you will be in a better position to detect errors and mistakes. Additionally, the fact that you may get a computer printout commission statement does not mean that you are obtaining 100% accurate accounting. Duplicate invoices are often photocopied in error. In addition, some companies give each of their commission employees and agents a different computer number. If these numbers are fed into the computer incorrectly, other people may receive credit for your sales. Also, be careful if your invoices are delayed and the company informs you that you will receive supplementary sheets at a later date. Many people forget to tally these sheets and lose valuable commissions.
- Specify what happens to commissions if you resign or are fired. This is a common problem that is typically not addressed when the job begins. Try to negotiate the right to receive commissions for orders that are accepted prior to the termination or resignation but are shipped *after* the termination date. Additionally, you may wish to receive commissions for reorders through the end of the selling season customary in your industry and/or for blanket orders or purchases which are to be filled for a period of time after the termination date. Remember, if you don't ask for these things the employer will only pay you commissions up to the termination date.

■ Finally, if you successfully negotiate items discussed above, insist
on the right to receive copies of all orders and shipping information after the termination date while your commission arrangement is still in effect. Companies have a legal obligation to keep
records of all accounts, particularly when their employees and
sales agents are entitled to commissions. This duty is most
apparent after the individual resigns or has been terminated, since
it is virtually impossible to obtain information on sales figures
after you no longer work for the company.

Advance on Commissions   Ask if you are entitled to a *draw* or *advance*
against commissions. (This arrangement is not typically made with sales
employees but with independent sales representatives and agents.) Salespeople and employees are sometimes advanced money to be applied against
and reimbursed by future commissions. When advances are made which do
not exceed commissions earnings, you are *not* generally personally liable to
return the difference (no matter what the company tells you) unless you
promised before to do so. The reason is that courts generally consider
advances to be additional salary unless language in an employment agreement or conduct of the parties expressly indicates that such advances were
intended to be a loan. Even if you leave the company before commission
earnings exceed a draw, you will probably not be liable to return the excess.

Thus, at the hiring interview, never agree to be personally liable for
repayment and never acknowledge to anyone that you intend to repay any
excess advance. Additionally, to protect your rights in this area, do not sign
or endorse draw checks containing the word "loan" on the face of the check,
do not sign an employment contract which states that advances are not
considered part payment of salary but rather a personal indebtedness to be
repaid at some future date when commission earnings do not exceed the
draw and never sign a promissory note or letter to this effect.

Request that the employer cannot stop or reduce the draw at any time
without prior notice when commission earnings do not exceed draw. Since
you may be relying on a draw to pay your bills and expenses until
commissions are received, you don't want to be left "high and dry."

Job Security

■ Specify the start date.
■ Try to get as much job security as possible—for example, stipulate
that you can continue to represent the principal on a yearly basis
or as long as your sales volume exceeds x .
■ If you cannot get at least a one-year contract, negotiate to receive
as much notice of termination as possible (i.e., that you can only
be fired on six month's notice). Sometimes, reps negotiate addi-

tional notice periods as the amount of time representing the principal increases. For example, a 30-day notice period becomes 60 days after the first year and 90 days after the second year, etc.

- During this notice period, specify that you can continue representing the line and will be paid for all orders obtained by you or procured in your territory, even if shipped after the termination date of the contract.
- Specify that any notices of termination must be sent certified mail, return receipt requested so you will be sure to have received such notice. (Note: If notice is sent by regular mail, the company may be in breach of contract.)

Termination of Employment

- Clarify when commissions stop but *avoid* arrangements where they cease immediately upon termination.
- Negotiate to receive commissions for a certain period of time after termination, i.e., through the end of the selling season or for a specified period of time thereafter (90 days after termination is a good figure).
- In addition to commissions, be aware that reps in certain industries are negotiating additional *severance* after termination. This means that if you are fired without cause you can receive the average monthly commission during the last year multiplied by the number of years worked.
- A fall-back provision using this concept can be to receive severance based on the increase of sales volume in your territory from your efforts. For example, if you took over a territory with a volume of $1 million annually and built that to $2 million annually, you would receive an additional three months' severance; volume exceeding $4 million annually would entitle you to six months' severance, etc.
- Specify when a final accounting will be made and commissions paid after termination.
- Discuss the handling of commissions on orders "pending" or "in the works" for sales expected but not yet consummated.

Proper Accounting

- Always request copies of all accepted orders and invoices within a certain period of time after shipment. Typically, you should negotiate to receive this information, together with an accurate commission statement and commission check, no later than the 30th day of the month following the month of shipment.

- Avoid arrangements where the company requires that you protest commission statements within a certain period of time after receipt (such as ten days), and if no notice regarding errors is received, they will be deemed correct.
- Demand the right for you, your accountant or your attorney to inspect the company's books and records at least once annually upon reasonable written notice at your own cost. If errors are discovered exceeding 5% of what you were told was owed, make the company pay for the cost of the inspection.

Points to Avoid

- Never accept an arrangement where you are paid commissions on a quarterly, semiannual or annual basis.
- Avoid agreeing that you will work exclusively and on a full-time basis for the company, unless this is financially in your best interests.
- Avoid arrangements where you must *personally* solicit the product and cannot hire a sales associate, partner, road salesperson or employee to assist in your selling endeavors.
- Avoid mandatory attendance at national sales meetings at your own expense.
- Resist arrangements where you must call on all accounts in your territory a certain number of times annually, service these accounts, and maintain accurate selling records and lead sheets.
- Be aware of situations requiring you to actively assist in any collection efforts requested by the company. If there is such a requirement, ask what activities will be included. For example, are you merely required to call on the account periodically to ask for payment, or must you hire and pay for a collection agency on behalf of the principal?
- Never sign contracts containing restrictive covenants prohibiting you from working for a competitor, calling on certain customers or revealing confidential information or trade secrets after termination, particularly before speaking to a lawyer knowledgeable in this area.
- Resist arrangements requiring you to maintain minimum general and automobile liability coverage in excess of $x per occurrence.
- Avoid signing contracts with clauses stating that any litigation must take place in the state where the principal resides.

Other Negotiating Points

- Ask the company to provide you with proof of product liability insurance naming your rep firm as a beneficiary on its policy and indemnifying you and holding you blameless in any liability or lawsuit (including the payment of legal fees incurred in defending yourself in a lawsuit) caused by injury to a customer by a product negligently designed or manufactured by the principal, or regarding patent, trademark or copyright matters affecting the principal or its products.
- Be sure your contract states that that there can be no modifications of any terms previously agreed upon unless reduced to writing and signed by both parties. This will eliminate the most flagrant abuses to reps—namely, sudden reduction of your commission rates and accounts in your territory without your approval.
- Be sure your contract states that it is binding on all successors and assigns. This way, if the company is sold, the new principal will be required to honor your contract and continue to engage you as the rep.

CONFIRMING THE AGREEMENT IN WRITING

Once you and the company have agreed to key terms, it is essential to confirm the deal in writing. Legal disputes usually arise in this area because principals hire reps on a handshake. A handshake, or oral agreement, indicates only that the parties came to some form of agreement; it does not say what the agreement was. Failure to spell out important terms often leads to misunderstandings and disputes. Even when key terms are discussed, the same spoken words that are agreed upon have different meanings from the salesperson's and company's perspective. Written words limit this sort of misunderstanding.

The following sample agreement was prepared by the National Electrical Manufacturers Representatives' Association (NEMRA). It illustrates many of the points described in the previous section and is the kind of formal agreement that should always be signed by both parties to avoid future problems. (Bear in mind that this is a "sample" agreement, and that it does not contain a number of favorable terms that salespeople must consider, such as an arbitration clause.)

SAMPLE PRINCIPAL–REP AGREEMENT

THIS AGREEMENT made this_____day of_____, 19_____by and
between_____a corporation incorporated under the laws of the State
of_____having its principal office at_____hereinafter referred to as
"Manufacturer,"

and

a corporation incorporated under the laws of the State of _____ having
its principal office at_____hereinafter referred to as "Representative,"
as follows:

Appointment and Acceptance.
Manufacturer appoints Representative as its exclusive selling representative to sell products (enumerated in Provision No. 3 hereof) in the
territory (defined in Provision No. 2 hereof); and Representative accepts
the appointment and agrees to sell and promote the sale of the
Manufacturer's products.

Territory.
Representative's territory shall consist of the following:_____

Products.
The products of the Manufacturer to be sold by the Representative
are:_____

Amount of Compensation.
Representative's compensation for services performed hereunder shall
be_____% of the "net invoice price" of the Manufacturer's product
shipped into Representative's territory. However, when engineering,
execution of the order, or shipment involves different territories, the
Manufacturer will split the full commission among the Representatives
whose territories are involved. The Manufacturer will make this determination and advise the interested Representatives at the time the order is
submitted to the Manufacturer. The sum of the split commission shall add
up to a full commission and no Representative whose territory is involved
shall receive less than_____% of the full commission.

Computation and Payment of Commission.
    a) Commissions are due and payable on or before the_____day of
       the month following the month in which the customer is invoiced;
       and if not paid when due, the amount not paid will accrue interest
       at_____% per annum from the date due until paid.
    b) Manufacturer will send Representative copies of all invoices at
       the time Manufacturer invoices customer, and each invoice shall
       indicate the amount of commission due Representative.
    c) At the time of payment of commissions to Representative, Man-
       ufacturer will send Representative a commission statement show-
       ing:
       1. the computation of all commissions earned during the ninety
          (90) day period prior to its issuance (listing all invoices
          covered by the statement), and
       2. commissions paid during that period (listing the invoices on
          which commissions are being paid), and
       3. commissions due and owing Representative.

d) "Net invoice price" shall mean the total price at which an order is invoiced to the customer, including any increase or decrease in the total amount of the order (even though such increase or decrease takes place after the effective date of termination), but excluding shipping and mailing costs; taxes; insurance; and any allowances or discounts granted to the customer by the Manufacturer.

e) There shall be deducted from any sums due representative:

1. an amount equal to commissions previously paid or credited on sales of Manufacturer's products which have since been returned by the customer or on allowances credited to the customer for any reason by the Manufacturer, and

2. an amount equivalent to commissions previously paid or credited on sales which Manufacturer shall not have been fully paid by the customer, whether by reason of the customer's bankruptcy, insolvency, or any other reason which, in Manufacturer's judgment, renders the account uncollectible (if any sums are ever realized upon such uncollectible accounts, Manufacturer will pay Representative its percentage of commission applicable at the time of the original sale upon the net proceeds of such collection).

f) "Order" shall mean any commitment to purchase Manufacturer's products which calls for shipment into Representative's territory or which is subject to split commission in accordance with Provision No. 4 hereof.

Acceptance of Orders.

All orders are subject to acceptance or rejection by an authorized officer of Manufacturer at its home office and to the approval of the Manufacturer's credit department. Manufacturer shall be responsible for all credit risks and collections.

If Manufacturer notifies customer of its acceptance or rejection of an order, a copy of any written notification shall be transmitted to the Representative. At least once every month, Manufacturer shall supply Representative with copies of all orders received directly by the Manufacturer, copies of all shipping notices, and copies of all correspondence and quotations made to the customers in the territory.

Terms of Sale.

All sales shall be at prices and upon terms established by the Manufacturer and it shall have the right, in its sole discretion, from time to time, to establish, change, alter or amend prices and other terms and conditions of sale. Representative shall not accept orders in the Manufacturer's name, make price quotations or delivery promises without the Manufacturer's prior approval.

Representative's Relationship and Conduct of Business.

a) Representative shall maintain a sales office in the territory and shall devote such time as may be reasonably necessary to sell and promote the sale of Manufacturer's products within the territory.

b) Representative will conduct all of its business in its own name and in such manner as it may see fit. Representative will pay all expenses whatever of its office and activities and be responsible for the acts and expenses of its employees.

c) Nothing in this agreement shall be construed to constitute Representative as the partner or employee or agent of the Manufacturer, nor shall either party have any authority to bind the other in any respect, it being intended that each shall remain an independent contractor responsible only for its own actions.

d) Representative shall not, without Manufacturer's prior written approval, enlarge, or limit orders, make representations or guarantees concerning Manufacturer's product or accept the return of, or make any allowance for such products.

e) Representative shall furnish to Manufacturer's credit department any information which it may have from time to time relative to the credit standing of any of its customers.

f) Representative shall abide by Manufacturer's policies and communicate same to Manufacturer's customers.

g) Manufacturer shall be solely responsible for the design, development, supply, production and performance of its products and the protection of its trade names. Manufacturer agrees to indemnify and hold Representative harmless from and against and to pay all losses, costs, damages or expenses whatsoever, including reasonable attorney's fees, which Representative may sustain or incur on account of infringement or alleged infringement of patents, trademarks, or trade names, or breach of warranty or claimed breach of warranty in any way resulting from the sale of Manufacturer's products. Manufacturer will indemnify Representative from and hold it harmless from and against all liabilities, losses, damages, costs or expenses, including reasonable attorney's fees, which it may at any time suffer, incur, or be required to pay by reason of injury or death to any person or damage to property or both caused or allegedly caused by any products sold by Manufacturer.

h) Manufacturer shall furnish Representative, at no expense to Representative, samples, catalogs, literature and any other material necessary for the proper promotion and sale of its products in the territory. Any literature which is not used or samples or other equipment belonging to the Manufacturer shall be returned to the Manufacturer at its request.

i) Whenever Representative, at Manufacturer's request, takes possession of Manufacturer's products for the purpose of delivering such products to customers for any other purpose, the risk of loss or damage to or destruction of such products shall be borne by the Manufacturer, and Manufacturer shall indemnify and hold Representative harmless against any claims, debts, liabilities or causes of action resulting from any such loss, damage or destruction.

Terms of Agreement and Termination.
This agreement shall be effective on the_____day of_____, 19_____, and shall continue for_____year(s) until the_____day of_____, 19_____. It shall be automatically renewed from year to year thereafter unless terminated by either party upon_____days notice to the other by registered mail or certified mail prior to the end of the initial term of this agreement, or any renewal term.

Rights Upon Termination.

Upon termination of this agreement for any reason, Representative shall be entitled to:

a) Commissions on all orders calling for shipment into Representative's territory which are dated or communicated to Manufacturer prior to the effective date of termination, regardless of when such orders are shipped; and

b) Its share of split commissions on orders dated or communicated to Manufacturer prior to the effective date of termination, regardless of when such orders are shipped.

c) Commissions referred to in this Provision No. 10 shall be paid on or before the_____day of the month in which the Manufacturer receives payment for the orders.

General.

This agreement contains the entire understanding of the parties, shall supersede any other oral or written agreements, and shall be binding upon, or inure to the benefit of, the parties' successors and assigns. It may not be modified in any way without the written consent of both parties. Representative shall not have the right to assign this agreement in whole or in part without Manufacturer's written consent.

IN WITNESS WHEREOF, the parties have executed this agreement the day and year above written in multiple counterparts, each of which shall be considered an original.

MANUFACTURER: _____

By: _____

  Title: _____

REPRESENTATIVE: _____

By: _____

  Title: _____

Although a written contract cannot guarantee that you will be satisfied with the company's performance, it can provide additional remedies in the event of a principal's nonperformance. That is why most reps in all industries within the past ten years are no longer accepting being hired on a handshake. They now recognize that they can be better protected by including favorable clauses in clearly drafted contracts. For example, by specifying *in writing* that commissions will continue to be paid on all orders accepted prior to termination but shipped thereafter, including reorders, many thousands of dollars in commissions can be obtained which typically would *not* be available in an oral agreement. Also, by specifying in the agreement that all changes must be *in writing* and approved by both parties, you can eliminate common areas of exploitation that would not be accomplished without a written agreement.

When written agreements are used, be sure that all changes, strikeouts and erasures are initialled by both parties and that all blanks are filled in. If additions are necessary, include them in a space provided or attach them to the contract itself. Then, note on the contract that addenda have been added and accepted by both parties. This prevents questions from arising if addenda are lost or separated, because it is difficult to prove there were any without mention in the body of the contract.

TURNING AN ORAL CONTRACT INTO A WRITTEN AGREEMENT

A formal agreement similar to the above is not always required to serve your purposes; in some cases an oral contract can be an acceptable substitute. Before I describe how this may be accomplished, a few words about oral contracts are appropriate. An oral contract is a verbal agreement between the salesperson and the company defining their working relationship. Such contracts may be binding when the duties, compensation and terms of employment are agreed to by both parties.

Salespeople often have oral agreements because their companies refuse to give them written contracts. Many principals like to use oral contracts because there is no written evidence to indicate what terms were discussed and accepted by both parties when they entered into their working arrangement. If disputes arise, it is more difficult for the salesperson to prove that the principal failed to abide by the terms of the agreement. For example, if a 5% commission rate was accepted verbally, a dishonest principal could deny this by stating that a lower commission rate on certain items had been accepted. The salesperson would then have to prove that both parties had agreed upon a higher commission figure.

When a legal dispute arises concerning the terms of an oral contract, a court will resolve the problem by examining all the evidence that the salesperson and company offer and weighing the testimony to determine who is telling the truth. Thus, to avoid problems, all salespeople should try to obtain a written contract to clarify their rights. However, if your company refuses to sign a written agreement, there are ways to protect yourself if you have an oral contract. Your chief concern should be directed towards obtaining written evidence indicating the accepted terms (i.e., concerning such areas as your commission rate, assigned territory, job security, notice-of-termination requirements and proper accounting).

If your company refuses to sign a written agreement, it is advisable to write a letter to the principal whenever you reach an oral agreement relating to your job.

Whatever the deal that is agreed upon, the letter should be drafted similar to the following.

SAMPLE LETTER AGREEMENT

Name of Rep Firm; Address
Date

Name of Company Officer
Title
Company Name
Address

Dear (Name of Company Officer),

It was a pleasure meeting with you yesterday. Per our discussion, this will confirm the terms of my engagement as a sales representative for your Company commencing (date) under the following terms and conditions:

I agree to represent the Company in: (specify states or territory). The above territory will be covered exclusively by me with no other sales reps covering this territory, and there will be no house accounts in this territory.

I will receive a commission of (specify) percent of the (specify) gross (net) invoice amount for all orders shipped in my exclusive territory regardless of how the order is obtained or received by you or your company.

There will be no deductions from my commission except for (specify). Commission checks together with accurate statements will be sent to me on or about the (specify) day of the month following the month of shipment and the Company agrees to send me copies of all invoices of shipments in my territory on a weekly basis.

(**Optional**: In addition, the Company will contribute a showroom participation fee of ($x) payable on the first day of each month of this Agreement, which is a separate charge and not to be deducted or collected against any commissions due me.)

I will be considered an independent contractor and will be responsible to pay all applicable social security, withholding and other employment taxes.

To cancel our Agreement, either party must send the other written notice no less than thirty (30) days prior to the effective termination date. Upon termination for any reason, I shall be paid commission on all shipments made for a period of six (6) months after the effective termination date for orders in house before the effective termination date.

If any of the terms of this letter are ambiguous or incorrect, please advise me immediately in writing, otherwise, this letter shall set forth and constitute our entire understanding of this matter which may not be modified or changed to any extent, except in writing, signed by both parties.

Very truly yours,

(Name of Rep; Firm Name)

SENT CERTIFIED MAIL, RETURN RECEIPT REQUESTED

Be as specific as possible when referring to subjects that you and the company have agreed upon. Write the letter with precision, since ambiguous terms are resolved against the letter writer. Be sure to keep a copy of the letter for your own records and save the certified mail receipt. If at a later date the terms of the oral agreement are changed (for instance, additional territory is assigned to you) write another letter specifying the new arrangement that has been reached. Keep a copy of this letter and all correspondence sent to and received from your company.

DETERMINING YOUR STATUS FOR TAX PURPOSES

Many salespeople lack knowledge as to what constitutes independent contractor versus employee status for tax purposes. The IRS generally opposes independent contractor status since employers are not required to withhold income and employment taxes. Additionally, since independent contractors can manipulate their earnings and deductions (they are entitled to claim all of their business-related expenses on Schedule C where expenses offset gross business income), many dollars of compensation income often go untaxed. This section will examine the legal distinction between being treated as an independent contractor and being treated as an employee for tax purposes, and will offer strategies to avoid problems in this area.

There is no precise legal definition that explains what an independent contractor is. In fact, each state has its own laws in determining whether a salesperson is an employee or an independent contractor. When the courts attempt to determine the difference, they analyze the facts of each particular case. The most significant factors that courts look at when making this distinction are:

1. The company's right of control over the salesperson;
2. Whether or not the company carries indemnity or liability insurance for the salesperson; and
3. Whether the parties have a written agreement which defines the status of the salesperson.

The company's right of control is best explained by the use of examples. Courts have found people to be employees if their employers:

- Had the right to supervise the details of their operations; i.e., required salespeople to collect money owed from accounts on behalf of the company
- Provided the salesperson with a company car or reimbursement for some or all expenses
- Restricted the person's ability to work for other companies or jobs (i.e., devote full-time efforts to this job)

- Required the person to call on particular customers
- Provided the person with insurance and Worker's Compensation benefits
- Deducted income and FICA taxes

This list is not meant to be all-inclusive; these factors are listed to help you determine whether the law in your state treats people as employees or independent contractors.

Since the law is so unsettled and frequently varies from case to case and state to state, federal legislation was introduced in the Senate several years ago to standardize this problem. Unfortunately, the bill was not passed; however, the bill is instructive since it outlined a set of rules to be applied. By following these rules, it is suggested you can minimize problems or document your position in the event of an audit.

According to the bill, an independent contractor:

1. Controls his own work schedule and number of working hours;
2. Operates from his own place of business or pays rent if an office is provided;
3. Risks income fluctuation since his earnings are a result of output and results (i.e., sales), rather than number of hours worked; and
4. Has a written contract with an employer before he begins working that states he is not considered an employee for purposes of the Federal Contributions Act, or the Federal Unemployment Tax Act; and income is not withheld at the source, and the contract states that the salesperson must pay his own self-employment and Federal Income Tax.

Following these rules will go a long way toward applying the correct status determination if it is contested by the IRS. In addition, a properly drafted contract with all of your principals and sales associates can protect you in many other areas as well. Don't forget to implement this if possible.

STEPS TO TAKE WHILE WORKING

While representing a principal, there are a number of steps you can take to reduce the chances of being exploited. These include checking your commission statements carefully and notifying the company immediately when you detect errors, saving all correspondence, records and documents to confirm all deals and actions, reviewing your contract periodically to be sure both parties are complying with all of its terms, and documenting all promises made to you. (Example: "You are the best salesperson around here so we would never fire you without notice except for a good reason.")

Proper accounting is vital for any salesperson who works on a commission basis. Most reps rely on the honesty and integrity of their principals as to the accuracy of the figures that are presented to them. In most instances companies do give a proper accounting. However, many principals use questionable methods of record-keeping. I have represented many sales clients who have been denied hundreds of thousands of dollars by dishonest principals who failed to record sales properly and to render credit for all shipped orders, and only paid these commissions after being threatened with legal action.

These are just a few of the abuses either intentionally or unintentionally practiced upon salespeople. The fact that you may get a computer printout commission statement does *not* mean you are obtaining 100% accurate accounting. Duplicate invoices are often photocopied in error. In addition, some companies give each of their salespeople a different computer number. If these numbers are fed into the computer incorrectly, other salespeople will receive credit for your sales. You should also be particularly careful if your invoices are delayed and the company informs you that you will receive supplementary sheets at a later date. Reps often forget to tally these sheets and lose valuable commissions.

Additionally, in order to prove you have a justifiable reason to view your company's books and records during pretrial discovery, you may be asked to provide a court with information that reveals what you are looking for. Usually, these requests must be supported by written documentation so you will not be viewed as being disruptive and engaging in a "fishing expedition." For example, you may have to make specific references to accounts or be required to furnish the dates of the sale in addition to the products that were sold. Thus, save all of your records. Remember that companies have a legal obligation to keep records of all accounts, particularly if their salespeople receive commissions. This becomes important after the salesperson resigns or is fired, since it is often impossible for him or her to obtain information on sales figures for goods that were shipped and paid for after the salesperson left the company.

If the principal will not voluntarily turn over this information, it may be necessary to compel him to do so by means of discovery procedures. Discovery procedures play an important role in virtually every lawsuit, and both parties use them to obtain information before the case is brought to trial. It first must be established to the court's satisfaction that money may be due and owing before you are entitled to examine the records of your company. You cannot ransack your principal's books and records in the hope that something helpful will turn up. However, if you can show that the company's documents and records will help your case, extensive discovery is usually allowed by the court.

Thus, save your commission statements, copies of checks, letters, memos and other documents received from the company while you are still working. All of this information may prove useful to your attorney later.

Reps are also wise to accumulate documents to confirm all deals, actions and modifications of working arrangements. If the company decides to reduce your commission rate or draw, or change your territory, and your contract specifically forbids any changes unless in writing and agreed to by both parties, send a letter to document your protest. If you don't take steps to indicate your dissatisfaction, you may appear to have consented to such changes by conduct.

STEPS TO TAKE IF YOU ARE FIRED

Your principal may have the right to fire you, but you could be entitled to damages, depending on the circumstances. Implement the following strategies when you are fired or believe you are about to be fired:

1. Insist on receiving a final statement of commissions and other benefits to determine if you are owed any money.
2. Know the law regarding the prompt payment of commissions. Reps in 26 states are entitled to receive their final commissions shortly after being fired. These states have sales rep protection laws which can be used to your advantage because they provide damages up to three times the commission amount owed plus reasonable attorney fees, costs and disbursements when reps must resort to litigation in the event of a principal's noncompliance. Many of these state laws also require the parties to have written agreements specifying how commissions are earned and when they are due.

Spurred by Congress's failure to enact the *Sales Representative Contractual Relations Bill of 1984* and quietly lobbied by sales groups with little opposition or knowledge from business interests, certain states are now recognizing inherent problems in the principal–agent relationship and are correcting them by legal means; expect more states to follow this trend and pass similar legislation in the coming years. All reps and rep firms must be aware of the new laws in *each* state in which they sell to enhance their rights in this area.

Each state law differs regarding time requirements and penalties imposed. For example, the Minnesota law requires payment of final commissions within three days of the reps's last day of work. In New York, commissions must be paid to a rep covering accounts in the state within five business days after termination of the working relationship or when commissions are earned. Ohio mandates payment within 13 days of termination or after commissions become due, while the time limit for reps selling to accounts in Texas is 30 days after termination, but only if there is no written contract between the parties defining when commissions are earned and payable.

In the above states, the following penalties are imposed on companies not paying reps in timely fashion as specified. Minnesota—commission amount plus $1/15$ of the commission amount due up to 15 days plus attorney fees; New York—twice the commission amount plus reasonable attorney fees, costs and disbursements; Ohio—exemplary damages up to three times the commission amount plus attorney fees and costs; Texas—three times the damages sustained by the rep plus attorney fees and court costs.

While the time requirements and penalties may differ, all of the 26 state rep protection laws apply to principals (defined as a person or company who manufactures, produces, imports or distributes a product for wholesale) typically located out-of-state who hire independent contractor-sales reps to call on customers and solicit orders for commissions in another state. Some states do not allow local in-state manufacturers to be covered; others do. Also, multiple state laws may sometimes apply, giving reps the opportunity to *forum shop*, or use the state law that is most favorable under certain circumstances. That is why all reps should be knowledgeable about each state law in their selling territory for optimum advantage. The compendium on page 192 is a synopsis of state laws regulating manufacturer and rep agreements.

Insist on written contracts for protection   Some states, including Tennessee, Florida, Alabama, New York, Georgia and Texas, require companies to issue written contracts spelling out important terms and to give reps a signed copy for their records after being hired. For many years I have advocated negotiating and obtaining written agreements to avoid many problems frequently encountered by reps (including sudden termination, erosion of accounts into house accounts and reduction of commission rates without warning). Properly drafted, written contracts can eliminate many of these abuses and should be insisted upon whenever applicable. *If the principal refuses, remind him that this is the law.*

Be aware of contract terms which avoid the effects of these laws   Sophistica-ted principals are attempting to reduce the harsh effects of these laws by including a number of clauses in agreements with reps. Some include an arbitration clause requiring that all controversies be settled by arbitration in the city where the company's main office is located. This can have a chilling effect since many out-of-state reps are reluctant to travel to a distant locale and incur expensive travel and related costs to obtain a hearing. Arbitration can work favorably for a principal, since the arbitrators selected are usually no-nonsense attorneys and business people who are not as likely to be swayed by sympathy as juries are and are not required to make decisions strictly on relevant law. When principals are found liable, it is less likely that the arbitrators will tack on additional damages (i.e., triple commission payments).

Additionally, *never* agree to a clause similar to the following: "The parties agree that the law of *X* State (where the principal is located, but not your state) will apply and govern in any case, controversy or proceeding." If legal action becomes necessary to protect your rights, you will be forced to seek an attorney licensed to practice in the other state, you could be bound by the law of that other state and you will be forced to attend countless hours of proceedings in an out-of-state location. The cost to you in lost time and distraction may easily exceed the value of the award you are seeking from the principal.

Many reps, anxious to obtain a company's line, often fail to question or understand the effect of such language and waive valuable rights under the laws of *their* major sales territory or home state. Thus, avoid signing contracts containing such a clause. *Helpful hint*: Even if you do sign a contract waiving your favorable state's law, some rep acts make such clauses void and unenforceable.

Always send a detailed written demand for unpaid commissions   This should be done by certified mail, return receipt requested, to document your claim and prove delivery. Such a demand will "start the clock" for the purposes of determining the number of days that commissions remain unpaid and put the principal on notice that additional damages and penalties may be owed for a continued breach. Remember, a written demand is essential in enforcing your rights.

Consider litigation to collect what is due   I used to advise sales rep clients that it was not worth pursuing a claim when less than $5,000 in commissions was owed since legal fees, costs and disbursements typically ran more than $2,000 when a case was brought to trial. Now, however, even small claims are worth pursuing in view of the extra legal fees, costs and up to triple damages that are now being awarded. Since it is conceivable that a principal could be liable for $20,000 on an original $5,000 claim, do *not* be afraid to consider litigation where appropriate; you may be able to collect additional damages, costs and fees in the process.

If you are owed a small amount of money (i.e., less than $2,000), consider instituting proceedings in Small Claims Court. Recognize, however, that since you may only be permitted to bring suit in the county where the principal resides or has its main office, the travel and incidental expenses involved may not make it worthwhile to pursue your rights.

Seek legal advice before you take any action   This is essential so you can receive an accurate opinion regarding your chances of success and an estimate of damages that are recoverable. Also, the matter must be analyzed to determine which state's law will apply. For example, if you sell to customers located in Texas, Arkansas and Mississippi, can you apply Texas law (and triple damages) to your unpaid commissions from sales in Arkansas and Mississippi, or only for sales in Texas? Since many of these acts are new, the law is unclear; sound legal advice can guide you accordingly. Your lawyer may also help you draft a demand letter or a letter stating your position, or a response to a letter received from a manufacturer which could strengthen your position if litigation becomes necessary.

SYNOPSIS OF STATE LAWS REGULATING MANUFACTURE AND REPRESENTATIVE AGREEMENTS				
STATE	TIME LIMIT	NON-COMPLIANCE PENALTY	WRITTEN CONTRACT	LEGAL REFERENCE
Alabama	Within 7 working days after termination if no written agreement	Triple damages plus reasonable attorney fees and costs	Required	Code of Alabama 1975, Vol. 6, §§8-24-1 through 8-24-5
Arizona	Within 30 days after termination of contract[1]	Damages sustained by the sales representative plus cost of suit including reasonable attorney fees	Required	§ 1. Title 44, Chap. 11, Arizona Rev. Statutes, Art. 15, §§ 44-1798 through 44-1798.03
Arkansas	Within 30 working days after termination if no written agreement	Liable in civil action for three times damage sustained by sales rep plus attorney fees and costs	Required	Arkansas Code, §§ 4-70-301 through4-70-306
California	Within 72 hours after termination if no written agreement	Liable in civil action for triple damages	No	California Statutes 1937, c.90 p. 197, §202; 1963, c.1088, p. 2549, §§ 1,2
Florida	Within 14 days of termination	Commission amount plus exemplary damages up to twice commissions owed, plus reasonable attorney fees	Required	Official Florida Statutes, § 686.201
Georgia	Within 14 days after termination if no contract; within agreement time if a written contract	Commission amount plus exemplary damages up to twice commissions owed, plus reasonable attorney fees	Required	Official Code of Georgia Annotated, Article 24, §§ 10-1-700 through 10-1-704
Iowa	Within 30 days after commission earned; upon termination, within 30 days	Commission plus liquidated damages (5% of commission due times number of days past due), including court costs and attorney fees	No	Code of Iowa, Vol. 1, 1989, Chap. 91A, §§ 91A.1 through 91A.13
Kansas	Within 30 days after commission earned	The commission amount	No	Kansas Statutes Annotated, 1987 Cumulative Supplement, Chap. 44, Art. 3, §§ 44-341 through 44-347

Kentucky	Within 30 days after effective date of termination	Commission plus exemplary damages not to exceed two times commission due plus attorney fees and court costs; if sales rep action found frivolous, Principal will be awarded attorney fees and court costs	No	Kentucky Rev. Statutes, Chap. 371, §§ 371.370-371.375 and 371.380-371.385
Louisiana	Within 30 working days after termination if no contract; otherwise as in written agreement	Triple damages plus attorney fees and costs	No[2]	Louisiana Rev. Statutes (West 1988), Title 51, R.S. 51:441 through 445
Illinois	Within 13 days of termination or when commission earned	Up to three times commission amount plus reasonable attorney fees and court costs	No	Illinois Rev. Statutes, Chap. 48, ¶¶ 2251, 2252, 2253
Indiana	Within 14 days after payment would have been due under contract	Exemplary damages up to three times commission, plus reasonable attorney fees and costs	No	Indiana Code, 1988 Ed., §§ 24-4-7-1 through 24-4-7-6
Maryland	Within 45 days after payment would have been due if contract not terminated	Exemplary damages not to exceed three times commission plus court costs, provided Principal furnished written notice 10 days prior of intent to file civil action for exemplary damages	No	Annotated Code Maryland, Art. 100, §§ 127 through 131
Massachusetts	Within 7 days after termination or expiration of agreement, or within 14 days for goods shipped after termination or expiration of agreement	The commission amount	Required[3]	Massachusetts Gen. Laws Annotated (West, 1988), Chap. 104, §§ 7 through 9
Minnesota	Within 3 working days of salesperson's last day of work	Commission plus 1/15th of commission for every day of nonpayment up to 15 days, plus reasonable attorney fees and costs	No	Minnesota Statutes 1988, Chap. 181, §§ 181.13, 181.14, 181.145

Mississippi	Within 21 days after effective date of termination	Up to triple commission due plus reasonable attorney fees and costs	No	1988 Misissippi Gen. Laws, Chap. 588, §§ 75-87-1, 75-87-3, 75-87-5, and Notes
New Hampshire	Within 45 days after date of termination of contract	In civil action, damages, exemplary damages, plus reasonable attorney fees and costs	Required	Ammendments to RSA 339-E:1 through 339-E:4 to SB 16, New Hampshire
New Jersey	Within 30 days after payment would have been due under contract if contract had not been terminated	Commissions plus exemplary damages not to exceed two times the amount of the commissions due plus reasonable attorney fees and court costs[4]	Required	New Jersey Act concerning sales representatives supplementing Title 56 of the Rev. Statutes
New York	Within 5 business days after termination, or when commission earned	Two times commission, plus reasonable attorney fees, court costs and disbursements	Required	Labor Law Book No. 30, Chap. 451, §§ 191-a, 191-b, 191-c
North Carolina	Within 45 days after effective date of contract termination[4]	In civil action, amounts due plus exemplary damages not to exceed amount of commissions, plus reasonable attorney fees and court costs	Required	§ 1. Chapter 66, Art. 27, §§ 66-190 through 66-193
Ohio	All commissions must be paid within 13 days of when due, or as specified by contract[4]	Liable in civil action for triple damages plus reasonable attorney fees and costs	No, but strongly recommended	Ohio Rev. Code 1988, § 1355.1
Oklahoma	If contract, within 14 calendar days; without contract, according to past practice or industry custom and usage[1]	Commission plus reasonable attorney fees and court costs	No[5]	Oklahoma Statutes, Title 15 §§ 675 through 680
Pennsylvania	Within 14 days after payment due if contract not terminated[1]	In civil action, commissions plus exemplary damages not to exceed two times commission plus reasonable attorney fees and court costs[4]	Required[6]	Pennsylvania Laws of 1988, Act 184

South Carolina	As required by contract or upon termination if there is no contract	In civil action, all amounts due plus punitive damages not to exceed three times commissions plus attorney fees and court costs[4]	No	Cumulative Suppl. of Code of Laws of South Carolina, Vol. 13A, Chap. 65, pp. 59, 60, §§ 39-65-10 through 39-65-80
Tennessee	Within 14 days of salesperson's termination	Up to three times commission, plus reasonable attorney fees and court costs	Required	Tennessee Code Annotated, § 47-50-114
Texas	Within 30 working days after termination date, or as specified in contract	In civil action, triple damages plus reasonable attorney fees and costs	Required	Texas Business & Commerce Code Annotated (Vernon, 1987), §§ 35.81 through 35.86

[1]Commissions for goods ordered prior to termination but shipped after termination must be paid for within 14 days after payment would have been due.

[2]If you have a written contract, it must set forth the method of commission computation and payment, and the representative must be given a copy.

[3]Only if either party requests it.

[4]If the court finds the sales representative's action frivolous, the Principal can be awarded attorney fees and court costs.

[5]If there is no written contract, the usual and customary practice between Principals and sales representatives shall prevail.

[6]This law applies to all current at-will contracts and to all contracts entered into or renewed after the effective date.

Obviously, *never* sign a release unless you know exactly what you are owed before settling a claim with a principal. Also, whenever you receive final commission checks, never cash them if they contain language such as "in full and final payment" without first speaking to a lawyer. In some states, you can write a restrictive endorsement on the back of the check. Example: "Under Protest. Endorsement of this check does not constitute a waiver of any and all claims for commissions owed" and you will still be able to sue for the balance. In other states, your cashing the check will *preclude* you from recovering anything further, despite any protest language. Thus, photocopy and save copies of all checks you receive and speak to a lawyer if applicable before endorsing and depositing such checks.

The lawyer you consult should be an experienced labor attorney with particular knowledge of problems typically encountered by salespeople and reps. At the initial interview, bring with you all pertinent written information including contracts, letters of intent, company memoranda, shipping lists, invoices, commission statements, etc. Tell the lawyer everything related to your problem since all communications are privileged and this will save time and make it easier for him or her to evaluate your case.

Once the lawyer receives all pertinent facts, he or she should then:

- Decide whether your case has a fair probability of success considering the law in the state in which the suit will be brought;
- Give you an accurate estimate as to how long the lawsuit will take; and
- Make a determination of the approximate legal fees and disbursements.

If the lawyer sees weaknesses in your case and believes that litigation will be unduly expensive, or if he or she desires to try to settle the matter without resorting to time-consuming litigation, he or she may send an initial demand letter similar to that on the opposite page. Many cases are settled by my office after the sending of such a letter.

In any event, the chosen course of action should be instituted without delay so you will be able to receive remuneration as quickly as possible. This will also insure that the requisite time period to start the action—the Statute of Limitations—will not have expired.

Strategies about how to hire a lawyer properly and work effectively with one are explained in more detail in the next chapter.

CONSIDERING ARBITRATION VERSUS LITIGATION

Arbitration is an alternative to formal litigation whereby disputes are settled without resorting to the court system. Cases are resolved by arbitrators who are not bound to make their decisions using strict rules of legal procedure. Since arbitration differs markedly from civil litigation, both the salesperson and the company must mutually agree upon the arbitration process.

Arbitration is faster and cheaper than litigation. While it may take a civil case up to four years to be resolved, the same case in arbitration might take four months from the date of filing the complaint to the day of decision. Those salespeople seeking a quick resolution of their problem will find this characteristic of arbitration to be very appealing. Also, there is far less preparation required for an arbitration case than for a full trial. The average arbitration lasts less than a day, in comparison to a trial, which may last several days. If you are paying attorney fees by the hour or by the hour plus a flat fee for trial work on a per diem basis (as opposed to contingency fees), the arbitration route affords you considerable savings. Also, some people favor arbitration because the arbitrators who are selected are usually familiar with the trade practices in your industry. This reduces court time because they are able to "trim the fat" and concentrate on the contractual provisions in dispute.

However, there are several disadvantages to the arbitration process for salespeople. If you opt for arbitration you may lose your most powerful weapon—that is, *the right to view your company's books and records.* In most states, the pretrial discovery procedures available in a court case are either

---

SAMPLE DEMAND LETTER

Date

Name of Principal Officer
Title
Name of Principal Company
Address
Address

Dear (Name of Principal Officer),

Please be advised that this office is General Counsel to the National Association of Sales Agents (NASA) and represents (name of rep, address).

Demand is hereby made for commissions totaling (specify), which have been earned by my client pursuant to the agreement between the parties and which remain unpaid despite due and diligent demand.

I also understand that you have failed to render a detailed, accurate accounting regarding additional orders and reorders procured by my client which have been shipped to his customers and orders which have been received directly by your firm and shipped to my client's accounts, resulting in additional commissions due.

In this regard, I suggest that you or your representative contact this office immediately in the attempt to resolve these issues in an amicable fashion to avoid expensive and protracted litigation which, under the laws of the state of (specify) may also include triple commission damages, reasonable costs, attorney fees and interest if the above stated amount of commissions are not paid within (specify) days of your receipt of this letter and a lawsuit is instituted.

Thank you for your prompt cooperation and attention.

Very truly yours,

Name of Attorney

SMS/nc

cc: (Name of Client)

SENT CERTIFIED MAIL, RETURN RECEIPT REQUESTED

---

limited or eliminated by arbitration. For example, you may not be able to force the company to turn over its books until after the arbitrator(s) has been appointed. The arbitrator has the power to decide what company records and documents you can view. His or her decision is discretionary and you can be denied. Also, if records are produced at the hearing (sometimes for the first time), you and your attorney may have little time to analyze them before proceeding. Thus, in cases where the salesperson must rely on the company to demonstrate what is owed, and when such records are not available to the salesperson "going into" the dispute, litigation may be a better forum than arbitration. Conversely, when you know exactly what is owed and don't need the company to produce its records, then arbitration may be more advantageous.

Also, be aware that arbitrators are less sympathetic than juries (who are more likely to rule on the side of the independent rep rather than the large company), especially if you are fired suddenly without cause, right before procuring a large order to which a claim for commissions is being made.

For all of these reasons, deciding if arbitration should be used to resolve your dispute is not a simple matter. Always discuss the pros and cons applicable to your particular case with your lawyer before agreeing to it.

10

■■

HIRING A LAWYER TO
PROTECT YOUR RIGHTS

Do you know how to get the most out of your lawyer and how to work effectively with one? This chapter will tell you how to avoid potential misunderstandings involving lawyer billing, what to include in retainer agreements, and how to recognize when your problem is not being handled competently or in a timely fashion. You will learn what to bring to the initial interview and what to say, how to negotiate a fair fee arrangement, and how to stay informed and keep your lawyer working on your case. Other portions of the book discuss how to protect your job before, during and after the employment relationship has ended; this chapter discusses your rights as a client.

▌ WHEN YOU NEED A LAWYER

The time to determine whether you need a lawyer is *before* action is considered. Common situations that might call for legal help include:

- Deciding to resign from a lucrative job
- Considering filing a discrimination case
- Threatening a lawsuit for breach of contract, commissions, wages or other monies owed
- Negotiating severance and other benefits resulting from a firing
- Reviewing the proposed contract received from a new employer

Your first step is to speak to an experienced labor attorney to determine if your problem warrants assistance. If it does, then a consultation should be scheduled so your problem can be reviewed in greater detail.

The place to start is to call a lawyer you have dealt with in the past and ask for the name of a labor law specialist. You should also inquire if your matter warrants a consultation. If the lawyer you speak to is willing to conduct the consultation, ask if he or she has sufficient expertise to provide you with competent advice. This is important. Most lawyers who represent clients in other fields are not qualified to represent people in labor matters because the law has become quite specialized. Just as you would not consult a heart surgeon about a skin problem, you should not consult a lawyer who does not regularly handle labor matters (i.e., does not devote at least 50% of his working time to representing individuals with employment-related disputes). If the lawyer tells you that he does not commonly handle your type of problem, ask for the names of other lawyers he is willing to recommend. Clients often receive excellent assistance through lawyer referrals.

If you don't deal regularly with a lawyer, you may have to ask friends and relatives for referrals. However, this may not be wise unless the person tells you about a lawyer who handled a *labor matter* (not a house closing or divorce) satisfactorily. You may also wish to call your local bar association and ask for the names of labor lawyers. Some associations maintain legal referral services and lists of labor lawyers who will not charge you more than $25 for a half hour consultation. Bar association personnel who handle incoming telephone requests are generally unbiased when referring names of lawyers. However, inquire whether the names supplied are experienced practitioners or inexperienced neophytes; be sure to ask for the names of experienced lawyers only.

After you obtain the names of a few lawyers, call them for the purpose of scheduling a consultation. At the initial consultation you should obtain a sound evaluation of your legal problem and decide if you should hire the lawyer. When scheduling the consultation, be sure to ask how much it will cost and what documents, including copies of your contract, letters, performance appraisals and reviews, should be brought to the meeting.

All discussions with the lawyer at the consultation are privileged and confidential, so don't be afraid to discuss your matter in great detail. After the consultation is over, you should have received a detailed analysis of:

- What your rights are
- Whether your case has a fair probability of success if additional action is taken
- What action should be taken by you to maximize your claim (examples include sending a letter of protest to document your position, collecting pertinent information, etc.)
- What action would be taken by him or her to protect your rights
- What your objectives should be in taking legal action
- Potential problems relating to federal and state statutes and case decisions in the state where a lawsuit would be brought
- Approximately how long the lawsuit will take
- The approximate legal fees and disbursements

If the lawyer sees weaknesses in your case and believes that litigation will be unduly expensive, or if he or she desires to try to settle the matter without resorting to time-consuming litigation, the lawyer may recommend sending a letter to the employer for negotiation purposes. The sample letter on page 139 is a good example of the kind of letter sent by my office after a client has been fired.

The vast majority of cases are settled out of court after such a letter is sent. Never underestimate the power of a lawyer's letter once it is received by an employer. In any event, the chosen course of action should be instituted without delay so you will be able to receive remuneration as quickly as possible. This will also ensure that your case falls within the requisite time period to start action—i.e., that the Statute of Limitations will not have expired.

A competent lawyer should give you a good feeling after you leave the consultation. During the initial meeting the lawyer should be attentive, not allow distractions or interruptions to disrupt the consultation, present an outward appearance of neatness and good grooming, not act in a boastful manner (beware of the lawyer who brags "I never lose a case") and should discuss fee arrangements up front. Some lawyers have a tendency to wait until all work is done and then submit large bills. The failure to discuss the fee arrangement at the initial interview may be a sign that the lawyer operates this way.

THE FEE ARRANGEMENT

Once you have decided to hire the lawyer, it is important to discuss the fee arrangement immediately so there will be no surprises. Questions to ask include the following:

- What is the lawyer's fee?
- If you are billed on an hourly basis, will the lawyer estimate the maximum amount of money you will be charged?
- How are time charges computed? Will you be charged for telephone calls with the lawyer? What kind of billing statement will you receive? Are costs and disbursements (telephone charges, travel, filing fees, photocopying expenses, etc.) included or are they extra?
- Is it better to be charged on a contingency basis? If so, what percentage of any money received in a settlement or lawsuit will be payable to the attorney? Are you required to pay an initial retainer to be applied against the contingency fee? Is this recoverable against the lawyer's fee if money is recovered?

To avoid problems and reduce misunderstandings, *always* insist on receiving a written retainer agreement before hiring the lawyer. The following are actual examples of retainer agreements given to my clients in various labor-related matters. The first letter is sent whenever a client retains my office to engage in settlement negotiations; the second letter, requiring the client's signature, is sent when negotiations are unsuccessful and litigation is necessary.

SAMPLE RETAINER AGREEMENTS

LAW OFFICES OF
STEVEN MITCHELL SACK
360 LEXINGTON AVENUE, 20TH FLOOR
NEW YORK, N.Y. 10017

(212) 983-6000

STEVEN M. SACK
JONATHAN S. SACK *

*ALSO ADMITTED IN N.J. & D.C.

NEW JERSEY OFFICES

920 NORTH BROAD STREET
ELIZABETH, NEW JERSEY 07208

Date

Name of client
Address
Address

Re: <u>Name of employer</u>

Dear Jordan,

This letter will confirm the terms of my engagement as your attorney regarding the above.

I met with you, reviewed your file and conducted preliminary research to learn the pertinent facts with respect to your current problems and drafted a letter of protest for you to protect your rights. For those and additional services to be rendered, you have paid me a retainer of Five Hundred Dollars ($500.00) which is my minimum fee in this matter.

I will now contact the above in the attempt to negotiate a favorable settlement to collect salary, severance pay and commissions allegedly owed for an additional period of time beyond the company's unilateral decision to only pay you only until (date). For my efforts, it is agreed that I shall be paid a contingency fee of Thirty Percent (30%) of all gross monies collected on your behalf, less the $500.00 previously paid, if a settlement can be effectuated.

All settlements will require your approval before I conclude same. Additionally, the aforementioned contingency fee arrangement is for legal work performed in <u>negotiations</u> only and does not cover work rendered in connection with a lawsuit. In the event you desire this office to assist you in formal litigation, both of us will discuss and agree upon a suitable fee arrangement at a later date.

Finally, you are aware of the hazards of litigation and that despite my efforts on your behalf there is no assurance or guarantee of the success or outcome of this matter.

As always, I look forward to serving you and will keep you posted with all developments as they occur.

Very truly yours,

Steven Mitchell Sack

SMS/nc
Enc.

LAW OFFICES OF
STEVEN MITCHELL SACK
360 LEXINGTON AVENUE, 20TH FLOOR
NEW YORK, N.Y. 10017

(212) 983-4000

STEVEN M. SACK
JONATHAN S. SACK *

*ALSO ADMITTED IN N.J. & D.C.

NEW JERSEY OFFICES

920 NORTH BROAD STREET
ELIZABETH, NEW JERSEY 07208

Date

Name of client
Address
Address

Re: <u>Name of employer</u>

Dear John,

This will confirm our agreement whereby you have retained this office to represent your rep firm in a lawsuit in the Supreme Court, New York County to collect commissions allegedly earned and due from the above conceivably worth in excess of One Hundred Thirty Thousand Dollars ($130,000.00).

In that regard, you have forwarded a retainer of Three Thousand Five Hundred Dollars ($3,500.00) which is my minimum fee in this matter. This retainer shall be applied against, and deducted from a contingency fee of Thirty Three Percent (33%) of all money collected in settlement, judgment or otherwise. In the event your matter proceeds to trial and an actual trial occurs, you also agree to pay an additional trial fee of Five Hundred Dollars ($500.00) per day or any part of a day thereof, which will be a <u>separate</u> fee and not deducted from the above contingency fee arrangement.

All settlements will require your approval before I conclude same. Additionally, the above fee arrangement only covers work rendered in connection with this lawsuit and does not cover any work in appellate courts, other actions or proceedings, or out-of-pocket disbursements. Out-of-pocket disbursements include, but are not limited to, costs of filing papers, court fees, process servers' fees, witness fees, court reporters' stenographic fees, and out of state travel and lodging expenses, which disbursements shall be paid for or reimbursed to me immediately upon my request. It is noted that you have forwarded the sum of Three Hundred Dollars ($300.00) for me to hold in my escrow account for such initial costs and disbursements.

Finally, I have advised you and you are aware of the hazards of litigation and that, despite my efforts on your behalf, there is no assurance or guarantee of the outcome of this matter, particularly with respect to your claim for reorders through the end of the selling season (since there was no written agreement confirming your right to receive such post-termination compensation). Also, you have assured me that there is no counterclaim exposure and no detrimental acts were committed on (name of employer), such as slander or breach of your fiduciary duty of loyalty or good faith while representing the line, and I have only agreed to represent you in this matter based on those assurances.

Kindly indicate your understanding and acceptance of the above by signing this letter below where indicated and returning the signed original to this office, keeping the copy for your files.

As always, I look forward to serving you.

Very truly yours,

Steven Mitchell Sack

I, (name of client), have read the above letter, understand and agree with all of its terms and have received a copy:

_____

Name of client

SMS/nc
Enc.

Be aware that there are distinct advantages and disadvantages in using different fee arrangements. For example, when you pay a flat fee you know how much will be charged, but you do not know how much care and attention will be spent on your matter. The hourly rate might be cheaper than a flat fee for simple matters, but some dishonest lawyers "pad" timesheets to increase their fees. Also, although contingency fee arrangements are beneficial to clients with weak cases or clients who cannot afford counsel's hourly rates, contingency fee arrangements often encourage lawyers to settle winning cases for less money rather than go to court. That is why no matter what type of fee is agreed upon, it is essential to hire a lawyer who is honest and has your best interests in mind at all times.

If you are paying the retainer in cash, ask for a receipt. Also, insist that you receive copies of all incoming and outgoing correspondence when it is sent or received so you will be able to follow the progress of your case. If the lawyer is reluctant to do this, think twice about hiring him or her.

It is also wise to ask for a monthly statement of services rendered, particularly if you are being charged by the hour. Request that billing statements be supported by detailed and complete time records including the date service was rendered, the time, type of service provided and names of people contacted. Some lawyers are reluctant to do this, but by receiving these statements on a regular basis, you will be able to question inconsistencies and errors before they get out of hand and keep billing mistakes to a minimum.

The following is an example of an hourly billing statement sent by my office to a client. Note that the client is only billed for a 5-minute telephone call where warranted. Some lawyers bill in minimum increments of 15 minutes. *Avoid* this arrangement, because if the lawyer is charging a high hourly rate (i.e., more than $200 per hour) the additional 10 minutes can be very expensive.

At the hiring interview you should also ask if the lawyer you are speaking to will handle the matter. When dealing with law firms, clients may think they are hiring one lawyer but their case is then assigned to another. To avoid this problem, specify in writing which lawyer will handle your case.

Additionally, specify in writing that the lawyer will return phone calls within 24 hours and will promptly pursue your rights. Some lawyers

---

SAMPLE MONTHLY BILLING STATEMENT

Date

Name of client
Company
Address

Current statement for all services rendered in the matter of the contract negotiation between (name of client) and (name of employer) at the rate of $200.00 per hour per agreement:

1. 1/05/92	Tel. conv. with Employer's Attorney	
	9:40-9:45 a.m.	5 min.
	Tel. conv. with Client	
	9:15-9:20 a.m.	5 min.
	Tel. conv. with Client	
	12:10-12:15 p.m.	5 min.
2. 1/04/92	Draft of Revised Agreement including	
	tel. conv. with Client	
	6:50 a.m.-8:05 a.m.	75 min.
3. 1/03/92	Meeting with Client	
	1:40-2:50 p.m.	70 min.
4. 12/19/91	Review of initial proposed Agreement	
	7:30 a.m.-7:55 a.m.	25 min.
	Tel. conv. with Client	
	9:35-9:40 a.m.; 3:40-3:45 p.m.	10 min.

Total time spent on Matter from December 19, 1991 through January 5, 1992 at standard rate of $200.00 per hour:

195 min. or 3.25 hours

Amount earned: $650.00

procrastinate once they are retained. The legal system is often a slow process. Don't stall it further by hiring a procrastinating lawyer. Also, to avoid problems down the road, be sure there are no conflicts of interest (such as that the law firm represented your employer several years ago). You should ask the lawyer up front if there are any such potential conflicts.

Finally, discuss the lawyer's escrow account arrangements. Escrow accounts are separate bank accounts that lawyers must maintain on the client's behalf. A lawyer must notify you immediately when funds are received on your behalf, and these funds must be deposited in a special account, separate from the firm's general business account. Insist on nothing less. Also, insist that all funds be deposited in an *interest-bearing account* and be sure you receive the interest together with your share of the settlement proceeds. Some lawyers fail to remit interest to the client.

HANDLING THE MATTER

If a settlement appears imminent, don't allow yourself to be intimidated by your lawyer into accepting it unless you are satisfied. Always remember that the lawyer works for you, not vice versa. If the lawyer believes a settlement is in your best interests, be sure you receive logical reasons why. Only accept his or her opinion if it makes sense.

If you are dissatisfied with your lawyer's conduct or with the way the matter is progressing, consult another lawyer. Do this before taking any action, including changing your lawyer, because you need a professional opinion to tell whether your lawyer acted correctly or improperly. Never fire your lawyer until you have hired a replacement.

CONCLUSION

If you have read this book carefully and thoughtfully, you now have a hands-on guide to avoiding many of the employment termination problems you may face, and, for those you cannot avoid, you have a guide on how to detect employer improprieties to protect your rights. Many of the items we have discussed in these pages encompass simple rules of common sense and reason.

The body of employment law has been created to further fairness and justice. It is there to protect you, but it will not help you unless you participate in your own defense. Before you make a major move, reread the appropriate portions of this book. Know the law. Discuss your situation with an attorney who specializes in labor law. And, above all, good luck.

Steven Mitchell Sack, Esq.

APPENDIX I

||||||||||||||||||||||||||||||||||||||||||||
GLOSSARY OF TERMS

The terms listed below are commonly known as "legalese." You can reduce your chances of being exploited in your personal and business dealings if you understand the meaning of the words contained in this glossary. In addition, you will be better able to communicate with your lawyer and use the legal system to your benefit.

Abuse of process A cause of action which arises when one party intentionally misuses the legal process to injure another.

Accord and satisfaction An agreement by the employee and his or her company to compromise disputes concerning outstanding debts, compensation or terms of employment. Satisfaction occurs when the terms of the compromise are fully performed.

Action in accounting A cause of action in which one party seeks a determination of the amount of money owed by another.

Admissible Capable of being introduced in court as evidence.

Advance Sometimes referred to as "draw," it is a sum of money which is applied against money to be earned.

Affidavit A written statement signed under oath.

Allegations Written statements of a party to a lawsuit which charge the other party with wrongdoing. In order to be successful, these must be proven.

Answer The defendant's reply to the plaintiff's allegations in a complaint.

Anticipatory breach A breach of contract that occurs when one party, i.e., the employee, states in advance of performance that he or she will definitely not perform under the terms of his or her contract.

Appeal A proceeding whereby the losing party to a lawsuit applies to a higher court to determine the correctness of the decision.

Arbitration A proceeding whereby both sides to a lawsuit agree to submit their dispute to arbitrators, rather than judges. The arbitration proceeding is expeditious and is legally binding on all parties.

Assignment The transfer of a right or interest by one party to another.

Attorney in fact A person appointed by another to transact business on his or her behalf; the person does not have to be a lawyer.

At-will employment *See* Employment at will.

Award A decision made by a judicial body to compensate the winning party in a lawsuit.

Bill of particulars A document used in a lawsuit which specifically details the loss alleged by the plaintiff.

Breach of contract A legal cause of action for the unjustified failure to perform a duty or obligation specified in an agreement.

Brief A concise statement of the main contentions of a lawsuit.

Burden of proof The responsibility of a party to a lawsuit to provide sufficient evidence to prove or disprove a claim.

Business deduction A legitimate expense that can be used to decrease the amount of income subject to tax.

Business slander A legal wrong committed when a party orally makes false statements which impugn the business reputation of another (e.g., imply that the person is dishonest, incompetent or financially unreliable).

Calendar A list of cases to be heard each day in court.

Cause of action The legal theory upon which the plaintiff seeks to recover damages.

Caveat emptor A Latin expression frequently applied to consumer transactions; translated as "Let the buyer beware."

Cease-and-desist letter A letter, usually sent by a lawyer, notifying an individual to stop engaging in a particular type of activity, behavior or conduct which infringes upon the rights of another.

Certificate of incorporation A document which creates a corporation.

Check A negotiable instrument; the depositor's written order requesting his or her bank to pay a definite sum of money to a named individual, entity or to the bearer.

Civil court Generally, any court which presides over noncriminal matters.

Claims court A particular court which hears tax disputes.

Clerk of the court A person who determines whether court papers are properly filed and court procedures followed.

Closely held business A business typically owned by fewer than ten co-owners.

Collateral estoppel *See* Estoppel. Collateral estoppel is where a prior but different legal action is conclusive in a way to bring about estoppel in a current legal action.

Common law Law which evolves from reported case decisions which are relied upon for their precedential value.

Compensatory damages A sum of money awarded to a party which represents the actual harm suffered or loss incurred.

Complaint A legal document which commences the lawsuit; it alleges facts and causes of action which the plaintiff relies upon to collect damages.

Conflict of interest The ethical inability of a lawyer to represent a client because of competing loyalties, e.g., representing both employer and employee in a labor dispute.

Consideration An essential element of an enforceable contract; something of value given or promised by one party in exchange for an act or promise of another.

Constitutional Recognized as legal or valid.

Contempt A legal sanction imposed when a rule or order of a judicial body is disobeyed.

Contingency fee A type of fee arrangement whereby a lawyer is paid a percentage of the money recovered. If unsuccessful, the client is only responsible for costs already paid by the lawyer.

Continuance The postponement of a legal proceeding to another date.

Contract An enforceable agreement, either written, oral, or implied by the actions or intentions of the parties.

Contract modification The alteration of contract terms.

Counterclaim A claim asserted by the defendant in a lawsuit.

Covenant A promise.

Credibility The believability of a witness as perceived by a judge or jury.

Creditor The party to whom money is owed.

Cross-examination The questioning of a witness by the opposing lawyer.

Damages An award, usually money, given to the winning party in a lawsuit as compensation for the wrongful acts of another.

Debtor The party who owes money.

Decision The determination of a case or matter by a judicial body.

Deductible The unrecoverable portion of insurance proceeds.

Defamation An oral or written statement communicated to a third party which impugns a person's reputation in the community.

Default judgment An award rendered after one party fails to appear in a lawsuit.

Defendant The person or entity who is sued in a lawsuit.

Defense The defendant's justification for relieving himself or herself of fault.

Definite term of employment Employment for a fixed period of time.

Deposition A pretrial proceeding in which one party is questioned, usually under oath, by the opposing party's lawyer.

Disclaimer A clause in a sales, service, or other contract which attempts to limit or exonerate one party from liability in the event of a lawsuit.

Discovery A general term used to describe several pretrial devices (e.g., depositions and interrogatories) that enable lawyers to elicit information from the opposing side.

District court A particular court that hears tax disputes.

Dual capacity A legal theory, used to circumvent Worker's Compensation laws, that allows an injured employee to sue his or her employer directly in court.

Due process Constitutional protections which guarantee that a person's life, liberty or property cannot be taken away without the opportunity to be heard in a judicial proceeding.

Duress Unlawful threats, pressure, or force that induces a person to act contrary to his or her intentions; if proved, it allows a party to disavow a contract.

Employee A person who works and is subject to an employer's scope, direction and control.

Employment at will Employment which does not provide an employee with job security, since the person can be fired on a moment's notice with or without cause.

Employment discrimination Conduct directed at employees and job applicants that is prohibited by law.

Equity Fairness; usually applied when a judicial body awards a suitable remedy other than money to a party (e.g., an injunction).

Escrow account A separate fund where lawyers are obligated to deposit money received from or on behalf of a client.

Estoppel Estoppel is a legal bar to prevent a party from asserting a fact or claim inconsistent with that party's prior position which has been relied on or acted on by another party.

Evidence Information in the form of oral testimony, exhibits, affidavits, etc., used to prove a party's claim.

Examination before trial A pretrial legal device; also called a "deposition."

Exhibit Tangible evidence used to prove a party's claim.

Exit agreements Agreements sometimes signed between employers and employees upon resignation or termination of an employee's services.

Express contract An agreement whose terms are manifested by clear and definite language, as distinguished from those agreements inferred from conduct.

False imprisonment The unlawful detention of a person who is held against his or her will without authority or justification.

Filing fee Money paid to start a lawsuit.

Final decree A court order or directive of a permanent nature.

Financial statement A document, usually prepared by an accountant, which reflects a business' (or individual's) assets, liabilities and financial condition.

Flat fee A sum of money paid to a lawyer as compensation for services.

Flat fee plus time A form of payment in which a lawyer receives one sum for services and then receives additional money calculated on an hourly basis.

Fraud A false statement that is relied upon and causes damages to the defrauded party.

General denial A reply contained in the defendant's answer.

Ground The basis for an action or an argument.

Guaranty A contract where one party agrees to answer for or satisfy the debt of another.

Hearsay evidence Unsubstantiated evidence that is often excluded by a court.

Hourly fee Money paid to a lawyer for services, computed on an hourly basis.

Implied contract An agreement that is tacit rather than expressed in clear and definite language; an agreement inferred from the conduct of the parties.

Indemnification Protection or reimbursement against damage or loss. The indemnified party is protected against liabilities or penalties from that party's actions; the indemnifying party provides the protection or reimbursement.

Infliction of emotional distress A legal cause of action in which one party seeks to recover damages for mental pain and suffering caused by another.

Injunction A court order restraining one party from doing or refusing to do an act.

Integration The act of making a contract whole by integrating its elements into a coherent single entity. An agreement is considered integrated when the parties involved accept the final version as a complete expression of their agreement.

Interrogatories A pretrial device used to elicit information; written questions are sent to an opponent to be answered under oath.

Invasion of privacy The violation of a person's constitutionally protected right to privacy.

Judgment A verdict rendered by a judicial body; if money is awarded, the winning party is the "judgment creditor" and the losing party is the "judgment debtor."

Jurisdiction The authority of a court to hear a particular matter.

Legal duty The responsibility of a party to perform a certain act.

Letter of agreement An enforceable contract in the form of a letter.

Letter of protest A letter sent to document a party's dissatisfaction.

Liable Legally in the wrong or legally responsible for.

Lien A claim made against the property of another in order to satisfy a judgment.

Lifetime contract An employment agreement of infinite duration which is often unenforceable.

Liquidated damages An amount of money agreed upon in advance by parties to a contract to be paid in the event of a breach or dispute.

Malicious interference with contractual rights A legal cause of action in which one party seeks to recover damages against an individual who has induced or caused another party to terminate a valid contract.

Malicious prosecution A legal cause of action in which one party seeks to recover damages after another party instigates or institutes a frivolous judicial proceeding (usually criminal) which is dismissed.

Mediation A voluntary dispute-resolution process in which both sides attempt to settle their differences without resorting to formal litigation.

Misappropriation The unlawful taking of another party's personal property.

Misrepresentation A legal cause of action which arises when one party makes untrue statements of fact that induce another party to act and be damaged as a result.

Mitigation of damages A legal principle which requires a party seeking damages to make reasonable efforts to reduce damages as much as possible; for example, to seek new employment after being unfairly discharged.

Motion A written request made to a court by one party during a lawsuit.

Negligence A party's failure to exercise a sufficient degree of care owed to another by law.

Nominal damages A small sum of money awarded by a court.

Noncompetition clause A restrictive provision in a contract which limits an employee's right to work in that particular industry after he or she ceases to be associated with his or her present employer.

Notary Public A person authorized under state law to administer an oath or verify a signature.

Notice to show cause A written document in a lawsuit asking a court to expeditiously rule on a matter.

Objection A formal protest made by a lawyer in a lawsuit.

Offer The presentment of terms, which, if accepted, may lead to the formation of a contract.

Opinion letter A written analysis of a client's case, prepared by a lawyer.

Option An agreement giving one party the right to choose a certain course of action.

Oral contract An enforceable verbal agreement.

Parol evidence Oral evidence introduced at a trial to alter or explain the terms of a written agreement.

Partnership A voluntary association between two or more competent persons engaged in a business as co-owners for profit.

Party A plaintiff or defendant in a lawsuit.

Perjury Committing false testimony while under oath.

Petition A request filed in court by one party.

Plaintiff The party who commences a lawsuit.

Pleading A written document that states the facts or arguments put forth by a party in a lawsuit.

Power of attorney A document executed by one party allowing another to act on his or her behalf in specified situations.

Pretrial discovery A legal procedure used to gather information from an opponent before the trial.

Process server An individual who delivers the summons and/or complaint to the defendant.

Promissory note A written acknowledgment of a debt whereby one party agrees to pay a specified sum on a specified date.

Proof Evidence presented at a trial and used by a judge or jury to fashion an award.

Punitive damages Money awarded as punishment for a party's wrongful acts.

Quantum meruit A legal principle whereby a court awards reasonable compensation to a party who performs work, labor or services at another party's request; also referred to as "unjust enrichment."

Rebuttal The opportunity for a lawyer at a trial to ask a client or witness additional questions to clarify points elicited by the opposing lawyer during cross-examination.

Release A written document which, when signed, relinquishes a party's rights to enforce a claim against another.

Remedy The means by which a right is enforced or protected.

Reply A written document in a lawsuit conveying the contentions of a party in response to a motion.

Restrictive covenant A provision in a contract which forbids one party from doing a certain act, e.g., working for another, soliciting customers, etc.

Retainer A sum of money paid to a lawyer for services to be rendered.

Service letter statutes Laws in some states that require an employer to furnish an employee with written reasons for his discharge.

Sex harassment Prohibited conduct of a sexual nature which occurs in the workplace.

Shop rights   The rights of an employer to use within the employer's facility a device or method developed by an employee.

Slander   Oral defamation of a party's reputation.

Small claims court   A particular court that presides over small disputes (e.g., those involving sums of less than $2,500).

Sole proprietorship   An unincorporated business.

Statement of fact   Remarks or comments of a specific nature that have a legal effect.

Statute   A law created by a legislative body.

Statute of frauds   A legal principle requiring that certain contracts be in writing in order to be enforceable.

Statute of limitations   A legal principle requiring a party to commence a lawsuit within a certain period of time.

Stipulation   An agreement between parties.

Submission agreement   A signed agreement whereby both parties agree to submit a present dispute to binding arbitration.

Subpoena   A written order requiring a party or witness to appear at a legal proceeding; a subpoena duces tecum is a written order requiring a party to bring books and records to the legal proceeding.

Summation   The last part of the trial wherein both lawyers recap the respective positions of their clients.

Summons   A written document served upon the defendant giving notification of a lawsuit.

Temporary decree   A court order or directive of a temporary nature, capable of being modified or changed.

Testimony   Oral evidence presented by a witness under oath.

"Time is of the essence"   A legal expression often included in agreements to specify the requirement of timeliness.

Tort   A civil wrong.

Unfair and deceptive practice   Illegal business and trade acts prohibited by various federal and state laws.

Unfair discharge   An employee's termination without legal justification.

Verdict   The decision of a judge or jury.

Verification   A written statement signed under oath.

Void   Legally without merit.

Waiver   A written document that, when signed, relinquishes a party's rights.

Whistleblowing   Protected conduct where one party complains about the illegal acts of another.

Witness   A person who testifies at a judicial proceeding.

Worker's compensation   A process in which an employee receives compensation for injuries sustained in the course of employment.

APPENDIX II

::

EEOC DISTRICT
AND AREA OFFICES

District offices (DO) are full-service units, handling all charge processing and all compliance and litigation enforcement functions. Area offices (AO) generally handle charge intake and initial investigations, with some of them also performing various compliance and litigation activities.

ALBUQUERQUE, AO
505 Marquette, NW, Suite 1105
Albuquerque, New Mexico 87102
(505)766-2061

ATLANTA, DO
75 Piedmont Ave., NE
Atlanta, Georgia 30335
(404) 331-6093

BALTIMORE, DO
711 West 40th St., Suite 210
Baltimore, Maryland 21211
(301) 962-3932

BIRMINGHAM, DO
1900 3rd Ave. N.
Birmingham, Alabama 35203
(205) 254-1166
        731-0083

BOSTON, AO
150 Causeway St., Suite 1000
Boston, Massachusetts 02114
(617) 223-4535

BUFFALO, AO
28 Church St., Rm. 301
Buffalo, New York 14202
(716) 846-4441

CHARLOTTE, DO
5500 Central Avenue
Charlotte, North Carolina 28212
(704) 563-2501

CHICAGO, DO
536 South Clark St., Rm. 910A
Chicago, Illinois 60605
(312) 353-2713

CINCINNATI, AO
550 Main St., Rm. 7015
Cincinnati, Ohio 45202
(513) 684-2379

CLEVELAND, DO
1375 Euclid Ave., Suite 600
Cleveland, Ohio 44115
(216) 522-7425

DALLAS, DO
1900 Pacific, 13th Floor
Dallas, Texas 75201
(214) 767-7015

DAYTON, AO
550 Main St., Rm. 7015
Cincinnati, Ohio 45202
(513) 684-2851

DENVER, DO
1845 Sherman St.
Denver, Colorado 80203
(303) 866-1300

DETROIT, DO
477 Michigan Ave.
Detroit, Michigan 48226
(313) 226-7636

EL PASO, AO
Common 4171, N. Missa Bld., C100
El Paso, Texas 79902
(915) 543-7596
       534-6550

FRESNO, AO
1313 P St., Rm. 103
Fresno, California 93721
(209) 487-5793

GREENSBORO, AO
324 West Market St., Rm. B-27
Greensboro, North Carolina 27402
(919) 333-5174

GREENVILLE, AO
300 E. Washington St., Suite B41
Greenville, South Carolina 29601
(803) 233-1791

HOUSTON, DO
1919 Smith St., 7th Floor
Houston, Texas 77002
(713) 653-3320

INDIANAPOLIS, DO
46 East Ohio St., Rm. 456
Indianapolis, Indiana 46204
(317) 226-7212

JACKSON, AO
207 W. Amite St.
Crossroads Fielding
Jackson, Missouri 39201
(601) 965-4537

KANSAS CITY, AO
911 Walnut, 10th Floor
Kansas City, Missouri 64106
(816) 374-5773
       426-5773

LITTLE ROCK, AO
320 West Capitol, Suite 621
Little Rock, Arkansas 72201
(501) 324-5060

LOS ANGELES, DO
3660 Wilshire Blvd., 6th Floor
Los Angeles, California 90010
(213) 251-7278

LOUISVILLE, AO
600 Dr. Martin Luther King Jr. Pl.
Rm. 268
Louisville, Kentucky 40202
(502) 582-6082

MEMPHIS, DO
1407 Union Ave., Suite 621
Memphis, Tennessee 38104
(901) 722-2617

MIAMI, DO
Metro Mall
1 NE 1st St., 6th Floor
Miami, Florida 33132
(305) 350-4491
       536-4491

MILWAUKEE, DO
310 W. Wisconsin Ave., Suite 800
Milwaukee, Wisconsin 53203-2292
(414) 297-1111

MINNEAPOLIS, AO
220 2nd St. S., Rm. 108
Minneapolis, Minnesota 55401-2141
(612) 370-3330

NASHVILLE, AO
50 Vantage Way, Suite 202
Nashville, Tennessee 37228
(615) 736-5820

NEWARK, AO
60 Park Pl., Rm. 301
Newark, New Jersey 07102
(201) 645-6383

NEW ORLEANS, DO
701 Layola Ave., Suite 600
New Orleans, Louisiana 70113
(504) 589-3842

NEW YORK, DO
90 Church St., 15th Floor, Rm. 1501
New York, New York 10007
(212) 264-7161

NORFOLK, AO
252 Monticello Ave.
Norfolk, Virginia 23510
(804) 441-3470

OAKLAND, AO
1333 Broadway, Suite 430
Oakland, California 94612
(415) 273-7588

OKLAHOMA CITY, AO
531 Couch Dr.
Oklahoma City, Oklahoma 73102
(405) 231-4912

PHILADELPHIA, DO
1421 Cherry St., 10th Floor
Philadelphia, Pennsylvania 19102
(215) 597-7784

PHOENIX, DO
4520 North Central Ave., Suite 300
Phoenix, Arizona 85012
(602) 261-3882
     640-5000

PITTSBURGH, AO
1000 Liberty Ave., Rm. 2038
Pittsburgh, Pennsylvania 15222
(412) 644-3444

RALEIGH, AO
1309 Annapolis Dr.
Raleigh, North Carolina 27608-2129
(919) 856-4064

RICHMOND, AO
3600 W. Broad St., Suite 229
Richmond, Virginia 23230
(804) 771-2692

SAN ANTONIO, AO
5410 Fredericksburg, Suite 200
San Antonio, Texas 78229
(512) 229-4810

SAN DIEGO, AO
880 Front St., Rm. 4521
San Diego, California 92188
(619) 293-6288
     557-6288

SAN FRANCISCO, DO
901 Market St., Suite 500
San Francisco, California 94103
(415) 744-6500

SAN JOSE, AO
84 West Santa Clara Ave., Rm. 300
San Jose, California 95113
not listed

SEATTLE, DO
2815 Second Ave., Suite 500
Seattle, Washington 98121
(206) 553-0968

ST. LOUIS, DO
625 North Euclid St., 5th Floor
St. Louis, Missouri 63108
(314) 425-6585

TAMPA, AO
501 E. Polk St.
Timberlake Annex Bldg.,
  Suite 1020
Tampa, Florida 33602
(813) 228-2310

WASHINGTON, AO
1801 L St. NW
Washington, District of
  Columbia 20507
(202)663-4264

INDEX

ABOUT THE AUTHOR

Steven Mitchell Sack maintains a private law practice in New York City devoted primarily to representation in contract and severance negotiations, labor disputes and litigation, and general labor law. A Phi Beta Kappa graduate of Stony Brook University and a graduate of Boston College Law School, he is a member of the American Bar Association, the New York State Bar Association and the New York County Lawyer's Association Labor and Employment Divisions, and is admitted to practice before the United States Tax Court.

Mr. Sack is the author of several legal books geared for the layman, including *The Salesperson's Legal Guide; Don't Get Taken: A Preventive Legal Guide to Protect Your Home, Family, Money and Job;* and the recently published *The Complete Legal Guide To Marriage, Divorce, Custody and Living Together.*

A disseminator of the law in a variety of media, Mr. Sack has been quoted and interviewed frequently in *The Wall Street Journal, The New York Times,* and other national publications due to his extensive experience in labor law. Mr. Sack has also appeared on numerous television shows, including "The Oprah Winfrey Show" and "The Sally Jessy Raphael Show."

He serves as a commercial arbitrator in employment-related disputes for the American Arbitration Association and conducts corporate and private seminars and conferences on labor-related subjects nationwide. Mr. Sack also serves as Labor Counsel for the National Association of Printers and Lithographers and for many sales associations composed of independent sales representatives, including, among others, the National Association of Independent Publisher's Representatives, the Office Products Reps Association, and the New York Boot and Shoe Traveler's Association.